The Economics of Derivatives

ENDORSEMENTS

'Derivatives are beneficial in small quantities and toxic in large volume. This book, rooted in deep knowledge of both markets and policy-making, shows how to handle the dilemmas this creates.'

John Kay, London School of Economics

'I find derivatives fiendishly hard to understand. This excellent book goes a long way to demystifying them. Simple yet lucid, comprehensive without being unmanageable, and practical while retaining analytical rigor. It is an absolute must for those trying to make sense of derivatives and also for those trying to regulate them, and ensuring that they don't again become weapons of mass destruction.'

Arvind Subramanian, (formerly, Peterson Institute for International Economics), Chief Economic Adviser, Government of India

'Even as derivatives markets have exploded in size and complexity, their 'value add' remains a contentious issue. At one end of the spectrum is the view that they enhance market efficiency, and at the other, the view that derivatives are largely 'financial weapons of mass destruction'. This is a debate that has largely frowned on moderation. This book by two outstanding professionals synthesizes that debate and presents a much needed balanced view that should inform policy-making in both advanced economies and emerging markets. Authoritative, comprehensive and insightful, this is at once a work of deep scholarship as well as rich real world experience.'

D. Subbarao, Former Governor, Reserve Bank of India

'This unique, fascinating and eminently readable book presents a synthesis of theory, empirical evidence, market practices and case studies and provides an outstanding analytical framework for policy-making and implementation. Drawing on the diverse professional experiences, deep scholarship and multiple institutional perspectives of the authors, it adds enormous value, in terms of clarity and perspectives, even for those like me who are familiar with this complex and controversial subject – as an academic or as a practitioner.'

Y. V. Reddy, Former Governor, Reserve Bank of India

'Everybody talks about financial derivatives and how they contributed to the 2007–2008 global financial crisis, but very few people have taken the time to provide us with a thoughtful account of the role of financial derivatives in today's global markets. While hundreds of books have been written on the valuation and hedging of financial derivatives, no book has taken a step back to look at the big picture and offer a framework for analyzing the societal cost and benefits of these products. This is a unique book that fills this very important gap. Any academic, practitioner, policy maker or serious student of financial history must find a place for this on their bookshelf.'

Hossein Kazemi, University of Massachusetts

'Are derivatives the elixir of financial innovation and creativity or weapons of mass destruction? Somanathan and Nageswaran have written a much-needed book that helps emerging market policy-makers think through the complexities of financial derivatives. Derivatives are of course financial tools which are double-edged – creative in the hands of the artist and destructive in the hands of the artful. This book raises the standard on realistic, professional assessment of a much misunderstood subject. It both surveys the literature and brings pragmatic views on how to use the tools effectively. I totally recommend it as both a textbook and handbook for policy-makers.'

Andrew Sheng, former Chairman, Securities and Futures Exchange Commission, Hong Kong

The Economics of Derivatives

T. V. Somanathan
V. Anantha Nageswaran

CAMBRIDGE
UNIVERSITY PRESS

CAMBRIDGE
UNIVERSITY PRESS

4843/24, 2nd Floor, Ansari Road, Daryaganj, Delhi - 110002, India

Cambridge University Press is part of the University of Cambridge.

It furthers the University's mission by disseminating knowledge in the pursuit of
education, learning and research at the highest international levels of excellence.

www.cambridge.org
Information on this title: www.cambridge.org/9781107091504

© T. V. Somanathan and V. Anantha Nageswaran 2015

First published 2015
Reprint 2015

Printed in India by Shree Maitrey Printech Pvt. Ltd., Noida

A catalogue record for this publication is available from the British Library

Library of Congress Cataloging-in-Publication Data

Somanathan, T. V.
The economics of derivatives / T.V. Somanathan, V. Anantha Nageswaran.
     pages cm
Includes bibliographical references and index.
Summary: "Discusses both the benefits and the drawbacks of derivatives trading and tries to
take a broad view of both theory and practice"-- Provided by publisher.
ISBN 978-1-107-09150-4 (hardback)
1. Derivative securities. I. Nageswaran, V. Anantha.
II. Title.
HG6024.A3S663 2015
332.64'57--dc23
2014034731

ISBN 978-1-107-09150-4 Hardback

To my mother, and my uncles T. S. Balaraman and T. S. Srinivasan, to whom I owe more than I can acknowledge

T. V. S.

To the various teachers in my life – past, present and future

V. A. N.

Contents

List of Tables, Figures and Boxes

Tables

Figures

Foreword

The term 'derivative' is one of a number of finance terms which immediately conjures up a wide range of reactions from people. Some will quickly blame the proliferation of the instrument for many of the global economy's woes whilst others view it as an instrument which has helped in risk mitigation and economic development. Unpicking the prejudices and drilling down to the fundamental drivers and uses of derivatives is critical. Looking from all sides enables the reader to gain a clearer understanding away from the noise related to finance in the post global financial crisis world. *The Economics of Derivatives* takes great strides in achieving this, taking the reader through an accessible yet sufficiently detailed and technical assessment, so as to provide the reader with a much better understanding.

Some participants and observers of the financial markets have understandably focused on the role derivatives played, most recently in the global financial crisis. Indeed, it has been argued that derivatives were key contributors which enabled excessive risk taking which resulted in rogue traders such as Nick Leeson and Jerome Kerviel. Of course, with all of these things, the reality is much less straightforward and fraught with complexity.

What is agreed is that the use of derivatives and the impact of them on the global economy are of great importance. The impact on the developed economies has been well documented. What receives less coverage is the significant benefit that derivatives have had on the emerging economies. The ability to unpack the different components of risk have directly enabled countries to manage risk more effectively and allocate it in ways which have resulted in improved economic outcomes. This book examines in detail these critical aspects and grounds them well in economic theory. By examining the impact of the use of derivatives on the developed and the emerging markets, the book rightly shines a light on both the positive aspects as well as the challenges the derivatives markets and its participants face. Further, the authors' judicious use of case studies provides the reader with the ability to observe the real-life uses of derivatives and judge for themselves the clear economic impact derivatives have had. The case studies are wide ranging, up to date and rich in their relevance; they enable the reader to gain a more rounded understanding of how such instruments have had direct economic benefit to emerging economies. The authors draw on contemporary experience and adeptly step the reader through the salient points in an unbiased way.

By providing additional risk tools, countries have been able to move forward on budgetary and planning decisions with much greater certainty which has in turn led to stronger economic benefits. Recent examples where countries have used derivatives in the context of commodities markets or natural events are explained to the reader in a way which illustrates the positive elements of the use of derivatives and their economic impact. The authors, however, do not shy away from discussing some of the very serious issues and perverse incentives that have also arisen as these tools have evolved. It is important to understand both sides of the story. The application of this balanced approach by the authors takes the reader through the broad spectrum of discussion whilst also expressing their own views, leaving the reader well positioned to make a much more informed judgement.

The Economics of Derivatives also, importantly, seeks to address the regulatory aspects of the markets. Whilst some market observers have been highly critical of the regulatory environment, some with the benefit of hindsight, this book takes a step back to make its assessment. It examines the flaws of the system, but also presents interesting perspectives on the pros and cons of seeking perfection in an inevitably imperfect world. Further, the authors rightly pose the questions and put forward their views for a more refined approach by the regulatory authorities in terms of the different types of markets in economies at different stages of development. The authors look at how regulation could be thought about in order to encourage financial innovation in developing economies versus developed economies. As they rightly observe, blunt instruments are not always appropriate and can result in unintended consequences. The regulatory spectrum and the degrees of respective complexity need closer examination, something which the authors set out. It is vital that the regulatory conundrum is fixed.

An adjunct to the regulatory conundrum is the performative nature of, and some market participants' approach to, the use of models. The authors' layout, well the issues we face as blind confidence, has sometimes been placed in models which in turn contributed to a number of market failures. The complications that have evolved around the modelling of derivatives and the consequential impact on being able to assess in an effective way the true underlying positions and their effect on the markets, adds a further layer of issues for the regulators and users of derivatives.

As someone who was at the heart of the financial world during the global financial crises and now working with emerging economies in particular, I have seen the various facets of derivatives and their impact. The power of good that can be brought to bear by the effective use of such instruments is immense and should not be underestimated. It is important that the positive elements of derivatives are reacquired and that we move away from the negative stereotyping that inevitably follows economic and financial shocks; we cannot let an unrefined framework stymie the positive application of derivatives. It is, of course, imperative that lessons are learned and the use and regulation of derivatives evolves in the most effective way. *The Economics of Derivatives* provides an excellent foundation for the assessment; irrespective of prejudices, good or bad, we must not be indifferent.

Bertrand Badré
Managing Director and Group Chief Financial
Officer, The World Bank Group
Washington, DC

Preface

Are derivatives markets beneficial to the economy? If so, how and in what circumstances? Can they be harmful to the economy? If so, how and in what circumstances? These are questions that interested us when we (separately and unbeknownst to each other) were doing our doctoral research in the late eighties and early nineties. In the years since then, these questions have become more important because derivatives trading – relatively small when we were students – has grown enormously in size, widened greatly in scope and expanded vastly in geographical spread. In recent years, derivatives have alternately been lauded for boosting prosperity and condemned for causing crises.

As economists who have done research on the subject and (at one time or other) traded derivatives, we have felt the absence of a balanced, concise and comprehensible examination of the economic effects of derivatives markets and their implications for public policy and regulation. This book is a contribution to filling that gap.

Writing this book has broadened and deepened our knowledge, but also made us even more aware of the gaps that remain in the economics of derivatives. Increased volumes of research have not necessarily narrowed these gaps. The field of derivatives has sometimes suffered from spurious precision and doctrinaire overconfidence. While this book will hopefully add to the reader's understanding of the subject, it is important to understand that that understanding will remain incomplete.

T. V. Somanathan
V. Anantha Nageswaran

(N.B. The views expressed in this book and the foreword are the personal views of the authors and the writer of the foreword respectively, and should not be construed as representing the views of any organizations they may be affiliated to.)

Acknowledgements

We are very grateful for the contributions of the many people who have helped us with this book. In particular, we would like to express our thanks to:

- Dr Srinivas Thiruvadanthai, Dr Mathias Denzler and Srivatsa Krishna for their valuable inputs;

- Harsh Gupta (our co-author on another book) for research assistance;

- Bertrand Badre for kindly writing an erudite and valuable foreword that provides a better introduction than we could have done;

- Professor John Kay, Professor Hossein Kazemi, Professor Arvind Subramanian, Dr Y. V. Reddy, Dr D. Subbarao and Andrew Sheng for their kind and invaluable comments on the book;

- Dr Willem Buiter, Professor Donald Mackenzie, Professor Jeffrey Frankel, Professor Markus Brunnermeier, Professor Avinash D. Persaud, Professor Charles A. Goodhart, Professor Hyun-Song Shin, Professor Richard G. Lipsey, Professor Thomas Philippon, Professor Ariel Reshef, Professor Alan Taylor, Lord Adair Turner, Tim Price, Professor Stephen Cecchetti, Professor Enisse Kharroubi, the Federal Reserve Bank of St. Louis, The World Bank, the Bank of Japan, the Bank for International Settlements, the Institute of Economic Affairs, Oxford University Press and Haver Analytics for kindly allowing us to use published material;

- *The Financial Times* and *Stringer Science + Business Media* for licences granted;

- Dr Emanuel Derman and Dr Paul Wilmott for kind permission to reproduce the 'Financial Modeller's Manifesto';

- Dhiraj Pandey, Ranjini Majumdar and Debjani Mazumder of Cambridge University Press for their outstanding professional support at every stage of the publishing process;

- K. S. Balachandren and G. Raguraman for able secretarial help and logistical support in many ways.

1

Introduction

[T]hese new financial instruments are an increasingly important vehicle for unbundling risks ... [They] enhance the ability to differentiate risk and allocate it to those investors most able and willing to take it ... a process that has undoubtedly improved national productivity growth and standards of living.

Alan Greenspan (1999)[1]

I view derivatives as time bombs, both for the parties that deal in them and the economic system ... these instruments will almost certainly multiply in variety and number until some event makes their toxicity clear. Central banks and governments have so far found no effective way to control, or even monitor, the risks posed by these contracts. In my view, derivatives are financial weapons of mass destruction, carrying dangers that, while now latent, are potentially lethal.

Warren Buffett (2002)[2]

Derivatives in modern economics are like nuclear energy in modern science; a source of immense power, which can also be the cause of enormous destruction. Derivatives (albeit not by that name) have been in existence for a long time, with forward trading in rice in Japan in the seventeenth century, being the first documented example, but their economic significance has increased enormously in recent years.

As of June 2013, according to data from the Bank for International Settlements (BIS), the total notional amount outstanding on derivative contracts was $762 trillion[3], i.e., $762,000 billion or $7.62 × 10^{14} (see Table 1.1). This includes 'Over The Counter' (OTC) contracts between two counterparties and contracts traded in recognized exchanges ('Exchange Traded Derivatives' or ETD). At $52.5 trillion , the notional amount of derivatives contracts traded in recognized exchanges amounted to just over 8 per cent of the total with OTC contracts making up 92 per cent. However, the BIS data excludes exchange-traded futures and options on *commodities*, and on individual *shares* for which data on a reliable comparable basis was not available. This figure therefore substantially underestimates the total volume of derivatives trading.

Table 1.1: Notional amounts of derivative contracts outstanding at year-end: 1995 to 2012 (selected years)

Type	Trillions of dollars of notional amounts outstanding							
	1995	2000	2005	2007	2008	2011	2012	2013
ETD	9.3	14.2	57.3	79.1	57.8	58.3	54.1	69.1
OTC:								
Foreign exchange options	–	15.7	31.4	56.2	50.0	63.4	67.4	73.1
Equity and commodity derivatives	–	2.6	11.2	16.9	10.9	9.1	8.8	9.3
Interest rate derivatives[4]	17.7	64.7	212.0	393.1	432.7	504.1	489.7	561.3
Credit default swaps[5]	–	0.9	13.9	58.2	41.9	28.6	25.1	24.3
Unallocated	–	12.3	30.8	61.4	62.7	42.6	41.6	24.9
Sub-total: **OTC derivatives**	**17.7**	**96.1**	**299.3**	**585.9**	**598.1**	**647.8**	**632.6**	**692.9**
Total	**27.0**	**110.3**	**356.5**	**665.0**	**655.9**	**706.1**	**686.7**	**762.0**

Source: BIS and Authors' calculations

As Figure 1.1 shows, global Gross Domestic Product (GDP, an approximation for national income) at current prices increased from approximately $10 trillion in 1980 to $72 trillion in 2012.

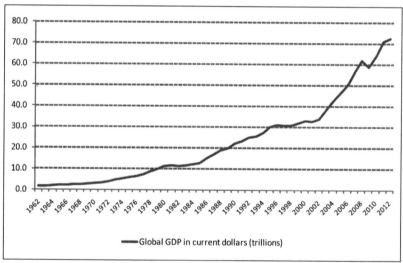

Figure 1.1: Global GDP 1962 to 2012
Source: World Bank Data Tables

Because the figures are at 'current' prices (i.e., the prices prevailing at each point of time) this increase represents a combination of inflation and real growth. In 2012, as Table 1.1 shows, the outstanding notional value of derivatives contracts was $686.7 trillion.[6] Hence, the notional amount outstanding in derivative contracts is now over nine times the size of the global GDP. Figure 1.2 shows how this multiple has evolved between 1995 and 2012.

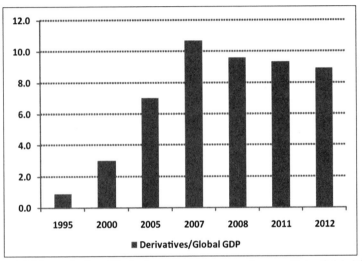

Figure 1.2: Notional value of derivative contracts at year end as a multiple of global GDP
Sources: BIS, ISDA and Angus Maddision Global GDP database

Figures 1.3 and 1.4 depict the changes in the notional value of different classes of OTC derivatives between 1998 and 2013. Foreign exchange and interest rate derivatives have continued to grow even after the financial crisis of 2008, while credit default swaps and equity and commodity OTC derivatives have declined.

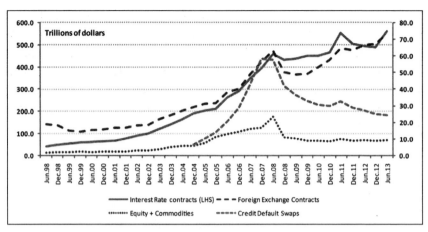

Note: Interest rate contracts are depicted on the left-hand scale and all others on the right-hand scale.

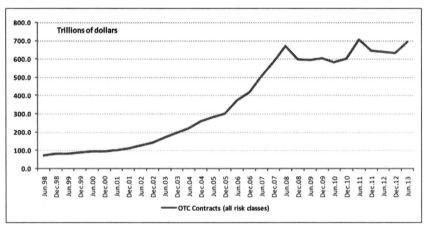

Figures 1.3 and 1.4: Trends in different classes of OTC contracts and total OTC volume (1998–2013)
Source: BIS

However, notional amounts are an exaggeration of the true value of the derivative contracts because many of these transactions cancel out (when the buyers' position is offset against the sellers') and, more importantly, because the actual amounts which are paid or received are far less than the notional value. (For instance, a futures contract can be entered into by putting up a small fraction of the notional value, typically 5 to 10 per cent, as margin.) Nevertheless, even if one makes the assumption that the market value is just a twentieth of the notional value, the resulting figure is now about half of the global GDP – an enormous sum. In 1995, the corresponding figure was about 4 per cent of global GDP. Derivatives markets have become so large over just two decades that they can no longer be ignored, or treated as a peripheral issue, by policy makers.

Aims and organization of the book

There are two broad streams of writing on derivatives. The first and larger stream (which can loosely be termed the 'financial' stream) is concerned with questions of *how the derivatives markets work*, with techniques for making profits or managing risks through derivatives and with methods for making the markets work better. The second and smaller stream (which can loosely be called the 'economic' stream) looks at the *contributions of derivatives to overall economic well-being*. Economists have contributed to the financial stream and non-economists have contributed to the economic stream. This book deals with the economic stream.

Within this economic stream, there are highly divergent opinions, as the quotations at the beginning of this chapter (from two of the 'highest priests' of finance) show. One school of thought holds that derivatives, by (*inter alia*) enabling the unbundling of risk and allocating it to those best able to bear it, make a major positive contribution to the economy. Another school of thought condemns derivatives as dangerous and unnecessary; some members of this school also opine that they are a source of price de-stabilization and even a cause of inflation.

There are few writings in the economic stream which attempt to take a wide-ranging look at *both* sides of the argument on the economic effects of derivatives and synthesize them. *This book is a modest attempt to do that.* It looks at the beneficial and adverse effects of derivatives trading from the point of view of economic theory and from the perspective of empirical evidence and recent economic history. The book aims to present the different points of view in a non-mathematical and simple, but not simplistic, manner with minimal jargon and then to present the authors' own synthesis. While primarily based on the discipline of economics, it also draws economic insights from relevant work in other disciplines, particularly sociology and law. It does not present any original empirical evidence but does present some new theoretical ideas.

The ultimate objective is to provide the reader a *basic conceptual framework from which to form his or her own informed judgment on whether, when and how derivatives are beneficial or harmful to the economy.*

The book does not contain a description of what the main derivative securities are, or how they work. It assumes that the reader has some elementary knowledge about how the simple derivatives (futures, options and swaps) are traded, but does not assume or require any detailed understanding of the workings of these markets.[7]

After this introductory chapter, Chapter 2 presents a definition and a typology of derivatives, which introduces readers to the different kinds of derivatives. Different derivatives have varying features and modes of classification and an understanding of the typology is useful especially from a regulatory perspective.

Chapter 3 discusses the extent to which derivatives markets perform socially useful economic functions. Chapter 4 continues this discussion with specific reference to the issue of 'market completion', which some economists regard as an important function of derivative markets.

Chapter 5 sets out the theoretical arguments and empirical evidence indicating that futures and other derivatives markets tend to have a price *stabilizing* effect on spot (cash) markets. Chapter 6 examines the arguments and evidence for the opposite view that derivatives have a *destabilizing* effect. Chapter 7 provides the authors' synthesis and reconciliation between these contradictory strands of thinking.

Chapter 8 presents a brief historical perspective of the factors leading to the extraordinary increase in the volume of derivatives trading in recent decades and Chapter 9 examines the contribution of derivatives to the global financial crisis of 2008.

Chapter 10 outlines the issue of models and how they affect derivatives markets.

Chapters 11 and 12 examine (in two parts) the role of derivatives with reference to emerging markets in particular and developing countries in general. They deal not only with derivatives markets *in* emerging economies, but also with the use of derivative markets *by* emerging market entities, and the effects *on* emerging economies of derivatives which have emerging market risks as the 'underlying'. They present case studies from Brazil, Chile, China, India, Mexico, Uruguay and Kazakhstan.

Chapter 13 deals with financial regulation in general, with particular reference to derivatives. It looks at the economic arguments for and against regulation and de-regulation.

Chapter 14 assesses the role of derivatives, and finance more generally, in economic development.

Chapter 15 presents the authors' recommendations towards a pragmatic and practical approach for public policy makers.

Notes and References

[1] Speech on *Financial derivatives* before the Futures Industry Association, Boca Raton, Florida, 19 March 1999. Available at: http://www.federalreserve.gov/boarddocs/speeches/1999/19990319.htm. Accessed on 11 July 2014.

[2] Edited excerpts from the *Berkshire Hathaway Annual Report for 2002*. Available at: http://www.fintools.com/docs/Warren%20Buffet%20on%20Derivatives.pdf. Accessed on 11 July 2014.

[3] Throughout this book, the $ symbol, unless otherwise indicated, denotes US dollars.

[4] 1995 figure includes foreign exchange derivatives.

[5] 2000 figure is an estimate based on 2001 data.

[6] Excluding exchange traded futures and options on commodities and individual shares – this figure is, therefore, an underestimate of the total volume of derivatives trading.

[7] Readers interested in understanding the derivatives markets can turn to many titles available in the markets including *Derivatives (2nd Edition)*, T. V. Somanathan, V. Anantha Nageswaran and Harsh Gupta, McGraw Hill Education, New Delhi, forthcoming.

2

Definition and Typology

In chemistry, a derivative is defined ... as a 'substance related structurally to another substance and theoretically derivable from it' or 'a substance that can be made from another substance'. Derivatives in finance work on the same principle.

Rene M. Stulz[1]

For all its current importance in finance, the term 'derivative' is of recent origin. Just a generation ago, readers may have assumed that the term related to mathematics (as in 'second derivative of a function') or chemistry (as in 'derivatives of carbon'). The acclaimed book *Inside the Financial Futures Markets* by Mark J. Powers and D. Vogel, published in 1984[2] and dealing exclusively with (what are now called) derivatives, did not use the word even once. This chapter looks at what derivatives are, how they may be classified and finally, what they are not.

Definition of derivative

A conventional and commonly used definition is as follows:

A derivative security is a contract designed in such a way that its price is *derived* from the price of an underlying asset.

Thus, a gold futures contract derives its price from the price of gold, which is the 'underlying' asset; an option on crude oil derives its price from the price of crude oil; a currency swap derives its value from the exchange rate of the currencies involved.

The first, and minor, problem with this definition is that the 'underlying' may not be an asset in the conventional sense: the underlying may be a liability (such as a bond) or an index (like the Standard & Poors or S&P 500 share index). However, this is a semantic issue. Mathematically, a liability is a negative asset. An index is the average value of a set of assets or liabilities. Whether something is an asset or liability also depends on whose perspective is involved.

The second and bigger problem is that certain instruments now widely considered as 'derivatives' are based on the occurrence of events (such as a debt default), which do not themselves have a 'price' in the common sense meaning of the term.

A more comprehensive version of this definition would run as follows:

A derivative security is a contract designed in such a way that its price is *derived* from the value of an underlying asset, liability, index or event. ['Derivative security' and 'underlying asset, liability, index or event' are usually shortened to simply 'derivative' and 'underlying' respectively.]

The main improvement here is the addition of the word 'event'. This definition is not perfect, as will be discussed later in this chapter, but it forms a good starting point to understand the different kinds of derivatives.

The price of the derivative is linked to the value of the underlying in a predictable way. Because of this, transactions in derivatives can be used:

- as a *substitute* for a transaction in the underlying asset – an investor who seeks to speculate on share prices may, instead of buying a basket of shares, buy a stock index futures contract;

- to *offset the risk* of price or value changes in the underlying – a person who holds a commodity and wants to protect against the risk of that commodity falling in value may buy a call option on that commodity.

Typology

Derivatives can be classified on the basis of:

- type of contract;
- nature of underlying;
- manner of trading;
- possibility of delivery; and
- nature of price relationship.

These modes of classification are not mutually exclusive.

Type of contract

Derivatives can be divided into the following types:

- Forwards: A forward contract is one where a buyer and seller agree *on a price now for the delivery of an asset at a predetermined future date.* The price remains constant regardless of fluctuations in the interim or the market price on that future date.

- Futures (a subset of forwards): A futures contract is a forward contract *traded on an organized exchange* rather than on a bilateral basis. Futures contracts are entered into and executed through a clearing house, which becomes the intermediary between the buyer and seller and guarantees performance of the contract by both parties.

- Options: Options are one-sided contracts where one party acquires the right, *but without the obligation,* to buy or sell the underlying asset at a predetermined price on a predetermined date; a premium is paid for acquiring this right. It is entirely the discretion of the option buyer whether or not to actually buy or sell on the predetermined date. A one-sided right to buy is called a call option, while a one-sided right to sell is called a put option.

- Swaps: Swaps are (in essence) transactions where two parties *exchange one stream of cash flows for another.* One party, which has an asset that earns a fixed rate of interest, may exchange this income stream with another party, which has an asset earning a floating rate of interest. Or, a party with an income stream in rupees may exchange this with another party having an income stream in dollars.

- Other derivatives, which may be called complex or exotic derivatives. These may:

  (a) be a mix of the above types (for example a 'swaption', which is an option to enter into a swap);

  (b) involve underlyings that are not simple or 'real' assets or liabilities but are indices or events – for example, the underlying on a weather forward contract may be the rainfall level at a particular place and the underlying on a credit default swap may be the event of a default by a particular borrower.

Nature of underlying (risk class)

Derivatives can be classified based on the nature of the underlying into:

- commodity derivatives (gold, silver, corn, wheat, jute, cotton, pepper, copper, electricity etc.);
- financial derivatives (equity, interest rate /debt instrument, currency, volatility, inflation etc.);
- weather or catastrophe derivatives (e.g. derivatives based on rainfall or other weather conditions);
- credit derivatives (e.g. credit default swaps); and so on.

Another basis of classification by underlying is between:

- real (sometimes called tradable[3]) underlying; and
- notional (sometimes called non-tradable) underlying

A notional underlying is one, which does not exist, and cannot be traded as such, in the spot market. For instance, one can buy futures contracts in gold and it is also possible to physically buy gold. Hence, gold is a real underlying. However, while one can buy futures and options on the Nifty or the Financial Times Stock Exchange (FTSE) Index, one cannot buy the index itself – by definition, it is an abstract mathematical expression of the prices of various shares. Even the composition of the index may change from time to time. Hence, the index is a notional underlying.

While an index-based underlying is often a proxy for a real underlying (e.g. the Nifty index is based on the prices of real shares that can be purchased), there are other notional underlying types, which do not exist at all. There are now derivatives based on 'volatility' of prices (itself an abstract concept). There are also derivatives based on weather conditions, though clearly one cannot buy or sell heat or cold, or rainfall or snow. Thus, a notional underlying can be:

- based on a well-known index of actual prices (e.g. share price indices like the Nifty or FTSE 100 or S&P 500) which are called 'index derivatives'; or
- based on an indicator (usually called 'index') created specifically for the derivative contract (for example the volatility index or weather indicators used in weather derivatives).

There are also derivative contracts where the *underlying is another derivative* — this, in turn, may be real or notional. For instance, in the gold options markets, the underlying of a 100 oz. option contract is usually not 100 oz. of gold itself but 100 oz. of gold futures.

The distinction between real and notional underlying has no impact on the manner of trading or pricing, but it does have regulatory implications. Contracts with a real underlying are relatively easier to regulate because the spot market in the underlying acts as an anchor for valuation of the derivative and it is difficult for prices to diverge from the intrinsic value of the underlying. For example, when there is an active spot market in gold, it is difficult to have a futures price which is irrationally higher or lower. On the other hand, in notional derivatives, there is no market in the 'underlying' and the underlying is measured by some authority or agency. For this reason, *notional derivatives have a higher level of regulatory risk: it is possible for the calculation of the underlying to be manipulated.* In 2012, scandals emerged involving the 'fixing' (literal and figurative) of the London Interbank Offered Rate (LIBOR), which is set by banks among themselves and acts as the base for many derivatives. Reports of manipulation of the cost of living index by the official statistical agency in Argentina, also illustrate the potential risk even with government statistics.[4] Indices that are developed specifically for derivatives trading are even more vulnerable than indices that are widely used for other purposes.

Derivatives can also be divided into *price-based* and *event-based* underlying. Price-based derivatives are those where the price of the derivative is derived from the *price of the underlying*. Most futures and options, and conventional cash flow swaps (i.e., interest rate and currency swaps) are price-based and the price fluctuates in accordance with the price of the underlying. However, some derivatives are event based. Cash flows are triggered (or not triggered) by the occurrence (or non-occurrence) of *specified events* and the event is the (notional) underlying. Thus, in a catastrophe bond, the occurrence of an earthquake may lead to the waiver of the principal on the bond. In a credit default swap, the occurrence of a default by the borrower may trigger a payment to the swap holder. The price of the derivative will fluctuate in accordance with the expected probability of the event. In such cases, credit default swaps being a prime example, the price of the derivative sometimes becomes a proxy or public expression of the expected probability of the event.

Manner of trading

Derivatives may either be **exchange-traded** (i.e., traded on an organized exchange with the exchange being the intermediary) or may be OTC, meaning that they are entered into bilaterally between two parties without an exchange acting as an intermediary. Among OTC derivatives, some (e.g. many OTC swaps) may have several features of exchange-traded derivatives like standardized contract terms. Some OTC contracts may be purely custom contracts drawn up between two parties.

This distinction too has regulatory implications. Exchange-traded derivatives are generally more difficult to manipulate and exposures are more transparent because of the regular publication of aggregated data.

Another distinction in terms of manner of trading (within exchange-traded derivatives) is between *open outcry* (where prices are openly shouted out on the floor of the exchange) and online or *screen-based trading*, where prices are transmitted electronically on computer screens. Open outcry is the older and now less common method, although there are those who believe it had some advantages in transparency and price discovery.

Possibility of delivery

Some derivative contracts have the possibility of actual physical delivery of the underlying (whether a commodity or financial instrument). So, if one buys cotton futures, one can receive a physical quantity of cotton at the maturity of the contract; if one sells pepper futures, one can deliver an equivalent quantity of pepper in settlement of the contract (and most commodity futures are of this kind).

In other derivative contracts, delivery is not possible and contracts are settled by means of paying financial values equivalent to the underlying; instead of receiving or delivering the underlying, the market price is paid and actual physical delivery has to be arranged separately.

Obviously, delivery is not possible in contracts with notional underlying and all such contracts are settled financially. Among contracts with a real deliverable, some do not allow physical delivery. In some cases, especially in options markets, the underlying may be a futures contract and that contract may allow physical delivery. From a regulatory perspective, contracts where physical delivery is possible are more difficult to manipulate than those where delivery is not possible, for the reasons already mentioned above when discussing real vs. notional derivatives.

Linearity of price relationship

Derivatives can also be divided into groups based on the mathematical relationship between the price of the derivative and the price of the underlying, particularly whether the relationship is linear or non-linear. When the price of the underlying rises or falls, the price of a futures contract will usually rise or fall proportionately. For instance, if the price of gold in the spot market increases by 5 per cent at any price level, the futures price will rise by a very similar proportion. Since there is broadly a 'straight line' relationship between the price of the underlying and the price of the derivative, this is a 'linear derivative'.

However, a similar increase in the price of the underlying may or may not result in a proportionate change of an options contract on the same underlying. If the strike price (the price mentioned in the options contract in the event the option is exercised by the buyer) is far from the current spot price, a 5 per cent change in the price of gold may produce only a 0.2 per cent change in the price of the option. However, a 5 per cent change when the current gold price is close to the strike price, may produce a 5 per cent change in the price of the option. Thus, the relationship between the derivative price and the underlying price has discontinuities, though it approximates to linearity in some cases (for instances deep-in-the-money options).

Futures and swaps are normally linear derivatives while options are normally non-linear, but there are exceptional circumstances when these general rules may not hold. Event-based derivatives do not have an 'underlying price'; they may however exhibit a linear or non-linear relationship vis-à-vis the *probability of the occurrence of the event.*

The term linear should not be taken to mean that the mathematical relationship is exactly or precisely linear; it would be more accurate to say that linear derivatives are those where the relationship *approximates* to a linear one.

From a regulatory perspective, the implications of changes in the underlying market on the derivatives market are easier to predict and understand for linear derivatives.

Descriptions of derivative securities

When describing derivatives, some or all of the classes in the typology may be used, and this can be confusing to the uninitiated. The first three classes –

type, underlying risk class and manner of trading are the most important. For instance, if an instrument is called an 'OTC copper option' it signifies that:

- the type of contract is options;
- the underlying is copper; and
- the contract is OTC and not exchange traded.

If another instrument is called a 'non-deliverable rupee forward', it is a forward contract in Indian rupees against which rupees cannot actually be delivered and must be settled financially in the host currency (say, US dollars).

Table 2.1 presents some data showing the relative importance of different kinds of derivatives on the basis of the three main methods of classification (type of contract, nature of underlying risk class and manner of trading).

Table 2.1: Major derivative types by size in terms of notional amount outstanding [1]
(Figures in $ billion)

Underlying (risk class)	Type and manner of trading						
	Exchange traded futures	Exchange traded options	OTC options	OTC forwards	Swaps (OTC)	Others (OTC)	Total (all types)
Interest rate	23806	38372	50191	89434	437066	579	639448
Equity and commodity	1175[3]	5427	5329	2350	1403	2727[2]	18411
Foreign exchange	227	117	15077	39575	26318	56	81370
Credit default	–	N/a	348	27	24470	–	24845
Other	–	N/a	15	63	N/a	–	78
Total (all risk classes)	25208	43916	70960	131449	489257	3362	764452

Source: Authors' calculations from BIS data

Notes: (1) Data as of end-June 2013. (2) Gold and Other Commodities only. (3) Only on Equity indices; single stock futures and options and commodities not included as data in 'Notional Amount Outstanding' since these categories not available in BIS database.

Weaknesses in the conventional definition

The conventional definition of derivatives, while useful in explanation, remains conceptually unsatisfactory. One could argue, on a reading of the definition, that equity shares in a coal-mining company are 'derivatives' because the price of the share is 'derived' from the price of coal (at least in the short run when quantity of output is constant). One could argue that all bonds are derivatives with the corresponding interest rate as the underlying. Likewise, the price of a mutual fund or exchange traded fund (ETF), which mimics, say, the Dow Jones Industrial Average, is derived from the value of the index. Yet, these are not normally considered derivatives and should not be.

Interestingly, in the academic literature there are signs of definitional inflation with more and more financial and real instruments being labelled as derivatives of some kind. In an attempt to show the antiquity of derivatives, some authors have regarded bills of exchange to be 'derivatives'. Hammurabi's code from eighteenth century BC Babylon provided for crop loans to be waived in times of natural disaster and it is argued that this is a put option.[5] There are those who argue that the ownership of a mine is nothing but a 'real option' whose value depends on the extent of the reserves discovered. (Lynch, sarcastically, suggested that a painting is a derivative as it is 'an asset whose value is derived from the market's demand for such a painting and the acclaim of the painter' and cash is 'an asset whose value is derived from the trust people have in cash'.)[6]

Another issue is that the structure of some event-based derivatives appear to be little different from insurance contracts. A credit default swap (CDS) is an agreement whereby one party makes a periodic payment to another in return for a pay-off by the other party if (and only if) a specified event happens. In economic terms, how is this different from insurance? And if these are derivatives, should insurance contracts not be considered derivatives too? In economic terms, how different is a weather futures contract from an old-fashioned bet on the weather? If a weather futures contract is a derivative, should a bet not be one too? And if two people enter into a contract, which involves a payment based on which team wins a cricket match, that seems to fall within the definition – there is a 'contract'(albeit not enforceable in law) and the price depends on a particular outcome.

Lynch provided a more precise (if more academic) definition of derivatives:

All derivatives are contracts between two counterparties in which the payoffs to and from each counterparty depend on the outcome of one or more extrinsic, future, uncertain events or metrics – that is, they are 'aleatory' contracts – and in which each counterparty expects such outcome to be opposite to that expected by the other counterparty.[7]

He added that they are zero-sum transactions.

The key addition to the expanded definition earlier in this chapter is that the two parties have *opposite expectations* (or desires) on the direction in which the price will move. This definition has the merit of reducing the errors of inclusion inherent in the conventional definition. It would exclude equities, bonds and the like because the 'counter parties' do not expect opposite outcomes: the holder of a bond does not want or expect a default and nor does the issuer; the interest of the shareholder and the company are not opposite to each other.

The practical disadvantage with Lynch's definition is that it would potentially include all wagers and insurance contracts. Lynch argues in favour of this. The distinction (or lack of one) between hedging-through-derivatives and insurance on one hand, and between speculation-through-derivatives and gambling on the other, have important implications for public policy and financial regulation.

Are insurance contracts derivatives? Or are some derivatives actually insurance policies?

Credit default swaps are regarded as derivatives while insurance policies are not. Credit default swaps involve the payment of an annual or periodic sum to the swap writer in return for which the swap holder is guaranteed the payment of a pre-agreed sum in the event of a default on a debt security by the issuer of the security. *Prima facie*, this has the essential elements of an insurance contract: a fixed and assured premium in return for the payment of the 'sum assured' if and when a stipulated event occurs. There are, however, differences – some intrinsic to the concept and some imposed by regulators.

Firstly, insurance has traditionally operated in the realm of *risk* rather than *uncertainty*. Knight, in his classic on risk and uncertainty, divided the probabilities of uncertain events into three kinds:

1. *A priori* probabilities, which are derived deductively, such as in rolling dice.

2. Statistical probabilities, which are generated by empirical evaluation of relative frequencies, as in life insurance.

3. Estimates, in which there is *no valid basis of any kind*[8] for classifying instances.[9]

Knight classified the first two – *a priori* and empirical probabilities – as 'objective' probability and the third as 'subjective' probability. He used objective and subjective probability to distinguish between risk and uncertainty respectively.[10] He then used this distinction (between objective and subjective probabilities or risk and uncertainty) as the basis for distinguishing between 'insurable risks and non-insurable risks'.[11] The probability of rain on a particular day in a particular city can be measured from historical weather records – this is an objective probability. But if a person asserts – without reference to data – that 'there is a 90 per cent chance of rain today' that is a subjective probability. Price variability on most underlyings are not subject to reasonable calculation of objective probabilities. For example, it is not possible to estimate 'the probability of the stock market rising by more than 10 points tomorrow' without a large margin of error. This kind of risk (or more precisely, uncertainty) cannot be covered by insurance – but can be hedged against.[12]

Secondly, insurance often involves situations where the risks for individual policyholders are independent of each other – in most situations, an accident to one car is not correlated with accidents to another car. (This may not apply during natural disasters like Hurricane Sandy or the Asian tsunami of 2004 when thousands of cars may be affected at the same time: which is why insurance policies often exclude certain kinds of catastrophes or require specific additional premia.) This enables risks to be pooled so that the overall cost to the insurer is predictable and manageable. Price risks cannot be pooled – when the stock market falls, all holders of shares suffer a loss at the same time and when it rises they all benefit at the same time.

Thirdly, insurance contracts require the presence of an '*insurable interest*': the purchaser of an insurance policy must have an interest in the continued existence or well-being of the subject matter of the contract such that the purchaser *does not desire the contingent event to happen*. Thus, one cannot take out an insurance policy on a stranger's house or car or life. The primary purpose of this requirement is to prevent moral hazard: without it, one could take a policy on a stranger's house and then work towards damaging that house and then collecting money on it. This would create an incentive (or negative externality) that is clearly contrary to public policy. The requirement has been long-standing and is intrinsic to the concept of insurance, but is also enshrined in the law.

Fourthly, writers of insurance policies are required by law to *hold reserves* against the value of the policies they have issued and the extent of these reserves is broadly related to actuarial calculations based on historical experience of the probability of the event occurring.

Of these, the last two are the most important from a regulatory point of view. There are many who argue strongly that CDSs must be treated and regulated as insurance and not as derivatives. (While Lynch argued that, in concept, insurance contracts are derivatives, he did recommend that all credit derivatives should have an insurable interest and reserve requirement.) Some of these issues will be discussed further in the chapters on regulation.

How is speculation different from gambling?

Is speculation merely a more positive term for gambling? This was never an easy question to answer, and the expansion of derivatives into ever more esoteric areas has made it even more difficult. Gambling has been defined as 'a reallocation of wealth, on the basis of deliberate risk, involving gain to one party and loss to another, usually without the introduction of productive work on either side'.[13]

Baer and Saxon in their seminal work on futures trading in the 1940s[14] argued that speculation is based on price risks that exist anyway without having to be created, whereas in many forms of gambling (like horse racing or card games) the financial risk is deliberately created. Hieronymus[15] also emphasizes this difference. The risk of a change in commodity prices exists with or without speculation and is not 'created' to enable wagering. Speculation may merely transfer the risk from the hedger to the speculator. Baer and Saxon also argued that speculation was economically useful while gambling is not; the merits of this argument rest on the assumption that speculation is economically beneficial, a matter considered in greater detail elsewhere in this book. They also pointed out that speculative futures contracts are enforceable by statute while gambling agreements are not legally enforceable (and in many countries, prohibited). This is a legal rather than economic distinction, and the law is derived from an ethical principle.

Much of the ethical distinction would appear to depend on two tests: firstly, whether the derivative is *creating a new risk* and secondly, whether there is 'productive work' or *some larger economic purpose* served by the transaction even if the transaction itself is speculative. The advocates of derivatives markets argue that speculators in the markets are merely shifting existing risks and are doing productive work through superior analysis and their resultant contributions to market information and liquidity. (These issues are discussed in the ensuing chapter on the economic functions of derivatives.) On the other hand, there are persuasive arguments that a subset of derivatives transactions – those where both parties are speculators and there is no hedging interest – are no different in concept, intent or effect from wagers. Many of the new derivatives do appear to create new financial risks. They claim an economically useful purpose but it often appears to be far-fetched. There are now 'election derivatives, terrorism derivatives, airline seat derivatives, motion picture box office receipt derivatives ... Higgs Boson derivatives' etc.[16] This is an important and complex issue for regulators, which will be discussed further in the context of regulation.

Notes and References

[1] R. M. Stulz, *Should We Fear Derivatives?* NBER Working Paper No. 10574, June 2004.

[2] M. J. Powers and D. Vogel, *Inside the Financial Futures Markets* (2nd edition). John Wiley & Sons, New York, 1984.

[3] The terms tradable and non-tradable are not used for this purpose in this book because of the potential for confusion with the economic terms 'tradable and non-tradable goods and services' used in the context of international trade.

[4] 'Argentina's New Inflation Index: Pricing Power—Will the Country's Statisticians Now Be Allowed To Do Their Work', *The Economist*, 22 February 2014.

[5] S. Kummer and C. Pauletto, *The History of Derivatives: A Few Milestones*. EFTA Seminar on Regulation of Derivatives Markets, Zurich, 3 May 2012.

[6] T. E. Lynch, ,'Derivatives: A Twenty–first Century Understanding', *Loyola University Chicago Law Journal*, Vol. 43, No. 1, 1–51.

[7] T. E. Lynch, *ibid.*

[8] Emphasis his.

[9] F. H. Knight, *Risk, Uncertainty and Profit.* Houghton Mifflin, Boston, 1921, 224–25.

[10] F. H. Knight, *Risk, Uncertainty and Profit.* op. cit., 233.

[11] S. F. LeRoy and L. D. Singell, Jr., 'Knight on Risk and Uncertainty', *Journal of Political Economy*, Vol. 95, No. 2, 394–406, April 1987.

[12] T. V. Somanathan, *Derivatives.* Tata McGraw Hill, New Delhi, 1998.

[13] S. Borna and J. Lowry, 'Gambling and Speculation', *Journal of Business Ethics*, Vol. 6, No. 3, 219–20, 1987.

14 J. B. Baer and O. G. Saxon, *Commodity Exchanges and Futures Trading*. Harper and Row, New York, 1948.

15 T. A. Hieronymus, *The Economics of Futures Trading*. Commodity Research Bureau, New York, 1977.

16 T. E. Lynch, 'Gambling by Another Name: The Challenge of Purely Speculative Derivatives', *Stanford Journal of Law, Business and Finance*, Vol. 17, No. 1, 93, 2011.

3

The Economic Functions of Derivatives Markets

...[T]hrough risk management using derivatives and dynamic hedges, financial firms like banks and investment banks reduce the risk of their financing activities to acceptable levels. This allows them to raise money from investors and fund firms with risky but worthwhile projects, thus expanding access and spreading wealth.

Raghuram G. Rajan and Luigi Zingales (2003)[1]

As was seen in Chapter 1, derivatives markets are now so large that they exert a significant effect on the overall economy. A large number of people now directly or indirectly earn (or lose) money from trading on derivatives and for them, the interesting issue is 'how do these markets work'. This book is more concerned with the existential question of 'why should they exist' and the policy question of 'how should they work'. To that end, this chapter examines the economic (as opposed to financial) functions, which derivatives markets perform. The term 'economic functions' is used to imply *socially useful* functions, i.e., those that promote welfare, and some economists have used the term 'social functions' for these.

The 'conventional' view in the literature of economics has been that derivatives markets perform several useful functions. The function on which there is the least disagreement is the hedging or risk transference function.

Hedging or risk transfer: The primary function

The primary economic function of most derivatives markets, especially the simple derivatives, is the *hedging function* also known as the risk-shifting or risk transference function. Derivatives enable market participants to hedge themselves (i.e., indemnify themselves) *from adverse price movements in the underlying in which they face a price risk.*[2] The ability to hedge enables them to transfer unwanted risk to others who are willing to bear that risk.

In futures markets, hedging is accomplished by buying or selling the futures contract. If a hedger (say, a textile mill owner requiring cotton) wants to protect himself against a *rising* price, he would buy the futures contract. If the spot price rises, the price of the futures contract moves in the same direction as the spot price. By selling the futures contract at the higher price, the hedger makes a profit; this profit approximately offsets the loss incurred on the spot market. If the hedger (say, a cotton farmer) is seeking protection against a *falling* price, she/he would sell the futures contract. If the price falls as expected, the price of the futures contract will fall by approximately the same amount as the spot price. The hedger then buys back the contract at a lower price and makes a profit, which neutralizes the loss incurred on the spot market. In both cases, the hedger is effectively neutralizing risk – but favourable risk is also neutralized. Thus, if the spot price falls, the miller will lose on the futures contract and will have to forgo the favourable price risk that he would otherwise have benefitted from. The price of avoiding unfavourable risk in a futures contract is the forgoing of favourable risk.

Options contracts arguably perform the hedging function even better than the futures markets. In an options contract, the cotton miller would buy a call option while the cotton farmer would buy a put option. The options would only be exercised if the expected adverse price risk came true. Thus, hedging through options does not involve forgoing favourable risk. If the adverse risk does not materialize, the option buyer loses only the premium. Overall, *options are more effective but more expensive* than futures – they are lower risk and lower return hedges. In the case of other derivatives, likes swaps and complex derivatives, the exact cost-benefit trade-off varies depending on the specific characteristics of a particular contract but the broad principle is the same.

A derivatives market normally comprises hedgers (seeking to avoid risk) and speculators (seeking to take risk to earn profits). Therefore, a derivatives transaction could happen in three ways:

- Case I: between two hedgers
- Case II: between a hedger and a speculator
- Case III: between two speculators

In the first case, a hedger needing protection against a price increase (long hedger) deals with a hedger needing protection against a price decrease (short hedger). In theory, there could be a derivatives market where all participants are hedgers, but such a market may not 'clear' because there may be too many short hedgers or long hedgers. Except by coincidence, it is unlikely that the number of short hedgers and long hedgers would be equal. This would leave some hedgers unable to hedge. This is why the speculator's role becomes important.

In the second case, one party is a hedger and the other a speculator. The rationale for the speculator to enter into this deal and take risk can come from one of two sources. The first possibility is that the speculator may possess (at least in his own opinion) superior knowledge or information about future price movements and thus hope to earn a profit by taking a view opposite to that of the hedger. Thus, while the hedger may wish to avoid the risk of a price increase, the speculator may be confident the price will not increase. The second possibility is that speculators do not have any informational advantage, but receive an implicit price premium from hedgers in the terms of the contract. Therefore, in the long run, the speculator earns this premium as reward for assuming risk. (Keynes was the first to postulate that the speculator might require a premium for this and hence predicted that on average, the futures price – ignoring carrying costs etc. – would display a 'normal backwardation' *vis-à-vis* the spot price. Empirical evidence on the existence of a normal backwardation has been inconclusive.)

However, when a market allows speculation, it could obviously also have transactions of the third type – between one speculator and another. (Lynch calls this third kind of transaction a 'purely speculative transaction'.)[3] Here the two speculators may have opposite expectations about the market or one of them may be simply interested in earning the normal 'premium' by trading repeatedly while the other has (in his own opinion) an informational advantage.

Of these three cases, the first two are welfare-enhancing from an economic point of view. In the first case, even though the transaction is zero-sum (in that one party's gain from the hedge is the other party's loss) neither of them is seeking the gain, and risk is reduced for both. Both are benefited (receive positive utility) and no one is harmed.

In the second case, risk is transferred from one unwilling to bear it to another who seeks it and who may, by specializing in that activity, be more efficient in bearing it. While in theory there can be markets where risk is simply exchanged between those with opposite hedging needs, in most markets there is a net transfer of risk from hedgers to the speculators who come forward to assume it (in the hope of profiting from price changes). To the extent risks are shifted towards those willing to bear them, this is clearly beneficial to the economy and welfare increasing, in the same way that trade is beneficial. (This is sometimes called the 'gains-from-trade' argument for speculation.[4])

In the third case (i.e., the purely speculative transaction), one speculator gains at the expense of another. The welfare effects of this case are more complicated to assess. *Per se*, this is a zero-sum activity with no increase in welfare. It has some indirect effects which may be positive. It increases liquidity in the market (see liquidity function below), which benefits hedgers too. Secondly, the purely speculative transaction may be adding new information and thus aiding price discovery. These effects, in turn, lead to the third effect: there is a case in economic theory (which will be discussed in detail in Chapter 5) that speculation leads to derivatives having a *stabilizing effect on the prices of the underlying*.

However some, like Lynch, argue that the third case (purely speculative trading) is in fact welfare-decreasing because it creates risk where none existed before, it is nothing but gambling and it may have negative externalities including the creation of systemic risk and the diversion of scarce human and financial resources, which could otherwise have been used for more productive purposes.

Secondary functions

Other functions which some (but not all) derivatives markets may perform are the following:

The specialization function

Since derivatives typically require a speculator to deposit only a fraction of the value of the contract, they facilitate speculation. Speculators willingly take on risks that hedgers want to offload. The speculator takes a position in the market not to reduce risk but to take risk and to profit thereby. These speculators specialize in acquiring knowledge about these markets. This produces the efficiencies of specialization and thereby increases overall economic efficiency to the extent that speculators are more capable of bearing risk. This is sometimes identified separately from the risk transfer function as the *specialization* or *division of labour* function.

Price discovery function

Derivatives markets provide a mechanism by which diverse and scattered opinions of the future are coalesced into one readily discernible number which provides a 'consensus of knowledgeable thinking.'[5] Even critics concede that derivatives markets are faster at capturing new information.[6] Exchange-traded futures improve price discovery in two ways:

- Firstly, not all underlying commodities or financial instruments have active spot markets with transparent price disclosure. In some cases, the spot market is divided into so many fine varieties of one commodity that a single number is not available. In such cases, the futures market – with its standardized deliverable variety – establishes, more quickly and clearly, a transparent benchmark for the current price.

- Secondly, even where there is a transparent and active spot market, the spot market does not provide any information about future prices. Thus while well-organized spot markets, like the stock market or the tea auction, perform a price discovery function too, they do so only in respect of the spot (i.e., current) price. The futures markets help in *discovery of the expected future price*. Futures prices are not identical to expected prices in the future, because they reflect carrying costs and/or the convenience of holding a commodity and/or the premium speculators charge for providing the hedging service. Nevertheless, futures prices provide an expression of the consensus of today's expectations about some point in the future.

The process of future price discovery also leads to the *inter-temporal resource allocation function,* by which market participants are able to compare the current and future prices and decide the optimal allocation of their stocks (inventories) between immediate sale and storage for future sale.[7] This signal tends to reduce price fluctuations from one period to another.

The relationship between options markets and the price of the underlying is much weaker than that between a futures market and its corresponding spot market. This is because options are contingent claims – e.g. a call option may or may not ultimately increase the demand for the commodity. It is only when exercise is carried out, or likely to be carried out, that the options market affects demand or supply in the underlying market. Therefore, options do not perform any useful price discovery function for the underlying.

Swaps do not help in price discovery for the underlying, but do perform the function of *discovering the 'price' of interest rate and currency risks.* Thus the 'swap rate' in an interest rate swap establishes the extent to which the market expects interest rates to fluctuate.

Complex derivatives generally do not perform a price discovery function *for the underlying*, but some of them – for instance, CDSs – may perform the function of *discovering the price of hedging*. Prices of event-based derivatives, when combined with data on historical average probability of the event can be used to 'discover' the probability of the event occurring. For example the price of the CDS on a particular type of credit may be 6 per cent; that level of market interest rate may correspond with a credit rating of CCC which, in turn, would (from historic data kept by credit rating agencies) indicate a particular probability of default. During the 2012 Eurozone financial crisis, for instance, the prices of credit default swaps were frequently cited as 'probabilities' of various countries defaulting.

By publishing and disseminating the prices that are 'discovered', derivatives markets also perform an *information function*.

Financing function

Swaps and similar derivatives widen borrowers' access to finance by allowing them to raise resources in different currencies or different interest rate formats (fixed vs. floating), while avoiding unwanted currency or interest rate risk. Thus, they perform a *financing function*. Without currency and interest rate swaps, it would be far more risky for companies in developing countries to raise external borrowings in foreign currency since the currency and interest rate risks might make them too risky. Thus, these instruments clearly do facilitate the movement of capital across borders towards the most productive use and thereby promote welfare. Credit default swaps also increase the willingness of financial institutions to lend to borrowers in remote markets and thus widen borrowers' access to credit.

Most derivatives markets operate on a *fractional margin* whereby the buyer and seller deposit only a fraction of the contract value (say 10 per cent) at the time of entering into it. Thus, derivatives transactions and futures contracts in particular, provide 'gearing' or 'leverage'. This is in itself a means of financing.

It has been argued that the use of standardized futures contracts makes it easier to raise finance against stocks of commodities, since lenders have an assurance of standardized quality and quick liquidity. This ease of financing helps increase the overall level of economic activity and is thus welfare-increasing. This claim is however weakened by the fact that this is not unique to futures or options: organized and well regulated spot markets could perform this function just as well.

Complex derivatives may also perform a useful financing function by making finance available for productive purposes that would otherwise not have been financed. While rigorous evidence is hard to come by, there are several anecdotal examples – one is referred to by Rajan and Zingales[8] viz. the privatization of Rhone Poulenc in France. The availability of a derivative instrument enabled the government to offer shares in the company to workers but with a guaranteed return, thereby overcoming workers' resistance.

Liquidity function

The fractional margin in derivatives markets (referred to above) enables traders to buy and sell a much larger volume of contracts than in a spot market. Standardization also means that transactions relating to many different varieties in the spot market may be channeled into one futures or options contract (e.g. transactions to hedge 10 different types of crude oil may be channeled through the Brent Crude futures contract). This makes derivatives markets very liquid and usually more liquid than the spot market in the same underlying, so that large transactions can be put through with ease. This *liquidity function* performed by derivatives makes the market more efficient as a whole with a lower gap between 'bid' and 'ask' prices.

The importance of the liquidity function depends partly on whether the credit markets in a given country are efficient. In India, for instance, it is not easy to finance spot market commodity or equity transactions through bank lending. The difficulties, which a trader would have to undergo to get approval for a loan against either shares or stocks of physical commodities, are considerable. The fractional margin system affords such traders a simple and automatic liquidity mechanism. This results in the overall volume in the market increasing considerably. The additional volume makes the market deeper and thus helps all participants put through their transactions quickly and at low spreads. This function is not performed by spot markets even if well organized and regulated. (This appears to be the main reason for the extraordinary popularity of single stock futures in India.)

Market completion function

Economic theorists have shown (through formidably complicated mathematics in what is known as the Arrow-Debreu theorem, named after the Nobel prize winning economists Kenneth Arrow and Gerard Debreu), that economic welfare is maximized through a perfectly competitive equilibrium. Such an equilibrium can only exist if, *inter alia*, markets are 'complete', i.e., *if markets exist in which to enter all possible types of contracts including insurance contracts and investment contracts linking the present and future.*

Derivatives trading creates new markets and, thereby, increases the extent of market completion. Since completeness of markets is an ideal situation, the incremental increase in completion represented by derivatives markets – it is argued – must (by bringing reality closer to the theoretical ideal) be a good thing and must be a source of greater economic welfare. Indeed a fairly large body of literature on derivatives and financial innovation is based on the assumption that incremental market completion is *ipso facto* a welcome and desirable outcome. This view was highly influential in the 1990s and the early years of the twenty-first century. This validity of this view is addressed separately in the next chapter.

Price stabilization function

The speculative activity on futures markets is widely believed to exercise a stabilising influence on spot prices by reducing the amplitude of short-term fluctuations. On the other hand, there are many who argue that these markets destabilize prices (and, in some cases, are causes of inflation in food prices). This is dealt with in greater detail in Chapters 5 to 7.

Socially useful functions of derivatives – an assessment

Having enumerated the functions that these markets are theoretically expected or believed to perform, it is useful to assess how effective and useful these functions are in practice.

The primary function of hedging or risk transference, is largely non-controversial. Most derivatives markets demonstrably do perform this function successfully most of the time. There is no dispute that futures, options and swaps are in fact used as hedges by many economic entities. It is intuitively obvious and empirically proven that hedging serves a useful economic purpose. For a simple example of a sector where hedging is the predominant motive for derivatives transactions and has a beneficial effect, one need not look further than import-export trade. Derivatives in their simplest form (forward contracts) have fulfilled for many decades the need of both exporters and importers for protection against the risk of currency fluctuation. A large proportion of import and export transactions involves short-term forward currency contracts to hedge the exchange rate variations between the time of sale and the time of payment. Even the worst critic of derivatives would not argue that this is speculation; indeed in the absence of forward cover, exporters and importers would effectively become unwitting and unwilling speculators in currency markets.

In many other markets too, ranging from commodities to equities and financial instruments, *some* participants are clearly using the markets for hedging. However, especially among financial derivatives, there are many markets where the hedging volume is very small relative to speculative volume. In these markets, *hedging is a mere side effect of what is really a market of the speculators, by the speculators and for the speculators.* In recent years there is evidence that many new financial derivative instruments have been created with the primary intent of acting as speculative vehicles. In such markets, purely speculative (i.e., speculator-to-speculator) transactions predominate by a large margin. If indirect and disputable benefits (like possible better information and possible price stabilisation) are excluded, such purely speculative transactions are at best, welfare-neutral and at worst, welfare-reducing. Because welfare reduction stems partly from diversion of productive resources and partly from the creation of systemic risk, the *likelihood of welfare-reduction increases with market size.* In such cases, a credible case can be made that the overall effect of the market – notwithstanding some benefit from the hedging function – is negative. This is one of the areas where regulators may have to make difficult choices.

A different issue is that derivatives markets sometimes fail to achieve the primary purpose of risk transfer. This occurs when the derivative price does not move in the same direction or to the same degree as the price of the underlying. The 'basis' (e.g. the difference between the spot and futures prices) may fluctuate so much that this change outweighs the hedging benefit – i.e., the volatility of the basis exceeds the volatility of the price itself. For example, a cotton mill may seek to hedge upward price risk by buying a futures contract whose deliverable variety (variety A) is not identical to the kind of cotton the mill needs (variety B). There is a price difference (called the 'basis') between A and B, but the normal expectation would be that the price of A and B would be closely correlated. But there may be a situation – say, an unexpected crop failure in the region where B is cultivated but not elsewhere – where A falls in price while B rises in price. In this case, the hedge might actually worsen the risk. This is a situation where the basis risk exceeds or is comparable to the price risk. While rare, this is not unknown especially in markets where delivery conditions allow a lot of variability in what is delivered and in markets with inadequate volume.

While even critics hardly ever question the existence of a useful risk transference function for derivatives, the secondary functions are more debatable.

The specialization function clearly appears to have validity when the speculator is an institution or experienced trader. Through their superior knowledge of the market and their ability to manage risks, they improve overall economic efficiency. However, the benefits of specialization may not hold in reality when many of the speculators are poorly informed persons who treat these as gambling vehicles and rely on the predictions of others without any clear understanding of the risks. In such cases, there is no *a priori* certainty that the shifting of risks from the hedgers to the speculators promotes economic welfare; it may merely shift the risk and affect the sharing of gains and losses.

The price discovery function (and its concomitant, the inter-temporal inventory allocation function) are clearly ones that futures markets do perform, but are more difficult to establish for other derivatives. The price discovery function is performed well only by derivatives traded openly, especially on organized exchanges. In recent years, a large volume of complex financial derivatives are traded OTC where the price discovery function is often not performed since prices are often not publicly disclosed. Further, the price discovery function assumes that speculators bring in useful (i.e., better) information. There is a view and some evidence that this is not necessarily the case; closely related to this is credible evidence that derivatives markets actually destabilize spot prices in certain circumstances and at certain times. To the extent this happens, derivatives markets are arguably leading to mis-discovery or the 'discovery of a wrong price'— in the manner that Columbus discovered 'India'. (These issues are discussed in greater detail in Chapter 6.)

The financing function is not seriously disputed. Fractional margins *ipso facto* are a form of financing. There is clear evidence that the presence of derivatives does make it easier to raise finance for productive activities, thus increasing welfare. However, critics argue that the leverage generated in some of these instruments is large *but often not visible to regulators*. It is, therefore, a source of high financial risk (when markets move unexpectedly) and this risk, it is argued, is disproportionate to any economic benefits – as illustrated by the global financial crisis.

The high levels of liquidity provided by active derivatives markets through standardization and fractional margins do increase market efficiency and this is not disputed. However, as will be seen in Chapter 6, the liquidity afforded by derivatives can also play a negative role in certain circumstances and indeed has been blamed for inflating commodity prices at certain junctures.

There is no doubt that market completion is increased by derivatives markets. However, whether this is a genuine 'function' at all (i.e., is market completion necessarily a useful thing) is a different question. This issue is dealt with at length in Chapter 4.

The price stabilization function (or alleged destabilization effect) is the most controversial of all. This is dealt with in detail in Chapters 5 to 7.

Notes and References

[1]   R. G. Rajan and L. Zingales, *Saving Capitalism from the Capitalists*. Crown Business, New York, 2003.

[2]   T. V. Somanathan, *Derivatives*. Tata McGraw Hill, New Delhi, 1998.

[3]   T. E. Lynch, 'Gambling by Another Name: The Challenge of Purely Speculative Derivatives', *Stanford Journal of Law, Business and Finance*, Vol. 17, No. 1, 68–130, 2011.

[4]   Jeremy C. Stein, 'Information Externalities and Welfare-Reducing Speculation', *Journal of Political Economy*, Vol. 95, No. 6, 1124, December 1987.

[5]   T. V. Somanathan, *Derivatives*. Tata McGraw Hill, New Delhi, 1998.

[6]   T. E. Lynch, *op. cit.*, 112.

[7]   C. L. Culp, 'The Social Functions of Derivatives', in *Financial Derivatives: Pricing and Risk Management*, edited by Robert Kolb and James A. Overdahl. John Wiley & Sons, New Jersey, 2010.

[8]   R. G. Rajan and L. Zingales, *Saving Capitalism from the Capitalists*. Crown Business, New York, 2003, 47–48.

4

Market Completion

The world is always second best, at best.

Avinash Dixit[1]

The preceding chapter on the economic functions of derivatives mentioned the concept of 'market completion' as a possible socially useful economic function of derivatives. A detailed examination of the Nobel Prize winning Arrow–Debreu theorem on which the market completion concept is based, would be beyond the scope of this book. However, the implications of market completion theory for derivatives, especially for regulation, are substantial. Therefore, this chapter explores this issue in greater detail. The Arrow-Debreu theorem and the various arguments it involves are extremely complex and abstruse, so (in the interest of the non-specialist reader) this chapter takes a highly simplified approach in order to enable the reader to grasp the essentials.

Kenneth Arrow and Gerard Debreu postulated that under certain conditions a welfare-maximizing *general equilibrium* could be attained.[2] This would be a welfare maximizing equilibrium in the sense that it would be Pareto-optimal, i.e., no change could be made to this equilibrium made without making at least one person worse off. This theoretical conclusion rests on a number of assumptions that do not obtain in real life. Two of the conditions required for this general equilibrium, and the most difficult to attain in practice, are the presence of perfect competition and the existence of complete markets. The Arrow–Debreu theorem has for many years been used as a philosophical basis for advocating free markets and *laissez faire* on the grounds that a perfectly competitive system will maximize welfare.

Apart from perfect competition, the utopian situation of the Arrow–Debreu equilibrium requires 'complete markets'. The term 'complete markets' or 'complete market' is used as a short form for the more accurate term a 'complete system of markets'. A complete system of markets is one where there is a market for every good. But the definition of 'good' for this purpose includes both a time element and a 'state-of-the-world' or prevailing environment. For example, conventionally one may define 'candles' as a good. For the purpose of complete markets, this is not a sufficient definition. The following are all theoretically different 'goods':

1. candles **on the night of 21st June** *if there is no power cut(outage)*
2. candles **during the day time on 21st June** *with or without a power cut*
3. candles **on the night of 21st June** *if there is a power cut*
4. candles **on Christmas Day** *with or without a power cut*

The underlined portions refer to time, while the italicized portions refer to the prevailing environment. Normally one may speak of the demand and supply of candles. However, if one thinks more carefully, one can see that the demand and supply of candles could be very different in each of the above situations – so much so that they are effectively 'different goods'. Item (1) is (in the Northern Hemisphere) a summer night with late sunsets and no power cuts. Item (2) is a summer day. Item (3) is a summer night but demand would clearly be higher because of the power cut. Item (4) is a case of a winter day (with an earlier sunset) and a festive occasion when more candles may be lit for decorative purposes than on other days. Complete markets would imply that there is a competitive market and price for each of the above goods. Thus, the participants in the market would quote different prices for each of these 'different goods'. The different situations are called 'states-of-the-world' and claims based on these different states are called state-contingent claims. By defining 'good' to include the date and the environment in which the commodity is consumed, economists are able to consider consumption, production and investment choices in a multi-period, uncertain world using largely the same utility theory developed to analyse timeless certainty.

One of the most lucid explanations of the market completion theory and its benefits is from Flood and is worth quoting *in extenso*:

> In the real world, systems of markets are not complete. The notion of completeness, however, is of interest for two reasons. First, it serves as a theoretical benchmark relative to which incompleteness can be assessed; such a comparison might, for example, suggest whether incompleteness implies inefficiency in a particular model. Second, although the notion of market completeness appears most often in theoretical discussions, the ideas involved can also be applied to more realistic problems. For example, in the state–preference context, markets for so–called 'derivative' securities—futures

and options—add value by providing investors with flexibility in fashioning their portfolios; thus, they make systems of markets less incomplete.[3]

... First and foremost, completing the system of markets makes everyone better off (or at least not worse off) by allowing risk to be transferred from the farmer to the speculator. Second, there is more than one way to complete an incomplete system of markets. Third, some means of completing a system of markets may be more cost-effective than others. One might even plausibly conjecture that all missing markets result from such transaction costs that render them cost-ineffective.

Other economists like Merton[4] and Pyle[5] also argued that the increase in 'Market completeness' was one of the ways in which new derivative securities increased economic welfare. From the basic proposition that complete markets is the welfare-maximizing ideal, comes the intuitively (seemingly) logical feeling that if completion is optimal, then incremental movement towards that ideal must be welfare-increasing; if a utopian state is reached by perfect completion, then every step forward towards that utopia must be good. Derivatives contracts of increasing complexity involve more and more specific states-of-the-world, and so must be welfare-increasing.

This intuitive and seemingly unassailable belief in the value of incremental market completion has become very widely accepted after the 1990s. For example, even Lord Turner (former head of the Financial Supervision Agency in the UK and known to be a sceptical commentator on the practical effects of derivatives) had no doubts on the *theoretical* position:

...the idea [is] that complex securitisation and derivatives must have delivered value added because they completed markets, making possible particular contracts not previously available, and thus allowing investors to pick precisely that combination of risk, return and liquidity which best met their preferences. In theory these benefits of 'market completion' follow *axiomatically*[6] from the Arrow Debreu theorem. ...[7]

Thus, the incremental market completion function of derivatives has attained the status of an axiom. A large body of academic literature on derivatives and financial innovation is based on the assumption that incremental market completion is *ipso facto* a welcome and desirable outcome.

Unfortunately, the incremental market completion function is not readily susceptible to empirical testing or verification. However, the point of this chapter is not that the benefits have not been empirically established; it is much more fundamental. The point is that *it is not even good theoretical economics.* What is intuitive is not necessarily true: the market completion benefits do *not* follow axiomatically from the Arrow–Debreu theorem. This is because of the 'theory of second best'.

The general theory of second best

Lipsey and Lancaster[8] established in their seminal (but unfortunately insufficiently disseminated) 'General Theory of Second Best' that when the first best solution – in this case, the theoretical fully complete market – is not attainable, there is no mathematical certainty that incremental improvements or incremental removal of distortions will improve welfare; indeed the contrary could happen. The general theory of second best – like the Arrow–Debreu model – is a theorem, not a theory; it is a mathematically proven proposition in its stated form. To quote Lipsey and Lancaster:

> …It is well known that the attainment of a Paretian optimum requires the simultaneous fulfillment of all the optimum conditions. The general theorem for the second best optimum states that if there is introduced into a general equilibrium system a constraint which prevents the attainment of one of the Paretian conditions, the other Paretian conditions, though still attainable, are, in general, no longer desirable. In other words, given that one of the Paretian optimum conditions cannot be fulfilled, then an optimum situation can only be achieved by departing from all the other Paretian conditions …

> …From this theorem there follows the important negative corollary that there is no a priori way to judge as between various situations in which some of the Paretian optimum conditions are fulfilled but while others are not. Specifically, it is *not*[9] true that a situation in which more, but not all, of the optimum conditions are fulfilled is necessarily, or is even likely to be superior to a situation in which fewer are fulfilled. It follows therefore that in a situation in which there exist many constraints which prevent the fulfillment of the Paretian optimum conditions, the removal of any one constraint may affect welfare or efficiency either *by raising it, by lowering it, or by leaving it unchanged.*[10]

The most common illustrations for the theory of second best relate to international trade. For example, if one country has monopoly power over a commodity (violating the optimality condition of perfect competition), is it still optimal for all other countries to continue to pursue a policy of no tariff barriers? It is easy to see that it may be welfare-increasing for other countries to create another distortion by another tariff or by non-tariff measures; the two-distortion equilibrium may be welfare-increasing compared to the situation of only one distortion. Similarly, if product or factor markets are not perfect, then too there may be a place for welfare-increasing compensatory distortions. If in an economy, there are 100 sources of divergence from the theoretical ideal, it is not necessary that correcting any one or two or twenty or even ninety-nine of them is *necessarily* welfare-enhancing. And, some of them may not be capable of correction by policy – for instance, many economic activities have positive and negative externalities whereas the Arrow–Debreu equilibrium assumes their absence.

Criticisms of the theory of second best

By removing the theoretical basis for an advocacy of laissez faire, the theory of second best created a lot of anxiety among classical economists. There were many critical responses to the theory.[11] Some of these took the form of pointing out errors in the specific examples used in the original paper, but this did not affect the validity or generality of the theorem. Others attempted to show that the problems resulting from the theory of second best were relatively small or could be tackled in a fairly straightforward way by limited and targeted policy interventions. For instance, Bhagwati and Ramaswami showed (in the context of trade theory) that in tackling a second best situation, a general principle to follow is that the distortion must be corrected as close to the source as possible.[12] Thus, if the imperfection arises through an externality in the product market, then the corrective policy should be through a production tax/subsidy, if it arises through a consumption externality, it should be a consumption tax/subsidy, if it is through the factor (e.g. labour) market then it should be a factor tax/subsidy and if it is through monopoly power in trade, then it should be a tariff/import-export subsidy.[13] However, much of the literature that is critical of second-best theory assumes the presence of one distortion, that economists know a distortion when they see one and know what the ideal policy is to remove the distortion directly; but this is only possible in a one-distortion world. In practice, distortions usually exist in multiple sectors at the same time and in such cases approaches of the Bhagwati-Ramaswami type do not provide much practical guidance.[14]

Yet others attempted to show that there were situations where the first best solution was still desirable or that the extent of situations covered by the second best theory was relatively small. For instance, it was shown, in the narrow context of maximizing production efficiency, that the first best solution might still be worth pursuing even when some optimality conditions were not met. The perfect general equilibrium requires that an economy achieve aggregate production efficiency. (Production efficiency implies that an economy is operating at its production possibility frontier, i.e., an economic level at which the economy can no longer produce additional amounts of a good without lowering the production level of another product.) Aggregate production efficiency is desired as one part of attaining a Pareto optimum. An implication derived from the theory of second best is that if the optimum situation does not obtain, then the pursuit of production efficiency may not be desirable. Diamond and Mirrlees showed that production efficiency is still desirable *provided* there is an optimum level of taxation and an optimal tax structure. Thus in some specified circumstances, some requirements of a perfect market may be worth pursuing even when other requirements are absent.[15]

The many responses to the theory of second best did not refute its basic premise, and none of them detract from the main point being made in this chapter: *that when all the conditions of perfection are not present it is not axiomatic – and there is no certainty – that incremental improvements in the direction of perfection are welfare-increasing.*

Second best theory in the financial sector

While most studies relating to the theory of second best have either been very general or dealt with the specific contexts of trade or production efficiency, there have been some which examine the issue with specific reference to the financial sector. In the first study of its kind in 1975, Hart showed that opening new markets was not necessarily welfare-increasing and provided an example of circumstances in which could be welfare-decreasing.[16] This result was later extended to a broader class of examples by Newbery and Stiglitz[17] (albeit in the context of trade) and by Elul in the specific context of finance. Elul showed that in almost every incomplete markets economy it is possible to perturb the equilibrium and make *all agents worse off* by introducing a new market.[18]

Second best conditions and derivatives: An intuitive example

As a practical example of how the theory of second best may affect the derivative markets, consider the case of mortgage-backed securities and CDS. Individual mortgages were packaged ('securitized') into collateralized debt obligations (CDOs). These CDOs were then rated by credit-rating agencies. Hypothetically, assume a first best world. In this world, the rating agencies would have accurate information on the probabilities of default by different borrowers. The rating agencies would be operating in a competitive market where their ratings are paid for by users of ratings. Because users would – through competition – weed out agencies that make inaccurate ratings, the competitive market would have attained a situation where ratings accurately reflect the probabilities of default. These accurate ratings would then allow investors to make the optimal portfolio choices of risk and reward based on their utility functions and their risk appetites. Into this world, enters a new derivative instrument – the CDS. By creating the market for protection against or speculation on various types of default, the CDS results in incremental market completion. This new instrument would allow investors to transfer or receive default risk based on their risk appetite and utility function. The new derivative instrument would further increase welfare from the situation obtaining before the creation of CDS.

Consider a different scenario: the credit rating agencies are not operating in a competitive market. They also do not have perfect information. Instead they are oligopolists (because of regulatory preference for a specified set of agencies) and are paid by issuers not by users. In this situation, the ratings may not accurately reflect the probabilities of default. Now assume a CDS market is created. The pricing of CDS would be based on the credit ratings, but those ratings do not correctly reflect default probabilities. Is this incremental market completion welfare-increasing? It is unlikely to be. The purchase and sale of CDS based on perceived credit risks of the rating agencies may not match the actual rates of default. Thereby, welfare may be reduced from the pre-CDS situation because the actual level of risk may be different from the utility function of the investor. (Astute readers might have noticed that something approximating this unfolded in the financial crisis of 2007–08.)

Another example would be the effect of the creation of a market in junk bonds. Creating this market would certainly increase the access to finance of some corporations and thereby incrementally complete the financial markets. However, it has been shown that the introduction of junk bonds makes the market for labour more volatile (*inter alia*, since it promotes takeovers and restructuring involving retrenchments of staff etc.). The market for human capital is incomplete (one cannot buy and sell human capital for every possible future date and state of the world). The workers affected may not be able diversify away the risk that is introduced by junk bonds; thus the risk is borne by those least able to do so and they may be worse off as a result of the creation of the new market.[19]

Policy implications of the theory of second best

Having co-written the General Theory of Second Best at a young age, Lipsey had the rare privilege of attending a conference to commemorate the fiftieth anniversary of his own paper (and it came just a year before the global financial crisis, which some would argue was precipitated in part by the blind adherence to 'market completion ideology'). In an article on that occasion, the *Economist* magazine said:

> To say that we live in a second-best world is just to say we live in the real world, not a blackboard model. Good policy advice in the real world is at least as much applied moral philosophy, psychology, and anthropology as it is applied economics. And if piecemeal policy advising is an art, then a useful wonk is a sort of artist, but in the way a good surgeon is an artist, not the way a novelist is. The theorists are novelists, illuminating the real world by inventing false ones. The best policy-oriented economists, both left and right, are second best economists in the sense that they grasp the lesson of their fictions, but aim at truly feasible ideals, not blackboard utopias.[20]

In his commemorative paper, Lipsey himself recommended verbal or 'appreciative' theorizing in the style of Adam Smith, Thomas Schelling, and Milton Friedman, i.e., theorizing informed by formal theory, but not bound by it:

> According to the appreciative approach, since the competitive market economy is the best known method of allocating resources, departures from

it through either public policy or private behaviour are regarded as prima facie undesirable, unless justified by well-reasoned arguments and persuasive evidence. ... What is needed is a good appreciative understanding of how the price system works, as well as understanding the cautionary warning from second best theory that any policy may have unexpected and undesirable consequences in apparently unrelated parts of the economy that need to be watched for and mitigated where necessary. Useful piecemeal policy advising is not impossible; neither can it be determined purely scientifically; instead it is an art, assisted by good economics, both theoretical and empirical.[21]

This is very wise counsel that all economists engaged in policy advice do well to remember. The fact that there could be undesirable consequences in apparently unrelated parts of the economy suggests other things that economists or policy makers should do: they should read widely, consult broadly and do both with an attitude of humility and openness.

Rodrik, in the specific context of developing countries, argued that '[b]est-practice institutions are, almost by definition, non-contextual and do not take account [such] complications. Insofar as they narrow rather than expand the menu of institutional choices available to reformers, they serve the cause badly.'[22] Developing countries are often advised to adopt best practices based on experience in other countries. The existence of a 'best practice' model, however, may mean that they pay less attention to their own special circumstances and do not analyse options as thoroughly or consult as widely as they might in the absence of a 'branded' best practice.

Conclusion

Though market completion arguments (relying on the Arrow–Debreu model) were often used in finance, the contradictory theory in the same field of the same vintage (the theory of second best) has received little or no attention from protagonists of financial innovation. This is in spite of the existence of specific findings even within the context of the financial sector. This omission to consider what has been known for years, taken with the extent of support that the 'market completion argument' has enjoyed in finance, raises the question of whether the advocates of 'market completion' in the financial sector – some of them highly erudite – were unaware of the theory of second best or chose to ignore it. Given the extent to which the discipline of economics has been divided into narrow sub-specialisms, and within specialisms into ideological schools of thought which often talk 'past' (rather than to) each other, both hypotheses are plausible.

Suffice it to say that the market completion function does not stand the test of scrutiny. Market completion may in certain situations and contexts indeed be welfare-increasing, but the opposite is just as possible. There can be no *a priori* theoretical presumption. The actual effect of market completion has not received empirical attention and there is thus no empirical basis for assuming one outcome over the other. In the absence of either theoretical basis or empirical evidence, support for market completion as a socially useful function of derivatives is, at best, an ideological belief, not a scientific conclusion; at worst it may be a self-serving nostrum for the financial services industry.

Notes and References

[1] Quoted in Dani Rodrik, *The Economics of a Parable, Explained.* Available at: http://rodrik.typepad.com/dani_rodriks_weblog/2011/04/the-economics-of-a-parable-explained.html. Accessed on 14 July 2014.

[2] K. J. Arrow and G. Debreu, 'Existence of an Equilibrium for a Competitive Economy', *Econometrica*, Vol. 22, No. 3, 265–90, 1954.

[3] Mark D. Flood, *An Introduction to Complete Markets.* Federal Reserve Bank of St. Louis, March/April 1991.

[4] R. C. Merton, 'Financial Innovation and Economic Performance', *Journal of Applied Corporate Finance*, Vol. 4, No. 4, 12–22, 1992.

[5] D. Pyle, 'The Economic Functions of Derivatives: An Academician's Point of View', Finance Working Paper No. 29. Haas School of Business, University of California at Berkeley, July 1993.

[6] Emphasis added.

[7] A. Turner, 'What Do Banks Do? Why Do Credit Booms and Busts Occur and What Can Public Policy Do About It?', Chapter 1 of *The Future of Finance – The LSE Report.* London School of Economics and Political Science, 33–34, 2010.

[8] R. G. Lipsey and K. Lancaster, 'The General Theory of Second Best', *The Review of Economic Studies*, Vol. 24, No. 1, 11–32, 1956–1957. © Oxford University Press, reproduced by permission.

[9] Emphasis added.

[10] Emphasis added.

[11] For a description of, and specific rejoinders to, many of them see: Richard G. Lipsey, 'Reflections on the General Theory of Second Best at its Golden Jubilee', *International Tax and Public Finance*, Vol. 14, No. 4, 349–64, 2007.

[12] J. Bhagwati and V. K. Ramaswami, 'Domestic Distortions, Tariffs and the Theory of Optimum Subsidy', *Journal of Political Economy*, Vol. LXXI No. 1, 44-50, February 1963.

[13] Jagdish N. Bhagwati, *The Generalized Theory of Distortions and Welfare*, Working Paper No. 39. Department of Economics, Massachusetts Institute of Technology, 1969.

[14] R. G. Lipsey, 'Reflections on the General Theory of Second Best at its golden jubilee', *International Tax and Public Finance*, Vol. 14, No. 4, 349–64, 2007.

[15] P. A. Diamond and J.A. Mirrlees, 'Optimal Taxation and Production Efficiency-I', *American Economic Review*, Vol. 61, No. 1, 8–27, March 1971.

[16] O. D. Hart, 'On the Optimality of Equilibria When the Market Structure is Incomplete', *Journal of Economic Theory*, Vol. 11, No. 3, 418–33, 1975.

[17] D. M. G. Newbery and J. E. Stiglitz, 'Pareto-inferior Trade and Optimal Trade Policy', *Review of Economic Studies*, Vol. 51, No. 1, 1–12, 1984.

[18] R. Elul, 'Welfare Effects of Financial Innovation in Incomplete Markets: Economies with Several Consumption Goods', *Journal of Economic Theory*, Vol. 65, No. 1, 43–78, 1995.

[19] See Elul, ibid.

[20] 'Making the Second Best of It', Economics Focus, *The Economist*, 21 August 2007.

[21] R. G. Lipsey, 'Reflections on the General Theory of Second Best at its Golden Jubilee', *International Tax and Public Finance*, Vol. 14, No. 4, 2007.

[22] Dani Rodrik, *Second Best Institutions*, NBER Working Paper Series, Working Paper 14050, June 2008. Available at: http://www.nber.org/papers/w14050. Accessed on 14 July 2014.

5

Derivatives and Price Stabilization

...In this way, speculators transfer resources from less to more urgent uses. The difference between the prices at which they sell and buy is their margin, which must cover costs of storage and furnish their remuneration. The excess over storage costs is a payment for specialized skill in knowing when to buy and when to sell and perhaps also for bearing risk.

Milton Friedman[1]

For decades, the role of futures markets in stabilizing or destabilizing prices on the spot market has been a subject of much controversy, not only among economists but also with the general public. What used to be a controversy about futures trading has, with the growth of new and more complex derivatives, become a controversy about derivatives in general.

Price stabilization, as mentioned in Chapter 4, is claimed by some economists to be one of the useful economic functions of futures trading in particular and, by extension, of derivatives in general. This chapter looks at how derivatives influence spot prices and at the theoretical basis for derivatives to exercise a stabilizing influence on prices. It then touches upon empirical studies supporting this view.

Do derivatives affect spot prices?

The first question that arises is whether and, if so, how transactions in the derivatives markets affect prices on the cash (spot) markets. After all, the overwhelming majority of derivatives transactions does not result in receipt or delivery of the underlying. The transactions are settled between the two parties merely by paying up the net price difference. Many economists and laymen have often compared the derivatives markets to mere betting markets and indeed (as was seen in Chapter 2) there are good reasons to compare them. Let it be supposed that there are bookmakers who take bets on the outcome of a football match. Clearly – and assuming there is no 'match-fixing' by players or coaches – the bets on the game must have no effect whatsoever on the outcome of the game. The winner or loser of the game will be determined by the levels of skill of the teams, their performance on the day and sheer luck. Knowing the current odds should not influence the result. If so, why should the 'betting' on derivatives markets influence the actual physical (or spot) market in the underlying?

Firstly, even in the football match example, if the odds are known they may subtly, if only slightly, affect the outcome. The team that knows it is a heavy favourite might have its confidence bolstered and thus play better on the day of the match. Alternatively, it may become overconfident and players might forgo practice that they might have undergone if they were not aware of how likely they were to win. Similarly, the underdog might have its self-confidence undermined or, alternatively, might redouble its efforts and study the opponents' every possible move and tactic. Either way, these subtle changes by either or both teams might influence the result of the match. Thus, the *information* provided by the betting might have some influence on reality. (It should also be noted that in sporting bets, those who place bets are not the ones who are playing the game; in finance, they are sometimes one and the same.)

Secondly, the existence of the betting market may lead to manipulation and thus actually affect the game itself. The infamous examples in the early part of this century of match-fixing in cricket (leading to ignominious bans on the captains of the South African and Indian teams) show that this is not fanciful. This may not apply to betting on an actual market, because price risks exist anyway in that market and one can speculate on it (albeit less conveniently) even without derivatives. However (and while manipulation will be ignored in the rest of this chapter) the recent scandals regarding the manipulation of LIBOR, the London bullion market's gold 'fixing' (perhaps appropriately named?) and foreign exchange rates to profit from derivatives, shows that the risk of manipulation does exist.

Next, consider a betting market on an actual financial instrument or commodity. Thus, there could be a bookmaker taking bets on the price of gold. Would the placing of bets on this market influence the actual price of gold? If the betting volume were small, the market would probably ignore it. However, if gold market participants came to know that the volume of bets on gold prices was larger than the size of the physical market, it would be reasonable for them to want to know what the odds are on the betting market and for them to factor that information into their own decisions. If there is a sudden increase in the odds of, say a fall in gold prices, then traders on the physical market might assume there was some new information they were not aware of and react accordingly.

In short, it is easy to see that the information inherent in *even a mere betting market can influence prices of the underlying*. There are indeed now betting markets (known as 'prediction markets') which estimate the probabilities of uncertain events.[2]

Now consider a forward or futures market where traders have the option of actually physically delivering the underlying. In such a case, the futures market is an alternative to the physical market. If, on the date of delivery, the futures price is higher than the spot price for the same variety, a trader would have every incentive to buy spot and then deliver on the futures market and make a riskless arbitrage profit. Clearly, in this case, participants will constantly watch, and be influenced by futures prices and one can expect a direct link between them.

In short, *derivatives do influence spot market prices*. They do so in two ways: firstly, by providing spot market participants with additional information which may influence their spot market decisions and thereby change spot prices; secondly, in those cases where the underlying can be delivered through the derivatives contract, any unreasonable price differential between the derivative price and the spot price (i.e., a differential not justified by actual differences in the circumstances) will be whittled away through arbitrage thereby affecting the spot price.

The link between futures and spot prices

Because a futures or forward market usually allows physical delivery of the underlying, there are two influences on the forward price: one is the expected price in the future (which is similar to a pure betting situation) and the other is the cost of holding the asset from now until the future date (which will determine the possible advantages of delivery). A detailed description of the pricing mechanism through which futures or forward prices are related to spot market prices is beyond the scope of this book.[3] However, the following is an oversimplified summary based largely on commodities as the underlying.

The quantitative relationship between spot and forward or futures prices at a given point in time can be expressed in the following inequality:

Futures Price $\leq$ Spot Price + Carrying costs to the date of maturity of the futures contract

Carrying costs include interest on the funds deployed but may also include physical costs of storage, insurance and the like.

In a properly functioning market, the futures price can never *exceed* the sum of the spot price and the carrying costs – this is ensured by arbitrage. If the differential exceeds the carrying cost, speculators can make a riskless and guaranteed profit by simultaneously buying the spot, selling the futures and then storing the commodity and delivering it against the futures contract. Thus, there is an upper bound to the futures price.

The reverse is, however, not true; there is no lower bound to the futures price. There is often no riskless arbitrage on the short side: arbitrage would require the speculator to sell the spot commodity now but that would imply having the commodity to deliver; this runs into the problem of having to 'borrow' the physical commodity. Not only can the difference between the prices be less than the carrying cost, but, in fact the futures price can be lower than the spot level. (Somanathan, building on earlier work by Pavaskar showed that this asymmetry – namely, that the price difference cannot exceed carrying costs but can fall below it – leads to an 'inherent bias' in favour of long hedgers and against short hedgers[4].)

Futures prices can (and do) fall below the spot price, especially in commodity markets. This may happen for one of two reasons. It may happen because the expected price at the future date is influenced by changed circumstances (like a forthcoming harvest). Or it may happen because of a 'convenience yield'.

Convenience yields arise mainly in commodity markets. Industrial users of a commodity suffer a cost if they run out of stock – it may be in the form of lost sales or idle machinery and labour. Thus not having stock carries an opportunity cost. That cost is avoided by holding stocks. Therefore, holding of stock has a notional 'yield', namely the avoided costs that may have been incurred in the event of lack of stock.

A convenience yield does not always exist and may often be nil. The larger the level of overall stocks in a market, the lower the convenience yield. Convenience yields become large when stocks (inventories) are low.

For financial instruments, there is generally no convenience yield. They may sometimes have an actual yield (e.g. dividends or interest payments), but this is conceptually equivalent to a negative carrying cost.

In the case of storable commodities, the price difference between futures and spot (apart from the absolute price itself) often plays a part in stockholding decisions of producers and consumers. If the price difference fully reflects carrying costs (net of convenience yield if any), then there is an *incentive to store*. If the price difference is not reflective of carrying costs (net of convenience yield), there is a *relative disincentive to store* because the holder of the commodity is not assured of recouping storage costs. (For example, if the price difference increases, there is a greater incentive to store and this may reduce supply on the spot market and vice versa.) This is another way in which futures prices affect spot prices. For certain commodities, storage does not necessarily mean storage in a warehouse. For mining companies, simply leaving the commodity un-mined (to be mined at a future date) is a form of storage but one which will not show up in any published inventory data.

Since carrying costs and convenience yield per unit of time are constant in the short run, *spot prices influence futures prices and futures prices influence spot prices* for all the above reasons. In most circumstances, a price change in one is either the cause or the effect of a similar price change in the other.

Extent and nature of the links between spot and derivatives prices

To avoid obscuring the primary purpose, the preceding discussion on futures pricing was simplified and brief. In practice, there are more complicating factors to be considered – whether the underlying is 'produced' continuously or discontinuously and is capable of continuous storage or is subject to a discontinuous change (like a harvest), and so on.

The extent of the effect of futures prices on spot depend partly on the elasticity of demand for the underlying and on downstream products, which make use of the underlying as a raw material.[5]

Some economists argue that the effect of futures on spot is minimal or that the prices on the futures markets are largely independent of the spot market and do not 'cause' any changes in the spot market (i.e., they resemble the case of betting on the football match).

While there is not complete clarity or consensus on the degree of causality and the manner in which the influence works, it is sufficient for the purpose of this chapter to note that it is almost universally accepted that *forward / futures prices are closely linked to spot prices and that changes in one can, and in fact generally do, affect the other.*

Other derivatives and the price of the underlying

Most derivatives other than futures influence spot prices largely through the information effect. However, some (certain options markets, for example) may allow physical delivery and in those cases, the price may be influenced by arbitrage possibilities.

How derivatives facilitate speculation

In earlier chapters, it was seen that derivatives markets create new avenues for speculation,[6] i.e., for people to participate in a market for the purpose of *taking risks by creating an exposure* to an underlying where they currently have none, in the hope of profit. The following discussion will focus initially on futures to preserve simplicity, before extending the arguments to other derivatives.

In economic theory, the primary source of the stabilizing influence of futures trading is (contrary to the popular layman's view) the *increased volume of speculation* that these markets foster. No doubt, speculation exists without futures markets, as is the case with the stock market or the spot commodity markets, but futures trading greatly facilitates it and increases its volume. This is because trading in futures makes it much easier and less expensive to speculate.

Long speculation

Suppose a speculator expects a boom in cotton prices and wishes to speculate on it. In the absence of a forward or futures market, the speculative transaction would involve many steps. First, a supplier has to be found and the full price of the cotton has to be paid. Next, the speculator has to take delivery of the cotton, find a warehouse to keep it in, find a transporter to take the cotton, insure the consignment en route, and pay the warehouse for the storage and other carrying costs. When it is time to sell the cotton (whether at a profit or loss depending on whether the speculation was successful) the speculator has to find a buyer and arrange for the sale of the cotton. The administrative costs of executing the sale and giving delivery to the buyer also will have to be incurred. The time and costs involved in this chain of activities for the speculator have to be set off against gains, if any, from the speculation. The sheer physical difficulty of carrying out these transactions means that only persons already involved in the cotton trade are likely to undertake this kind of speculation.

Executing the same transaction in a futures market would be as simple as communicating by phone or email an order to a broker and paying the, say, 10 per cent margin required. At the end of the transaction, another instruction to the broker would suffice and the net gain or loss will be credited or debited to the speculator's account. The sheer ease of the transaction means that speculation on this market is now within reach of virtually anyone with the means to do it.

Short speculation

On the other hand, if the speculator is expecting a fall in the cotton price, to gain from it, he must sell now and buy back later. Theoretically, he could 'borrow' the cotton from someone who has cotton, on promise of returning the cotton at a specified future date. (Indeed, Williams has argued that futures markets are nothing but markets for borrowing and lending commodities.[7]) However, this is more difficult than buying cotton because not many cotton owners would be willing to 'lend in kind'. Assuming he finds a willing lender, he then has to pay the consideration for the loan (a 'commodity interest rate'), take delivery of the cotton and then simultaneously find a buyer to buy it from him. Later, when the transaction is over, the speculator would have to find the full amount of the consignment and buy an equal amount of cotton from someone else, and transport that cotton back to the original lender of the cotton.

This complicated sequence of transactions is even more difficult to execute than a 'long side speculation' (i.e., speculating on a rising price). It may be potentially feasible in countries like the US with speedy contract enforcement and advanced and reliable transport and logistics. In most developing countries, this kind of short speculation is almost impossible to execute successfully – the risks of any one of the intermediaries (lender, buyer, transporter etc.) failing to perform the contract in a timely manner are high. Timing is the essence of successful speculation. The slowness of the judicial system and/or legal uncertainties (say, differing attitudes of different courts at different times to the same transaction) mean that contract enforcement may either never happen or take years. These risks mean that short speculation is almost impossible even for those intimately involved with the cotton trade.

Short selling in a futures market is as easy as going long: a telephone call or email to the broker with a deposit of the fractional margin money.

Gearing (leverage) in futures markets

Another feature to note from the examples above is that both long and short speculation (without a futures market) involve at some stage *depositing the full cost of the commodity*. The gearing or leverage in a futures market means that speculation can be indulged in with a fraction of the capital required on the cash market. Again, theoretically the same gearing can be achieved by borrowing. In a developing country context, this too is easier said than done. Even in developed countries, the transaction costs of borrowing to finance speculation are larger than the automatic leverage provided by the fractional margin of a futures contract.

To sum up, futures trading results in a higher volume of speculation because:

• it reduces transaction costs of long speculation;

• it either reduces the transaction cost of short speculation or enables short speculation where this may not have been possible;

• it allows fractional margin and thereby provides ready and automatic financing for speculation; and

• it enables parties unconnected with the market to engage in speculation with ease.

The next question is what effect the increased speculation engendered by futures markets has on the prices of the underlying (cash) market.

The classical view: Constructive speculation

There has been a long-standing consensus among economic theorists that speculation in a competitive market has a stabilizing influence on prices.[8] Among those who have held and propounded this view are such stalwarts as Adam Smith, J. S. Mill and Alfred Marshall. The logic of this is simple: for any speculation to be successful, the selling price has to be higher than the purchase price. This implies that speculators tend to buy when something is cheap and to sell when it is costly. This further implies that they increase the level of demand at a time of lower price and increase the supply at a time of higher price. In short, they increase the demand during a glut and increase the supply during scarcity and this means the effect of their speculation is stabilizing. It raises the price when it is very low and reduces it when it is very high. Additionally, professional speculators expend time and resources in finding information on market conditions and prospects, in their own interests. They then use this information to buy cheap and sell dear, thereby reducing the extremes of price movements. This twin activity – collection of information and its use in a stabilizing manner – has been termed constructive speculation.[9] Futures markets give market participants a very liquid mechanism to use their knowledge of future events to make profits.

Milton Friedman[10] and others have argued that speculation can only be profitable if it is stabilizing in nature. Friedman's argument is based on certain assumptions, and in some conditions even destabilizing speculation can be profitable. However, in most circumstances, destabilizing speculation results in losses for the speculator. Over a period of time, destabilizing (loss making) speculators are then expected to be eliminated from the market.

Turnovsky examined, from a theoretical perspective, whether a definitive general conclusion could be drawn on the stabilizing effect of futures trading. He then considered a number of realistic specific situations and concluded that 'While we are unable to draw any definitive conclusions on this issue, we find that in all cases considered, the futures market stabilizes the spot price, as well as lowering its long–run mean'.[11] Danthine also presented models showing that futures markets have a stabilizing influence, based primarily on the improved information that speculators bring in.[12]

Other sources of stabilizing influence

Apart from the benefits of speculation *per se*, there are other reasons why futures trading may stabilize prices.

A stabilizing influence may arise from the future price discovery, specialization and information dissemination functions referred to in Chapter 3. By 'discovering' a future price, the futures market 'concentrates in the present, the influence of the future': *facts about future demand and supply are ascertained better and taken into account earlier and disseminated more widely than they would be without a futures market* and because of this, the *amplitude of price fluctuations may be reduced.*[13]

In her research on jute futures in India, Das described as an example a case where news of a bumper harvest in another country, of a crop exported by India, was gathered by professional speculators in a commodity futures market. To take advantage of this they would sell futures contracts in India and thereby drive down the futures price. When this happens, spot market traders notice that the attractiveness of holding stocks of the commodity is reduced, because the price which they can expect to get has come down. As a result, spot market traders move to reduce their stock holdings by discharging existing stocks onto the spot market. This lowers the spot price. When this happens, demand for the commodity expands since the price has fallen. (The extent of the expansion will depend on the price elasticity of demand for the commodity.) Because of the enhanced demand, the surplus at the time of the actual harvest will be less than it would otherwise have been. Accordingly, the post-harvest fall in the price will also be of a lesser magnitude than would have occurred in the absence of futures trading.[14]

In the opposite case, assume a bad harvest in the foreign country is expected, and this information comes to the notice of professional speculators who monitor price trends all over the world. Speculators buy up futures contracts for delivery after the harvest period. The act of buying pushes up the futures price, giving spot market traders a greater incentive to hold stocks since they can anticipate a better return from stockholding than expected earlier. This results in additional demand for spot, pushing up the spot price. The rise in the spot price will lead to a contraction in the demand for the commodity. (The extent of the contraction will depend on the price elasticity of demand.) Accordingly, when the crop is harvested, the reduced supply will meet a reduced demand. This will mean that the post-harvest price increase will be smaller than it would have been in the absence of futures trading.[15]

The noteworthy point in this example is that apart from speculation, the *future price discovery and dissemination that the futures market provides, accelerates the supply and demand adjustment in the spot market.*

There are occasions when prices are affected by exogenous shocks and then further destabilized by panics and herd reactions from producers and consumers (as distinct from speculators). There is evidence that *participants who are hedged are less likely to panic* and engage in destabilizing behaviour. Thus, they are less likely to sell against a falling price or buy against a rising price because their hedge will keep them protected from the consequences of rising or falling prices. Thus, the derivatives market (this effect goes beyond futures) arguably reduces the element of herd reactions and panics and the resulting destabilizing vicious circles, with a corresponding reduction in the amplitude of price fluctuations.

Das pointed out in the context of the 1970s Indian jute futures market that

> the sharp slump in prices immediately after harvest occurs because the supply from the farm exceeds the consumption demand. Therefore, the post-harvest slump in prices can be avoided if the excess of supply over demand is held

back. Futures trading enables the producers, merchants and stockists to carry stocks without assuming any undue risk of price fall as such risk can be shifted ... through hedging. In the absence of ... hedging, the different functionaries would have no alternative but to unload their stocks on an already depressed market ... Futures trading not only keeps prices higher during the post-harvest months, it also checks the sharp price rise during the off-season. Hedging facilities ... enable merchants to carry (inventory) till the lean months. As hedges are lifted and stocks released ..., a sharp upswing is averted ... The price then becomes lower than it would otherwise be.[16]

It is interesting that these factors also seem to imply that the greater the volume of activity (speculative or hedging), the better the price stabilizing influence of futures trading. This proposition is supported by some empirical evidence.[17] (However, Jeremy Stein[18] – see next chapter – disagreed and showed that an increase in speculation can in some circumstances be destabilizing.[19])

It must be noted that the price stabilizing influence of futures trading discussed here is of a short-term or seasonal character.

Empirical evidence

There is a large body of empirical evidence showing that futures trading has a stabilizing influence on prices. Studies by Working,[20] Gray,[21] Powers,[22] Cox,[23] Jerome Stein[24] and Jacks[25] in the USA and Naik,[26] M. G. Pavaskar,[27] Das,[28] R. Pavaskar,[29] and Somanathan[30] in India indicated a stabilizing influence for futures trading in various markets. While these studies date back several decades, there are also several recent ones. Bessembinder and Seguin[31] (for a variety of financial and commodity futures) Haigh et al[32] (for US natural gas and crude oil), Bandivadekar and Ghosh[33] and Nair[34] (for Indian equities), writing in the 1990s and 2000s, found futures trading to have a stabilizing effect.

Jacks' study examined this question at length over a very long historical period stretching from the nineteenth to the late twentieth century, covering many countries and concluded that 'futures markets are systematically associated with lower levels of commodity price volatility.' Jacks' methodology involved comparing periods with futures with periods without futures, since markets had been established and prohibited at different times. In most cases, futures markets had a stabilizing influence even when – at the time events were happening - there was a consensus that it was destabilizing.[35]

Other derivatives

A priori, one can see that some (though not all) of the factors pertaining to futures, particularly the informational effects of constructive speculation, are also theoretically applicable to other derivatives. The absence of destabilizing panic sales or purchases among those who are hedged is a factor which applies to all derivatives. While there are few empirical studies looking directly at this question, Chatrath *et al* did find a stabilizing influence for traded equity options on the S&P 100 share index.[36]

Derivatives and price stabilization: A summary

A substantial body of economic theory indicates that derivatives trading is likely to exert a stabilizing influence on spot prices, by decreasing the amplitude of short-term price fluctuations. There is also a body of empirical evidence in respect of futures trading which supports this view. The causative factors operating to produce this stabilizing influence are:

1. Enhanced speculation: Economic theory indicates that speculation is generally stabilizing in nature because speculators (to be successful) must buy at lower prices and sell at higher prices thereby adding to demand when demand is weak and adding to supply when demand is strong. Derivatives trading leads to enhanced speculation. This is a result of fractional margins and the fact that derivatives enable short positions to be taken. Since speculation is generally stabilizing and derivatives promote speculation, derivatives must be stabilizing in their effect.

2. Improved flow of information: Derivatives trading may lead to improved information flow because of the presence of professional speculators who specialize in gathering and analysing supply and demand; this results in better anticipation of future events.

3. Future price discovery: Futures markets (but not necessarily other derivatives) enable discovery of future (expected) prices, resulting in better anticipation of future events and thereby reducing the effect of the actual events themselves.

4. Avoiding panics: By providing hedging to market participants, derivatives trading may reduce the tendency to 'panic' or follow the herd and thus avert vicious circles of sharp price rises or falls.

Notes and References

1   M. Friedman, 'In Defense of Destabilizing Speculation', in *Essays in Economics and Econometrics*, edited by Ralph W. Pfouts, 133–41. University of North Carolina Press, Chapel Hill, 1960.

2   E. Servan-Schreiber, *Betting on a Better World—How Might Prediction Markets Benefit International Relations?*, paper presented at the annual meeting of the International Studies Association, New York, 2009. Available at: http://www.lumenogic.com/www/static/pdf/isa-servan-schreiber.pdf. Accessed on 14 July 2014.

3   For a detailed non-mathematical discussion, see T. V. Somanathan, *Derivatives*. Tata McGraw Hill, New Delhi, 1998.

4   T. V. Somanathan, *Derivatives*, Appendix 3.2. Tata McGraw Hill, New Delhi, 1998.

5   J. D. Hamilton, 'Causes and Consequences of the Oil Shock of 2007–08', *Brookings Papers on Economic Activity*, 234–38, Spring 2009.

6   Speculation can be defined as the acquisition of an asset or liability exclusively for resale motivated solely by the anticipation of capital appreciation.

7   J. Williams, *The Economic Function of Futures Markets*, (Second edition). Cambridge University Press, Cambridge, 1994.

8   For a concise overview of the classical theory of speculation, see B. A. Goss and B. S. Yamey, *The Economics of Futures Trading, Readings Selected, Edited and Introduced* (Second edition). Macmillan, London, 1978.

9   T. V. Somanathan, *Derivatives. Op.cit.*

10 M. Friedman, *Essays in Positive Economics*. University of Chicago Press, Chicago, 1953.

11 S. J. Turnovsky, 'The Determination of Spot and Futures Prices with Storable Commodities', *Econometrica*, Vol. 51, No. 5, 1363–87, September 1983.

12 J. P. Danthine, 'Information, Futures Prices, and Stabilizing Speculation', *Journal of Economic Theory*, Vol. 17, No. 1, 79–98, February 1978.

13 R. Pavaskar, *Efficiency of Futures Trading*. Popular Prakashan, Bombay, 120, 1977.

14 K. Das, *Futures Trading in Jute and Jute Goods: An Economic Analysis*. Unpublished PhD dissertation, Calcutta University, 1975.

15 T. V. Somanathan, *Derivatives, Op. cit.*

16 K. Das, *Futures Trading in Jute and Jute Goods: An Economic Analysis*. Unpublished PhD dissertation, Calcutta University, 119–20, 1975.

17 D. B. Sharpe, 'A S A Official's Response to Farmers Who Question Validity of Futures Market', *Financial Exchange*, International edition. – Chicago Board of Trade, Vol. 6, No 2, March–April 1987.

18 Not to be confused with Jerome L. Stein who has also written on futures markets.

19 Jeremy C. Stein, 'Information Externalities and Welfare–Reducing Speculation', *Journal of Political Economy*, Vol. 95, No. 6, 1123–45, December 1987.

[20] H. Working, 'Price Effects of Futures Trading', *Food Research Institute Studies*. February 1960.

[21] R. W. Gray, 'Onions Revisited', in *Selected Writings on Futures Markets*, Vol. II, edited by A. E. Peck. Chicago Board of Trade, Chicago, 1977.

[22] M. J. Powers, 'Does Futures Trading Reduce Price Fluctuations in the Cash Markets?', *American Economic Review*, Vol. 60, No. 3, 460–64.

[23] C. C. Cox, 'Futures Trading and Market Information', *Journal of Political Economy*, Vol. 84, No. 6, 1215–37, 1976.

[24] Jerome L. Stein, *The Economics of Futures Markets*. Basil Blackwell. Oxford, 146-47, 1986.

[25] D. S. Jacks, 'Populists versus Theorists: Futures Markets and the Volatility of Prices', *Explorations in Economic History*, Vol. 44, 342–62, 2007.

[26] A. S. Naik, *Effects of Futures Trading on Prices*. Somaiya Publications, Bombay, 1970.

[27] M. G. Pavaskar, *Effects of Futures Trading on Short Period Price Fluctuations* (mimeo.). University of Bombay, 1970.

[28] K. Das, *op. cit.*

[29] R. Pavaskar, *op. cit.*

[30] T. V. Somanathan, *Commodity and Financial Futures Markets: An Economic Analysis*. Unpublished PhD Dissertation, Calcutta University, 1987.

[31] H. Bessembinder and P. J. Seguin, 'Price volatility, Trading Volume, and Market Depth—Evidence from Futures Markets', *Journal of Financial & Quantitative Analysis*, Vol. 28, No. 1, 21–39, March 1993.

[32] M. Haigh, J. Hranaiova and J. Overdahl, 'Price Dynamics, Price Behaviour and Large Futures Trader Interactions in the Energy Complex', CFTC Working Paper, 2005. Available at: http://www.cftc.gov/files/opa/press05/opacftc-managed-money-trader-study.pdf.

[33] S. Bandivadekar and S. Ghosh, 'Derivatives and Volatility on Indian Stock Markets', *Reserve Bank of India Occasional Papers*, Vol. 24, No. 3, 187–201, 2003.

[34] A. S. Nair, *Impact of Derivative Trading on Volatility of the Underlying: Evidence from the Indian Stock Market*. Available at: http://www.igidr.ac.in/conf/oldmoney/mfc_10/Abhilash%20nair_submission_25.pdf. Accessed on14 July 2014.

[35] D. S. Jacks, *op.cit.*

[36] A. Chatrath, S. Ramchander and F. Song, 'Does Options Trading Lead to Greater Cash Market Volatility?', *Journal of Futures Markets*, Vol. 15, No. 7, 785–803, 2006.

6

Derivatives and Price Destabilization

For my part, I wish everyone of them[speculators] had his devilish head shot off.[1]

Abraham Lincoln

For as long as we fail to treat speculators the way they deserve—with a bullet in the head—we will not get anywhere at all.[2]

Vladimir Lenin
(Quoted by David S. Jacks[3])

The last chapter explained that classical economic theory indicates that derivatives trading has a stabilizing effect on spot prices and there is empirical support for this view. Nevertheless, derivatives markets have often been blamed for price destabilization. Contrary to the classical theory, there are also credible theories indicating that derivatives may destabilize spot prices. This chapter outlines the theoretical basis for a destabilizing influence and looks at empirical evidence. It first looks at 'conventional' (or older) theories on how derivatives may destabilize spot prices, spanning commodities as well as other types of underlying. It then looks at the more recent theory on destabilization of commodity prices through the use of commodities as an investment class, also known as 'financialization of commodities'.

Economic theory versus political fact: Perception of derivatives as destabilizing

Outside the rarefied world of economists, derivatives have often been accused of being a major agent of price *destabilization* through excessive speculation, and even of being a cause of inflation. Admittedly, a general feeling that speculation is bad and (since speculation is presumed to be bad) derivatives are bad, lies at the root of many of these criticisms. It was something on which Abraham Lincoln and Vladimir Lenin were in surprisingly close agreement.

Traditionally, the response of most 'mainstream' economists to such popular perceptions has been to dismiss them as being based on insufficient understanding of the market mechanism. Regulators 'have frequently expressed concern that futures and options markets can be price destabilizing and welfare

58

reducing...[but] theoretical economists, on the other hand, have tended to follow the spirit of Friedman.'[4]

The negative perception outside the economics fraternity has persisted and has led frequently to changes in government policy and public attitudes towards derivatives. After the 2008 financial crisis (which exposed the major weaknesses in some of the strongly held beliefs of conventional or 'mainstream' economists) the traditional response of 'the critics are ill-informed', no longer carries credibility. In several countries, there was a strong feeling that derivatives had exacerbated food price increases beyond what was justified by fundamentals. Governments and/or legislatures moved to inquire into and/ or restrict derivatives trading, particularly in commodities. For instance, the United States Senate's Permanent Sub-committee on Investigations launched an investigation of the wheat market. After taking a lot of expert testimony and direct evidence from market participants, it reached the bipartisan conclusion that there had been excessive and destabilizing speculation and that

> the unwarranted changes in wheat prices resulting from the large amount of index trading in the Chicago wheat futures market created an undue burden on interstate commerce. This undue burden was imposed on farmers, grain elevators, grain merchants, grain processors, and others by impeding useful hedging strategies, imposing significant unanticipated costs, and providing inaccurate indications of expected prices in the wheat markets.[5]

Issues related to food prices are obviously even more sensitive in poorer countries. In India, the government banned futures trading in several essential commodities in 2007 and set up an Expert Committee on Futures Trading (generally known as the Abhijit Sen Committee) specifically to 'examine whether and to what extent futures trading has contributed to price rise in agricultural commodities'. The Committee's report, after a long and elaborate consultative process involving economists and market participants, was inconclusive, provided few new insights and left open the possibility that futures trading might have been destabilizing.[6]

At the same time, the absence of credible, widely and well-understood theoretical explanations for how derivatives are destabilizing has made it difficult for economists and regulators to discard the conventional economic wisdom.

Actually, some credible theoretical explanations of the destabilizing potential of derivatives have been around for quite long. Partly the problem is one of their inadequate dissemination outside a narrow specialized circle. This may, in part, be due to the fact that the 'speculation is stabilizing' theories came from household names like Hicks and Friedman while the contrary ones were from less-famous scholars. Another reason is that those explanations have often been felt to be applicable only in rare or exceptional circumstances. Therefore, the gap between mainstream economists and public perception has not been bridged.

The conventional theoretical case for destabilization

Poorly informed speculators (negative information externalities)

Generally, the classical theory assumes that when secondary traders (speculators with no intrinsic interest in the market), enter the market, there is no negative informational effect. On the contrary, it assumes there is a positive informational effect because speculators are assumed to specialize in gathering information on the market. Consider however a situation where secondary traders come in with garbled or incorrect information. Jeremy Stein[7] showed that in such cases, the 'misinformation' effect brought in by the secondary traders may, by *misinforming the primary (spot) traders*, create a destabilizing and welfare-reducing effect. In his words:

> Introducing more speculators into the market for a given commodity leads to improved risk sharing but can also change the informational content of prices. This inflicts an externality on those trades already in the market, whose ability to make inferences based on current prices will be affected. In some cases, the externality is negative: the entry of new speculators lowers the informativeness of the price to existing traders. The net result can be one of price destabilization and welfare reduction. This is true even when all the agents are rational, risk-averse, competitors who make the best possible use of their available information.[8]

In essence, whereas the primary traders have direct access to correct or accurate information, the secondary traders may not necessarily add any information. In some cases – the scenario Stein referred to – they may in fact add misinformation. However, by virtue of their activity, this misinformation will affect the price which itself is new information for the primary traders.

This can be shown to be destabilizing. This is supported by the earlier theory of Grossman and Stiglitz[9] who also showed that imperfections in information may lead to inefficient markets. Hart and Kreps reached a similar conclusion and showed that speculation can be destabilizing if speculators get their predictions wrong some of the time.[10]

Momentum (or movement) trading

One of the oldest criticisms of the classical 'speculation-is-good' school was the presence of 'movement trading', now generally referred to as 'momentum trading'. Momentum trading is a situation where speculators *follow the movement* or *move with the trend*. (The following discussion uses the term 'movement trading' when referring to the older literature.)

The conventional theory on speculation assumes that speculators are contrarian – they buy low and sell high. Hart and Kreps observed that the classical way of describing speculation – as involving buying low and selling high – is itself misleading. Rather, it is more accurate to say that speculators *buy when the chances of price appreciation are high and sell when the chances of price appreciation are low.*[11] This is clearly a far more accurate reflection of reality than the classical view. This definition has the merit of more fully and reflecting the different kinds of speculation.

In momentum trading, instead of 'buy low and sell high', the *operating principle is 'buy high and sell higher' or 'sell low and buy back even lower.'* According to Irwin, one of the first economists to study this systematically as far back as 1937, movement traders use their superior agility in entering and leaving the market, to take profits before the movement comes to an end, but after attracting a lot of others into the market.

Movement trading involves buying as the price rises and selling as the price falls. As such it boosts demand when the price is high and increases supply when the price is low; in both cases it exacerbates volatility. Therefore movement trading is *a priori* destabilizing, and contrary to Friedman's presumption, movement traders do make profits through destabilizing speculation.[12] The conventional economic theory on constructive speculation does not hold in the face of movement trading.

An early defence of the classical theory of constructive speculation against the critique on movement trading came from Goss and Yamey. They argued that, even if movement trading were commonplace in real life, it does not negate the view that, in general, destabilizing speculators lose money. Goss and Yamey argued that:

> this theory does not imply that speculators *as a whole* make profits from their destabilizing activities; it implies no more than that one important category of speculators–the professionals and then only the agile ones–make profits in the circumstances.[13]

This is because eventually, prices return to the levels dictated by fundamentals. At that time the last batch of speculators, who bought at the peak or sold at the trough, loses heavily. In the arithmetic sense, if the profits and losses of the various speculators are added up, speculators as a whole cannot be winners from destabilizing speculation.

Goss and Yamey further argued that even if there is movement trading at one stage, the same movement traders may later engage in stabilizing behaviour. Assume that there is a bullish phase in a market and a professional speculator thinks (or knows) it is not justified by fundamentals, but feels that it will continue for some time due to the mass bullish psychology. In the futures market he can 'go with the market' by buying in the near futures contract and simultaneously go against the mass psychology and sell in a distant futures contract. If he is right, he can potentially gain twice–initially by joining the crowd in the near month, and later by reaping the benefit of the correction of the overvaluation. The 'second gain arises from "correct" behaviour which tends to off-set the results of the "incorrect" behaviour'[14]. Such simultaneous buying and selling is not possible in spot markets. The actions of the speculator in simultaneously buying near and selling distant futures will reduce the contango or increase the backwardation, which itself will send a signal to the market that the current price is overvalued and expedite a correction. This, argued Goss and Yamey, makes it difficult for inappropriate price levels to persist for long.

Overall, the defence of the classical theory of constructive speculation against the movement trading theory was twofold:

- firstly that, movement trading is not commonplace and is more of an aberration; and

- secondly that, even if it exists, it is not all but only some speculators who can profit from movement trading.

Both these assumptions do not seem to hold any longer. It is increasingly clear that, in the modern era, speculators often do not act in a contrarian manner and do attempt to go with the trend. The use of computerized algorithms based on charts and technical analysis strengthens this trend. Secondly, if the duration of movement trading is long enough, it is possible for a large number of speculators (especially institutions) to earn profits for a long time before losses are inflicted on others who may not necessarily be speculators.

Friedman himself in 1960 conceded the possibility of destabilizing speculation but argued that if it were happening, it implied that market participants were receiving positive utility from gambling.[15] In a micro-economic sense, this may be true, but from a normative public policy perspective, it is difficult to argue that derivatives should be allowed to destabilize market prices because they provide utility to gamblers.

Dynamic hedging

Another way in which derivatives markets can destabilize prices is through the practice of *dynamic hedging*, sometimes called *delta hedging*. This is of particular relevance to options markets. Market makers (institutional sellers) of OTC options write options on the basis of demand from their customers. Writers of options have to assume unlimited price risk, but the real intention of the institution may be only to earn the dealing commission or profit margin (the difference between bid and ask prices, known as the bid-ask spread). Having written an option, the market-making institution has to find a way of offloading the unwanted risk exposure. To some extent, the written options may cancel each other out. Usually, however, a net exposure will remain. If this exposure cannot be hedged by placing an exactly opposite transaction at a lower cost, the bank may engage in the practice known as dynamic hedging.

Dynamic hedging is a technique whereby the writer of an option hedges himself by continuously buying or selling a *fractional amount of the underlying asset itself* in order to simulate the effect of an options position. A full understanding of this will require a detailed understanding of options pricing which is beyond the scope of this book but a simple numerical example is given in Appendix 6.1.

The main point is that dynamic hedging, whether by call option writers or put option writers, *involves buying as the price rises* and *selling as the price falls.*

Thus, *dynamic hedging by option writers is destabilizing in nature.* The extent of the destabilizing influence would depend on the size of the net short position in options compared to the spot market volume.

It is interesting to note that at certain times, dynamic hedging can itself cause momentum trading when other participants note the behaviour of the dynamic hedgers and realize the predicament the hedgers are in.

Empirical evidence on the conventional theories on destabilization

There is a body of empirical evidence in recent years which supports the theories described above. Firstly, on the issue of potential misinformation as postulated by Stein, while there appears to be little specific empirical evidence, Sen[16] (in a supplementary note to the eponymous committee's report) states:

> ... But it is equally true that the main reason why futures exchanges have seen such spectacular growth is because they are serving contracts to meet a demand from speculators that has far outpaced the connection with the physical markets. The exact profile of these speculators is not known and, although many are located in smaller towns, it is unlikely that most of them come with informed knowledge of the commodity domain. Indeed the required domain knowledge is rather scarce even in the National Exchanges and with the Regulator. A likely consequence of this and the replacement of pit trading by screen trading is that easily available domain material, such as the plethora of news from international exchanges being served on many of the commodity portals that have mushroomed, is filtering into prices in futures exchanges more than other information relevant to the formation of local spot prices.

This is virtually a description of the theoretical scenario of misinformation that Stein had postulated. Considering that Sen and the report of the Committee he headed make no mention of Stein's theory, this completely independent observation based on first hand testimony from the exchanges and participants is significant. It strengthens the inference that Stein's theory does often hold good in practice.

Secondly, there is clear evidence of the persistence of momentum trading (and/or herd behaviour – see later in this chapter) over extended periods of time. Partly, this is connected to the growth of computerized algorithmic trading approaches where decisions are triggered automatically by price changes. Newman for instance, cites the long bull run in coffee prices from 2002 to 2007 as an example of a period 'where the dominant form of speculative activities act(ed) to drive prices away from that warranted by supply and demand over long periods of time'.[17] In December 2012, the *Financial Times* wrote on the dangers posed by momentum trading.[18]

Thirdly, the potentially large effects of the destabilizing tendency of dynamic hedging were illustrated when they played a role in the sudden crash of share prices on Wall Street's Black Monday in October 1987.[19]

Fourthly, several of the studies that concluded that there was a stabilizing influence did find that there were occasions when the influence of speculation was destabilizing. For example, Siopis and Lyroudi's study of the Greek stock market[20] and Somanathan's study of pepper and sacking futures in India did find a destabilizing influence in a minority of instances.[21]

Fifthly, in terms of a general comparison of price volatility with and without futures, new evidence has emerged in recent years. (The existence of voluminous data and statistical models for testing means this has become a fertile ground for masters and doctoral students to do projects on, and seems to be particularly popular with students of finance in business schools.) Jian, Balyeat and Leatham in the USA concluded that an unexpected increase in futures trading volume caused an increase in cash price volatility for most commodities. They also found a weak causal feedback between open interest and cash price volatility and their findings were generally consistent with a destabilizing effect of futures trading on agricultural commodity markets.[22] A study carried out for the Indian regulator, the Forward Markets Commission, by the Indian Institute of Management, Bangalore, came to a similar conclusion.[23] Sahi and Raizada found some destabilizing elements in a study of several Indian commodity futures markets.[24] Nath and Lingareddy in a study of the futures markets in India for gram, black gram (*urad*) and wheat found an increased volatility of prices in the case of black gram. In the other two commodities, the study was inconclusive.[25] (However, Pavaskar and Ghosh severely criticized the study by Nath and Lingareddy and similar analyses[26]. While there is merit in some of their methodological criticisms, they appear to overstate their case by arguing that volatility is not an issue at all and should not be a yardstick by which to judge futures trading. This is difficult to agree with from a policy perspective given the potential adverse effects that commodity price volatility has on the economy.) Kumar found a destabilizing (volatility-increasing) effect across a range of Indian commodity markets covering agriculture, metals, and energy.[27] The Abhijit Sen Committee set up by the Indian government, after reviewing various studies including several of those mentioned here, stated that '...it does suggest that speculative activity in futures markets can destabilize spot prices' and warned '...against aggressive attempts to expand futures trading, especially if driven not by those who manage price risks in physical trade by hedging in futures markets but by speculators or others based on exaggerated claims regarding futures markets efficacy'.[28] Fratzscher found that excessive derivatives trading was linked to increased volatility in the South Korean stock market.[29]

However, in terms of the number of studies, empirical support for the conventional theories of destabilization is weaker than the empirical support for the conventional theories suggesting stabilization.

Newer theories on destabilization

The 'conventional' theories on the destabilizing potential of derivatives are relatively of old vintage and have existed for at least 20 years (much longer as regards movement trading). Going purely by those theories, and the fact that the empirical evidence for stabilization seemed relatively stronger in quantitative terms, most economists have tended to see the possibility of destabilization by derivatives as an occasional aberration of academic interest that, from a regulatory perspective, was relatively insignificant.

There are some relatively new theoretical approaches which indicate that derivatives can destabilize prices of the underlying. The two main 'new' streams relate to:

- the concept of 'herd behaviour' (arising from research into 'behavioural finance'); and
- the concept of 'financialization' (i.e., the trend for commodities to become an investment class and be used as financial instruments rather than for their intrinsic worth as commodities).

Herd behaviour

Conventional theory ignores the behavioural impact on traders of the actions of other traders. In practice, individual traders may exhibit 'herd behaviour' whereby they copy the behaviour of other traders rather than take decisions based on their own well considered and rational cost-benefit calculations. If this were to happen, it would contradict the assumption of constructive speculation because speculators (instead of buying low and selling high on the basis of rational expectations) *would buy when others buy and sell when others sell.*

Herd behaviour may occur for different motivations and in different forms; the United Nations Conference on Trade and Development (UNCTAD) after reviewing several studies on the subject, provided a useful taxonomy which underpins the following description.[30]

Intentional herding

Intentional herding can occur for four motives. Firstly, groups of individuals, especially if they come from similar social and economic backgrounds are affected by peer behaviour and may like to conform. This is 'conformity-based herding'.

Secondly, there is safety in numbers: employees' reputations may be better safeguarded by imitating others than by taking a position contrary to them. If a trade fails, the employee's reputation may be tarnished if others at the same time did not carry out the same trade. On the other hand, if many others had done the same thing, employers are likely to consider the failure to be attributable to a change in market sentiment rather than to the poor judgement of the employee. This can be called 'reputation-based herding'.

Thirdly, the modern tendency is to measure the returns of investments against benchmarks, and traders' bonuses often depend on their *relative* performance vis-à-vis benchmarks. If the trader loses money, but only at a rate slightly below the benchmark, that is not a problem and may even be seen as 'good' performance. But if a trader loses money on an investment while the benchmark does not, that could have a more adverse impact on remuneration. Therefore, traders have an incentive to copy the movements of others so that they stay in line with the benchmark. This is another motive for herding, known as 'compensation-based herding'. In this respect, Keynes was prescient. He had likened professional investment to:

> … those newspaper competitions in which the competitors have to pick out the six prettiest faces from a hundred photographs, the prize being

awarded to the competitor whose choice most nearly corresponds to the average preferences of the competitors as a whole; so that each competitor has to pick, not those faces which he himself finds prettiest, but those which he thinks likeliest to catch the fancy of the other competitors, all of whom are looking at the problem from the same point of view. It is not a case of choosing those which, to the best of one's judgment, are really the prettiest, nor even those which average opinion genuinely thinks the prettiest. We have reached the third degree where we devote our intelligences to anticipating what average opinion expects the average opinion to be. And there are some, I believe, who practise the fourth, fifth and higher degrees.[31]

Fourthly, many participants follow others because they believe those others must be acting on new and relevant information not available to them. This belief may not necessarily be correct, but it is effective nevertheless. This is called 'information-based herding'.

It should be noted that in all the above examples, the trader who is imitating others is acting in a perfectly rational manner as an agent (though not necessarily from the point of view of the principal or employer).

Noise trading

Herding may be caused unintentionally because traders react to 'noise' or pseudo-signals rather than to true new information. A major reason for this is the use of technical analysis. Technical analysis is a method of predicting price movements by studying past patterns and essentially is based on 'following a trend'. A rise or fall in price may trigger a 'buy' or 'sell' signal respectively. The trigger may be activated sometimes because of actual new information but at other times 'by accident'. When technical analysis is implemented through computerized algorithms, many traders get the same signal at the same time and so a whole 'herd' of traders move together. In the short run, this herd movement also generates increased confidence in the validity of the technical analysis which can thus become self-fulfilling for a time. This form of herd behaviour is essentially the same as momentum trading.

Another example of noise trading is when portfolios are affected by a change in other unrelated markets. Assume that as a matter of strategy, all portfolios managed by a group of investment advisers are expected to have, say, 5 to 10 per cent invested in commodities. On a given day, assume that global equity markets rise by a large margin, thereby raising the overall value of portfolios.

The result is that portfolios have also risen in size; the portfolios now need to be re-balanced by buying more commodities (see Chapter 7 for illustrations). Since many investment advisers follow a similar approach, all of them, as a herd, may buy commodities thereby triggering a rise in prices of commodities completely unrelated to the fundamentals of those commodities.

In the above cases, there is *no new information* on the underlying market triggering the price move and hence the speculative action does not fit the classical assumption of constructive speculation. On the contrary, the actions of 'speculators' (who may be 'investors', see below) are actually destabilizing the market.

Many (but not all) forms of herd behaviour differ from momentum trading in motivation, but all are similar in their effects on markets because they imply that speculators would buy as the price rises and sell as the price falls. Thus, herd behaviour contradicts the assumption of constructive speculation.

It should be noted that herd behaviour does not occur just because all or many traders take the same position at the same time. If there is a change in fundamentals or an exogenous shock (for example, a sudden change of government in Ukraine which could disrupt energy supplies) that may occasion identical trades by many participants; but the trades are triggered by fundamentals rather than by an intention to mimic others. This can be called 'spurious herding' inasmuch as it is not really herding – it is a reaction to new information and does not destabilise prices.

Many of the examples cited above, i.e., reputation- and compensation-based herding, the effect of technical analysis, the prevalence of portfolio-rebalancing trades, are clearly and obviously part of the reality of modern financial markets and need little 'proof', but if proof were needed it is found in the form of a survey of market traders by UNCTAD (which confirmed the existence of such tendencies).

'Financialization' or the effect of commodities becoming an investment class

The classical view of speculation was that it was a short-term and opportunistic activity where the speculator was as ready to indulge in short speculation as in long speculation. This 'world view' fitted the facts quite well until fairly recently, but does not necessarily do so any longer because several institutions have taken to commodities as an 'asset class' in their investment portfolios.

Commodities as assets in financial portfolios

Modern portfolio theory, based on the Modigliani–Miller theorem and the capital asset pricing model, encourages investors to diversify their portfolios with investments that are not correlated with other instruments. The overall risk of a portfolio (for a given level of return) may be reduced by diversification of the portfolio. The portfolios of big financial institutions and the investors they advise are heavily weighted with financial instruments (stocks and shares, bonds etc.) Investments that do not belong to these classes make an attractive addition to a portfolio because they are not (or at least are presumed not to be) well correlated to stocks or bonds.

Precious metals (which, being precious, occupy little space and are compact to store and easy to transport as customs officers well know) have historically been easy to speculate on with or without futures. Non-precious commodities such as the pepper in Example 6.1 below are not easy to store or transport and speculation without derivatives is cumbersome for those not already engaged in the physical trading of the commodity. Derivatives enable a much larger circle of people to speculate. Between 2000 and 2010, many new futures and options markets in commodities and financial instruments opened in developing countries like China and India. These markets grew dramatically in turnover in a very short time. The availability of active futures and options markets is necessary for widespread speculation in these commodities, though it is not a sufficient condition.

Effect of loose monetary policy

Even after the push from modern portfolio theory to diversify, commodities were not until recently a very attractive 'asset' for investors because they offer no interest or dividends and thus incur a significant opportunity cost in terms of income forgone. This changed in the first decade of the twenty-first century.

Starting with the 'dot com bust' in 2000, interest rates have been at historically low levels both in real and in nominal terms. In several developed countries (like Japan and the US) the interest rate on bank deposits has been nil or close to nil. In a zero-interest rate environment, commodities (with a lower correlation with stock and bond prices) became more attractive as a long-term investment in anticipation of price rise. A paper by Gorton and Rouwenhorst published in 2006 indicated, using data over a long period of time, that portfolios would benefit from an asset allocation to commodities.[32] This proved to be quite influential.

Thus, in the first decade of this century, two new trends took hold:

- new futures markets were opened in developing countries like India and China, *increasing the potential* for speculation in commodities; and

- low interest rates prevailed, *reducing the opportunity cost* of investing in commodities.

Both the 'necessary' and the 'sufficient' conditions for commodities to become a portfolio asset were now fulfilled and commodities entered the portfolios of investors to an unprecedented extent. The oil market offers a good illustration of the spurt in the magnitude of commodity investing. Between 1983 and 2005, the growth in futures volume was moderate and consistent with the conventional assumption on speculative trading. Prices went up and down at different times during this period. However, from 2005 to 2008, volumes trebled. (This period also witnessed a massive increase in oil prices although there were many fundamental factors also at work.)

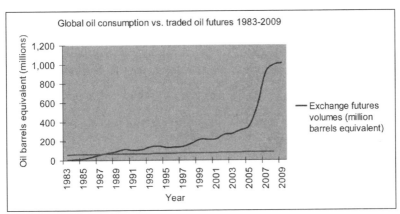

Figure 6.1: Speculators versus 'investors' in oil futures
Note: The grey line towards the bottom of the chart depicts global oil consumption.
Source: NYMEX (taken from Turner's paper – see Note 7 to Chapter 40)

The conventional theoretical analysis looks at market participants as hedgers and speculators (with arbitrageurs being a subset among speculators). Speculation – in the traditional analysis – is quintessentially short term. On that basis, speculation does not affect the price trend because each speculative transaction involves both a purchase and a sale. The effect of speculation on demand is illustrated in the following example.

Example 6.1:

The demand for pepper in a given market is 100 quintals per month, based on actual consumption needs. Initially there is no speculation. Then, in January, a speculator enters the market by purchasing 50 quintals and then storing it. He sells this holding in March. The total demand in the market is as follows:

Month	Consumption demand	Speculative demand	Speculative supply (negative demand)	Net demand
January	100	50	0	150
February	100	0	0	100
March	100	0	-50	50
Total	300	50	-50	300

The total demand for each month has three components: normal consumption demand, speculative demand and then speculative supply. (For simplicity, speculative supply is treated as negative speculative demand.)

Assume that consumption demand is steady at 100 quintals a month. In January, the speculator buys 50 quintals on the spot market and puts this quantity in storage. This results in an increase in total demand in the market from 100 to 150. Obviously, this increase in demand will raise prices above the level that would have prevailed without the speculative purchase.

In March, the speculator sells the stored quantity. This increases supply which for simplicity in the illustration, is treated as negative demand. The total pepper demand drops from 100 to 50 quintals. This will lead to a drop in the price of pepper vis-à-vis what it would have been without the speculative sale.

It will be seen that for the three-month period as a whole, the total demand has remained at 300 quintals i.e., 150 in January, 100 in February and 50 in March. In the absence of speculation, the demand over the same period would have been 300 quintals (100 per month). Thus the total demand remains identical to the consumption demand even though there has been speculation. In January, the total demand exceeded consumption demand but in March, the sale by the speculator offset the consumption demand. In January, speculation would have raised prices above the level that would have prevailed without the speculative purchase, but in March, the effect of speculation would have been to reduce the price below what it would have been without the speculative sale.

Example 6.1 illustrates classic short-term speculation. The speculator raises prices when starting the speculation and then reduces prices when ending the speculation. If the speculator made a profit, it follows that he sold in March at a higher price than he bought in January and thus he bought when prices were low and sold when prices were high. The speculation could have occurred either by buying physical stocks, storing and then selling (which is cumbersome) or by buying futures (against which delivery is possible) which is more convenient. As already noted in Chapter 5, in a futures market where delivery is possible, there is a strong link between the futures price and the spot price; so even if the speculation occurred through the futures market, it would also have influenced spot prices.

To the extent investors now look to hold commodities in their portfolios, they no longer represent a conventional short-term 'speculation'. The 'investment' is long term though often held through short-term derivative instruments because the transaction costs of holding the underlying may be high. For example, if an investor wishes to include crude oil in his investment portfolio, actually buying and storing a physical consignment of oil is cumbersome. Instead, it is easier to buy oil futures. Though each oil futures contract is short-term, the investment can be kept long term by routine 'rolling over' of the short-term contract: as soon as, say, the June contract nears expiry, the June contract is sold and the September contract is simultaneously purchased. (Rolling over entails some costs and 'basis risk' but in the long run the cost is fairly predictable.) The continuous rollover, which is necessary for an investor to hold a commodity produces a different pattern of demand from the conventional 'speculator' upon whom the theoretical edifice has been constructed. The following illustrations will make this clear:

Example 6.2:

Assume the same initial facts as in Example 6.1 viz. the demand for pepper in the same market is 100 quintals per month, based on actual consumption needs. Initially there is no speculation or investment. Then, in January, an investment fund decides to buy 50 quintals of pepper as a portfolio holding and stores it. It continues to hold the pepper indefinitely. The total demand in the market is as follows:

Month	Consumption demand	Speculative demand	Speculative supply (negative demand)	Net demand
January	100	50	0	150
February	100	0	0	100
March	100	0	0	100
Total	300	50		350

What happens in January is the same in Example 6.2 as in Example 6.1: demand increases because of the new speculative demand and becomes 150 quintals instead of 100. However, what happens in March is different. The drop in demand in March seen in Example 6.1 does not occur now. The total demand in March is now 100 whereas it was 50 in the previous example. In this situation, for the quarter as a whole, the total demand in the market has increased from 300 to 350 quintals – a very different outcome from Example 6.1 when (for the quarter as a whole) demand was not affected by speculation. In this case it stands to reason that prices will be higher than they would have been without speculation.

Example 6.3:

Assume the same initial facts as in Example 6.1 viz. the demand for pepper in the same market is 100 quintals per month, based on actual consumption needs. Instead of buying pepper on the spot market and storing it, the investment fund makes its investment through the futures market. It buys the March futures contract in pepper. At the end of March it rolls over the position by selling the March futures contract and simultaneously buying the June futures contract. The total demand in the market is as follows:

Month	Consumption demand	Speculative demand	Speculative supply (negative demand)	Net demand
January	100	50	0	150
February	100	0	0	100
March	100	50 (Buy June contract)	–50 (Sell March contract)	100
Total	300	100	–50	350

The situation in January is exactly as in the previous examples. In March, in this example, the investment funds sells 50 quintals of the March contract which has become deliverable but simultaneously buys 50 quintals of the June contract. The nett effect of the two transactions is that the total demand in March remains 100 quintals as in Example 6.2 (and unlike Example 6.1). In this case too, demand for the quarter as a whole has changed because of the speculative (or more precisely, investment) demand. The increased demand has manifested itself through the futures market but, as discussed in Chapter 5, in a futures market where delivery is possible, this will, through arbitrage relationships, raise the spot price above the level that would have prevailed without the investment demand.

The simplified illustration in the examples indicates how, *contrary to conventional economic wisdom, it is possible for prices to be driven up (or down) by futures trading when commodities become long term investment assets rather than vehicles of short term speculation.*

Effects of investment

As illustrated above, the fairly recent advent of funds which use commodities as an asset class (rather than as a short term speculation) may mean that the old theories on benign speculation no longer hold. In the old theory, since every speculative purchase of futures was eventually offset by a sale with no consumption, the net impact on supply/ demand was neutral; also since the sale price had to be higher than the purchase price (for speculation to be profitable), the overall effect must be stabilizing (sell high, buy low) as unprofitable speculation is unsustainable.

But if every such sale is immediately replaced by a new roll-over purchase (because it is now held for a long period as an 'asset class' *irrespective of price*) then the net bought position will increase and the period of time for which the price is influenced is longer. In this scenario, it is possible to create an asset bubble through futures, holding prices up for much longer than the duration of a futures contract and thereby commodity prices can be pushed up for a long period of time – till the bubble bursts.

In the traditional theory there were hedgers and speculators; now there are hedgers (who could be long or short), speculators (who could be long or short) PLUS 'investors' who are almost all net long rather than short. Unlike the hedger who offsets purchases by sales and the speculator who buys *and* sells opportunistically on the basis of price movements (and is thus highly influenced by fluctuations), the investor buys and holds to 'stay invested' in a particular commodity as a portfolio choice and *thus remains long through several contract periods irrespective of short-term price movements.* When commodity investors reduce the asset allocation to commodities, the reverse effect – of reducing prices below levels that would otherwise prevail – is also possible. Commodity investing greatly increases the risk of herd behaviour because of the need for portfolio re-balancing triggered by events completely unrelated to the commodity markets.

By metamorphosing from a market for hedgers and speculators interested in the specific factors affecting a particular commodity to a market for investors who regard the commodity as offering diversification *per se* irrespective of its intrinsic price movements, the effect of futures may now have changed. From being a market reflecting the stocks (in the sense of physical inventories) of a commodity, it has become a market in a new kind of stock (in the sense of share or security) and thus closely linked to stock prices.

Even experts who generally believe that commodity investing generally does not (in practice) destabilize spot prices, concede that in theory it may do so: for instance, Sanders and Irwin, who have produced a substantial amount of empirical work arguing against the proposition, state that:

> Given the allegations about the size and impact of speculators in agricultural futures markets that have again arisen within industry, government, and academia, additional research efforts are needed to better understand the market participation of speculators in general and long–only index funds in particular[33].

Empirical evidence on the effects of 'financialization'

While there is a clear *theoretical* basis to show that commodity investing can result in an increase in commodity prices, the more important question is whether it has actually done so. This area has attracted a lot of empirical studies in recent years. There is now a sizeable body of empirical evidence to support the hypothesis that the commodity investing has destabilized spot prices in recent years. Recent studies by Newman (of the coffee market),[34] Singleton (crude oil),[35] Hernandez and Torero (agricultural commodities),[36] Gilbert (agricultural commodities, metals and crude oil),[37] Mayer (covering agricultural commodities, metals, crude oil and natural gas),[38] Tang and Xiong[39] as well as Inamura *et al.*[40] (commodities included in the Goldman Sachs and Dow Jones UBS commodity indices), Buyuksahin and Robe (US equities and the commodities in the Goldman Sachs index),[41] the International Food Policy Research Institute (agricultural commodities)[42] and Henderson *et al.* (studying commodity-linked notes)[43] find evidence that financialization has had a destabilizing influence on spot commodity prices.

On the other hand several other recent empirical studies including those by Irwin and Sanders,[44] Korniotis[45] and Fattouh *et al.*[46] came to the opposite conclusion.

Appendix 6.1:

The destabilizing effect of dynamic hedging by option writers

An option is a contract which confers upon the buyer the right (without the obligation) to buy or sell an asset at a pre-specified 'exercise' or 'strike' price on or before a pre-specified date. The strike price specified may be quite different from the current market price. If the strike price is far removed from the current price such that the buyer does not get any immediate advantage from the option, the option would be called an 'out-of-the money' option. The opposite party (option writer or seller) has an obligation, without a right, to sell or buy the underlying at the strike price. The buyer of the option pays a premium for this right. The option itself can also be resold and so it has a market price. Therefore the terms premium and price are used interchangeably in this discussion. This price partly reflects the current market price of the underlying.

For example, if a person holds an option to buy gold at $2000 when the current price of gold is $1400, clearly the option has no intrinsic value at the current time since there is no benefit to exercising it. However, if the price of gold were to rise to $2500, then the option would become very valuable because the option holder could buy gold at $2000 and immediately sell it at $2500.

When the price of gold is much higher than the strike price, the option itself is not very valuable. But, when the price of gold moves closer to the strike price, the chance of the option becoming profitable increases. Therefore, the option itself becomes more valuable. In the gold example, the option would be worth more when the spot gold price is $1900 than when it is $1400.

It can be shown that the *change in price of an option can be approximately offset by holding a corresponding but fractional position in the spot or futures market.* A call option writer (who is exposed to upward price risk) will hedge by buying the underlying, while a put option writer will hedge by selling the underlying. It is not necessary for them to buy or sell the full quantity of underlying involved in the option contract. The option writer's exposure is to the option premium or market price. As already mentioned, other things being equal, the option premium varies with the underlying price. Quantitatively, the effect depends on the value of the 'delta', the delta being the *price sensitivity (rate of change) of the option premium for a given change in the price of the underlying.* Therefore, the option writer can replicate this price risk by buying or selling the underlying asset adjusted for the delta. However, since the delta itself undergoes change (the rate of change being the 'gamma'), the option writer has to continuously (dynamically) adjust his long or short position in the underlying to make sure the price risk on his position mirrors that of the option he has written.

As the price rises, the delta of a call option will rise. As the price falls, the delta of a put option will rise. This implies that when the price rises or falls, *the option writer has to hold a larger quantity of the underlying. This means they will have to buy more of the underlying when the price of the underlying rises and sell more of the underlying when the price of the underlying falls.* This is destabilizing. The numerical examples below will demonstrate this.

Example A6.1:

Dealer *A*, writes a call option on 50,000 oz. of silver at a strike price of 17500 cents per ounce when the price of spot silver is 15000 cents an ounce (i.e., the option is out-of-the-money). *A* is interested in earning a standard trading commission on the transaction and not in taking the speculative price risk. Assume the delta is 0.1 (i.e., the rate of change of the option premium is 0.1 times the rate of change of the price of silver). *A* will suffer a loss if the price of silver rises above 17500 cents because the buyer of the option will then exercise it. *A* hedges his exposure dynamically by buying

$0.1 \times 50,000 = 5,000$ oz. of spot silver.

Later, the spot price of silver on the bullion market rises to 16000 cents per ounce. The delta at this level is 0.2. *A* now needs to hold

$0.2 \times 50,000$ oz.$= 10,000$ oz. of spot silver.

He therefore buys a further 5,000 oz. of silver.

Later the price of silver on the bullion market rises still further to 16400 cents; at this level the delta also rises to 0.4. *A*'s required holding is now

$0.4 \times 50,000 = 20,000$ oz.

He therefore buys another 10,000 oz. The purpose of this process is to make up for the loss on the call option he has sold through the price appreciation on the spot silver he has bought. From an economic point of view, the point to note is that the more the price rises, the more silver the option writer has to buy.

Example A6.2:

B writes a put option on 5,000 oz. of silver at the same strike price of 17500 cents when the market price of silver is 15000 cents an ounce. Since this is a put, it is in-the-money. Assume the delta is -0.9 [N.B. Since the price of a put option varies inversely with theprice of the underlying, the delta is negative.] She hedges dynamically by selling

0.9 × 50,000 =45,000 oz. of spot silver.

Later, the price rises to 16000 cents per ounce. The delta at this level is -0.8. She now needs to hold

-0.8 × 50,000 oz.,

viz., a short position of 40,000 oz.

Therefore she buys back 5,000 oz. of silver. Later the price rises still further to 16400 cents and the delta is – 0.6. Her required holding is now

-0.6 × 50,000=-30,000 oz.

She therefore buys back another 10,000 oz. The purpose of this process is to make up for her gain on the put option she has sold, by her loss on the spot (since she is not interested in speculative profits). The point to note is that *as the price rises, B too (like A who had the opposite position) buys more and more silver.*

The main point that emerges is that dynamic hedging whether by call option writers or put option writers, involves buying against a rising price. It can be shown similarly that dynamic hedging by both put and call option writers involves selling against a falling price. Thus dynamic hedging by option writers is destabilizing in nature.

Notes and References

[1] Quoted in F. Carpenter, *Six Months at the White House with Abraham Lincoln*. Hurd, New York, 1866.

[2] V. I. Lenin, *Complete Collected Works*, Vol. 35. Moscow, 1964.

[3] Both quotations taken from David Jacks' paper cited in Chapter 5 (see Note 25).

[4] Jeremy C. Stein, 'Information Externalities and Welfare-Reducing Speculation', *Journal of Political Economy*, Vol. 95, No. 6, 1124, December 1987.

5   United States Senate, Permanent Sub-committee on Investigations, 'Excessive Speculation in the Wheat Market', *Majority and Minority Staff Report*, 2009.

6   Government of India, *Report of the Expert Committee on Commodity Futures Trading*, 48–9 (paras 11.7 to 11.9), 2008. Available at: http://www.fmc.gov.in//WriteReadData/links/Abhijit%20Sen%20Report-85542553.pdf. Accessed on 14 July 2014.

7   Not to be confused with Jerome L. Stein.

8   Jeremy C. Stein, *op.cit.* 1123–45.

9   S. J. Grossman and J. E. Stiglitz, 'On the Impossibility of Informationally Efficient Markets', *American Economic Review*, Vol. 70, No. 3, 393–408, 1980.

10 O. D. Hart and D. Kreps, 'Price Destabilizing Speculation', *Journal of Political Economy*, Vol. 94, No. 5, 927–52, 1986.

11 O. D. Hart and D. Kreps, *Ibid*.

12 H. S. Irwin, 'The Nature of Risk Assumption in the Trading on Organized Exchanges', *American Economic Review*, Vol. 27, 267–75, June 1937

13 B. A. Goss and B. S. Yamey, *The Economics of Futures Trading; Readings Selected, Edited and Introduced* (Second Edition), 35, Macmillan, London, 1978.

14 *Ibid.*, 57.

15 Milton Friedman, 'In Defense of Destabilizing Speculation' in *Essays in Economics and Econometrics*, edited by Ralph W. Pfouts, 133–41. University of North Carolina Press, 1960.

16 Abhijit Sen, 'Supplementary Note By Prof. Abhijit Sen, Chairman Expert Committee on Futures Trading', paragraph 11, 57–8, Abhijit Sen Committee Report (*Report of the Expert Committee on Commodity Futures Trading*). Government of India, 2008. Available at: http://www.fmc.gov.in//WriteReadData/links/Abhijit%20Sen%20Report-85542553.pdf. Accessed on 14 July 2014.

17 Susan Newman, 'The New Price Makers: An Investigation into the Impact of Financial Investment on Coffee Price Behaviour', *NCCR Trade Working Paper No. 2009/7*. Swiss National Centre of Competence in Research, 2009.

18 Gillian Tett, 'Momentum Trading Part of Wider Structural Flaw', *Financial Times*, 21 December 2012.

19 Brady Commission, *Report of the Presidential Task Force on Market Mechanisms*. U.S. Government Printing Office, Washington DC, 1988.

20 A. Siopis and K. Lyroudi, *Effects of Derviatives Trading on Stock Market Volatility– The case of the Athens Stock Exchange.* Available at: http://www.finance-innovation.org/risk08/files/5140943.pdf. Accessed on 14 July 2014.

21 T. V. Somanathan, *Derivatives*, Tata McGraw Hill, New Delhi, 1998, 120.

22 Jian Yang, R. B. Balyeat and D. J. Leatham, 'Futures Trading Activity and Commodity Cash Price Volatility', *Journal of Business Finance & Accounting*, Vol. 32, No. 1-2, 297–323, January 2005. Available at SSRN: http://ssrn.com/abstract=662001. Accessed on 14 July 2014.

[23] As cited in the Abhijit Sen Committee Report (*Report of the Expert Committee on Commodity Futures Trading*, Government of India, 2008), *op. cit.*

[24] G. S. Sahi, *Influence of Commodity Derivatives on Volatility of the Underlying*. December 2006. Available at: http://papers.ssrn.com/sol3/papers.cfm?abstract_id=949161. Accessed 14 July 2014.

[25] G. C. Nath and T. Lingareddy, *Commodity Derivative Market and its Impact on Spot Market*. January 2008. Available at SSRN: http://ssrn.com/abstract=1087904 or http://dx.doi.org/10.2139/ssrn. Accessed on 15 July 2012. Also see (by the same authors) 'Impact of Futures Trading on Commodity Prices', *Economic and Political Weekly*, Vol. 53, No. 3, 19 January 2008.

[26] M. G. Pavaskar and N. Ghosh, 'More on Futures Trading and Commodity Prices', *Economic and Political Weekly*, Vol. 43, No. 10, 8 March 2008.

[27] Brajesh Kumar, *Effect of Futures Trading on Spot Market Volatility: Evidence from Indian Commodity Derivatives Markets*. March 2009. Available at SSRN: http://ssrn.com/abstract=1364231 or http://dx.doi.org/10.2139/ssrn.1364231. Accessed on 14 July 2014.

[28] *Report of the Expert Committee on Commodity Futures Trading*, *op.cit*, paragraph 5.5, 26.

[29] Oliver Fratzscher, 'Emerging Derivative Markets in Asia', Chapter for *Asian Financial Market Development*. World Bank, March 2006, 17.

[30] United Nations Conference on Trade and Development and Arbeitkammer Wien, *Price Formation in Financialized Commodity Markets – The role of information*. United Nations, New York and Geneva, June 2011.

[31] J. M. Keynes, *The General Theory of Employment, Interest, and Money*, 1936, chapter 12. Available at: http://gutenberg.net.au/ebooks03/0300071h/printall.html. Accessed 6 November 2014.

[32] G. Gorton and K. G. Rouwenhorst, 'Facts and Fantasies About Commodity Futures', *Financial Analysts Journal*, Vol. 62, No. 2, 2006, 47–68.

[33] D. R. Sanders, S. H. Irwin and R. P. Merrin, 'The Adequacy of Speculation in Agricultural Futures Markets: Too Much of a Good Thing?', *Journal of Applied Economic Perspectives and Policy*, Vol. 32, No. 1, 77–94, 2010.

[34] Susan Newman, *Op. cit.*

[35] K. J. Singleton, 'Investor Flows and the 2008 Boom-bust in Oil Prices', 2011. Available at SSRN: http://ssrn.com/abstract=1793449. Accessed on 14 July 2014.

[36] M. Hernández and M. Torero, 'Examining the Dynamic Relationship between Spot and Future Prices of Agricultural Commodities', IFPRI Discussion Paper 00988, 2010.

[37] C. L. Gilbert, *Speculative Influence on Commodity Future Prices 2006-2008*, UNCTAD Discussion Paper 197, 2010.

[38] J. Mayer, 'The Growing Interdependence between Financial and Commodity Markets', UNCTAD Discussion Paper 195, 2009.

[39] K. Tang and W. Xiong, 'Index Investments and Financialization of Commodities', NBER Working Paper 16385, 2010.

40 Y. Inamura, T. Kimata, T. Kimura and T. Muto, 'Recent Surge in Global Commodity Prices – Impact of Financialisation of Commodities and Globally Accommodative Monetary Conditions', *Bank of Japan Review*, March 2011.

41 B. Buyuksahin and M. A. Robe, *Speculators, Commodities and Cross-market Linkages*, 2011. Available at SSRN: http://ssrn.com/abstract=1707103. Accessed on 11 July 2014.

42 International Food Policy Research Institute, *When Speculation Matters*, IFPRI Issue Brief 57, February 2009.

43 B. J. Henderson, N. D. Pearson and L. Wang, *New Evidence on the Financialization of Commodity Markets*. Available at SSRN: http://ssrn.com/abstract=1990828. Accessed on 11 July 2014.

44 S. H. Irwin and D. R. Sanders, 'The Impact of Index and Swap Funds on Commodity Futures Markets: Preliminary Results', OECD Food, Agriculture and Fisheries Working Paper No. 27, 2010.

45 M. G. Korniotis, *Does Speculation Affect Spot Price Levels? The Case of Metals with and without Futures Markets*, Finance and Economics Discussion Series. Divisions of Research and Statistics and Monetary Affairs, Federal Reserve Board, Washington, D.C., 2009.

46 B. Fattouh, L. Kilian and L. Mahadeva, 'The Role of Speculation in Oil Markets: What Have We Learned So Far?', *The Energy Journal* Vol. 34, No. 3, 7–33, 2013.

7

The Effects of Derivatives on Prices of the Underlying: A Synthesis

...a simple gains-from-trade argument ensures that consumers will always be better off when they are allowed to trade with speculators than when they do not have this option... Unfortunately, the question whether some speculation is better than none is probably not a very relevant one. In terms of real-world policy-making, it seems more interesting to ask: 'Is more speculation better than less?' Gains-from-trade arguments offer no help here.

Jeremy C. Stein[1]

Chapter 5 showed that conventional economic theory was that derivatives, through constructive speculation and improved information, would reduce spot price volatility. Chapter 6 looked at theoretical and empirical evidence that the opposite could be true: that derivatives may destabilize spot prices. This chapter brings together the opposing arguments and arrives at a coherent view.

Conventionally derivatives were thought to have a stabilizing effect because they:

- facilitate speculation and speculation was generally felt to have a stabilizing effect;

- increase the flow of information and in some cases, facilitate discovery of the future price; speculators – partly by specialization – bring in new and more accurate information; this allows better anticipation of the future and better inventory planning thereby reducing price volatility;

- allow spot market traders to hedge their risks and thereby reduce the chance that they would make panic sales at a low price or panic purchases at a high price, in response to an unexpected price change.

Set against these were the reasons why derivatives might have a destabilizing effect:

- momentum trading is destabilizing, so derivatives can destabilize spot markets to the extent such trading occurs;

- speculators may bring in inaccurate information and in that case their effect on the market is to reduce the level of information; this will worsen anticipation of the future, distort inventory planning and increase price volatility;

- though panics are indeed reduced, some hedging products – e.g. dynamic hedging by option writers – actually destabilize prices.

Until recently, the pro-stabilization arguments appeared to hold the upper hand. The possibility of momentum trading – as a destabilizing force – had been raised as far back as the 1930s, but this was thought to be a rare aberration and departure from the norm, of some theoretical interest but not a serious question for policy. Later came the theories that the additional information introduced by derivatives-based speculation might in fact be a negative rather than a positive externality because the information may in fact be misinformation. This too was seen as an interesting theoretical proposition with limited practical implication. Dynamic hedging was known to have destabilizing effects but its volume was relatively small. Empirical studies were far from unanimous, but using the very crude yardstick of quantity, a majority of studies indicated that futures prices had exerted a stabilizing influence on spot prices. Overall, in the mid-1990s, a reasonable economist taking a reasonable view of the theoretical framework and the empirical evidence could reasonably conclude that derivatives (or at least forwards and futures) were not a cause of instability in spot prices. This confidence among economists was not always shared by politicians or people in the street, and so the subject remained controversial. However, economists usually saw this as a case of ill-informed politics and felt that the remedy was to better educate policy makers and the public.

The events over the last 15 years have challenged that traditional view.

- There has been a big increase in algorithmic trading which is usually trend-following in nature. A rising market will typically trigger a buy signal when specific 'barriers' are breached and vice versa, and this is classic momentum trading and thus destabilizing.
- Long-term speculation through long-only investment in commodities is now quantitatively large. This has created additional demand in both forward and spot markets which makes the price higher than it would otherwise be.
- Commodities have become part of wider portfolios of financial (investment) assets. When the value of the portfolio changes, the targeted level of commodity investments within that portfolio also changes. A change in completely unrelated markets (which affects the portfolio size) results

in purchases or sales of commodities for reasons unconnected with the commodity itself. This activity (portfolio re-balancing) is not based on 'new' or 'better' information but rather on irrelevant and extraneous information. Speculators of this kind are clearly bringing in negative information externalities by introducing misinformation (see Example 7.1).

• Herd behaviour has become better defined in theoretical work and there is now clear evidence that herd behaviour (and the momentum trading that often goes with it) happens fairly frequently.

Example 7.1:

An investment adviser advises her clients to allocate 10% of their portfolio to commodities and keep the remaining 90% in equities. She manages $10 million of assets. This means a holding of $1 million of commodities. Now assume that the equity market falls by 10% while the commodity market remains unchanged. The value of equities in the portfolio she manages declines from $9 million to $8.1 million. The total portfolio is now worth:

$8.1 m (equities) + $ 1m (commodities) = $ 9.1 m

The 10% drop in equities has reduced the value of the portfolio by 9%. Commodities have now become 'overweight' in the portfolio because they constitute 11% (i.e., 1 out of 9.1 million). To restore the weight of commodities to the targeted level, 10% of the commodity holdings will have to be sold. Note that this sale is triggered by factors completely unrelated to the commodity market.

Other commodity participants, seeing this sale may (erroneously) conclude that she has some information about the commodity market and may also sell. This is the negative information externality: she has actually introduced misinformation into the market and moved prices away from what is justified by fundamentals. (If enough traders follow this 'signal', they may trigger sell orders in the algorithms of algorithmic traders.)

Figure 7.1 is a diagrammatic summary of the price stabilizing and /or destabilizing impact of derivatives on spot prices. The chart distinguishes between accepted facts, well-established theories and areas of disagreement. The major areas of disagreement relate to the extent and prevalence of momentum trading, of herd behaviour and of misinformation. This is largely a matter of circumstances and cannot be determined through theoretical arguments.

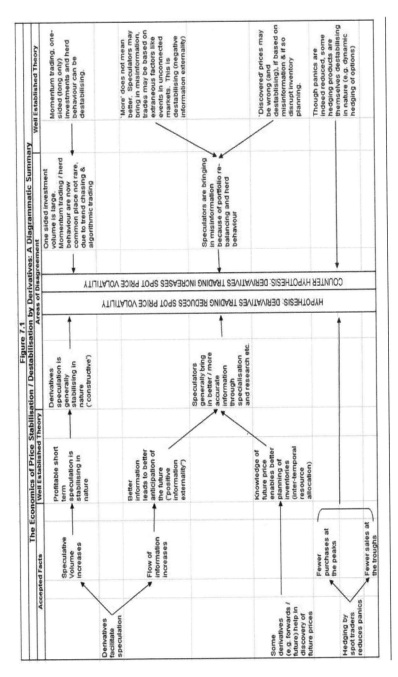

Figure 7.1: The economics of price stabilization /destabilization by derivatives: A diagrammatic summary

Destabilizing effect of regulatory restrictions on short-side speculation

The conclusions in the preceding paragraphs and Figure 7.1 were based on the normal functioning of derivatives markets – i.e., a situation where traders are free to engage in both long and short speculation (also known as short-side speculation)[2]. In practice, regulators have often tended to restrict short speculation (i.e., selling of assets in anticipation of falling prices, to buy back later). Such asymmetrical restrictions create an additional avenue for price destabilization.

Long speculation tends to drive prices higher while short speculation tends to drive them lower. Constructive speculation can only operate when speculators are able to do both so that they can correct undervaluation and overvaluation. Unfortunately, the attitude that is often taken selectively towards 'short speculators' is that they are evil, out to bite the hand that feeds them and destroy the economy. On the other hand, 'long speculators' get a free pass because their speculation boosts asset prices and that is considered good!

The combination of no restrictions on long speculation with restrictions on short speculation can impart an artificial upward push to prices beyond what is justified by fundamentals; when accompanied by a 'Greenspan put' (i.e., regulatory support to prevent large falls in prices – see Chapter 8) it helps to create asset bubbles.

Implications of rising correlation on commodity investing

Commodity investing was supposed to add to the efficiency of investor portfolios by offering diversification. Diversification is effective only to the extent that different assets are not correlated; the lower the correlation the better for diversification. However, the large increase in commodity investment and the fact that much of it is algorithmic and subject to portfolio re-balancing may mean that correlations between commodities and equities at the international level have increased significantly. Inamura *et al.* showed that the correlation between equity and commodity prices rose sharply during the period when financialization exploded (see Figure 7.2).[3]

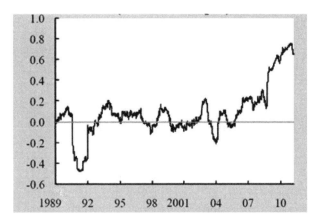

Figure 7.2: Correlation between returns on commodity index and equity index

Note: The figures show the one-year rolling correlation between the daily return of the MSCI-AC World global equity index and that of the S&P GSCI commodity index. Reproduced from Y. Inamura, T. Kimata, T. Kimura and T.Muto, 'Recent Surge in Global Commodity Prices–Impact of financialization of commodities and globally accommodative monetary conditions', *Bank of Japan Review*, March 2011.

They also found that correlation between commodities within the indices commonly used by investors had risen over the same period vis-à-vis correlations between commodities not in the index (see Figure 7.3), though they had been very similar in the pre-financialization era.

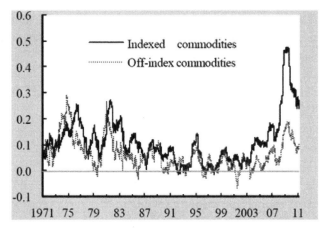

Figure 7.3: Average correlations of indexed and off-index commodities

Note: Reproduced from Y. Inamura, T. Kimata, T. Kimura and T. Muto, 'Recent Surge in Global Commodity Prices–Impact of financialization of commodities and globally accommodative monetary conditions', *Bank of Japan Review*, March 2011.

This has the interesting and paradoxical implication that the very growth of commodity investing may be reducing its effectiveness at least in so far as the investment occurs through commonly tracked indices. Lombardi and Ravazzolo[4] found that increased correlation between equities and commodities was removing much of the original rationale for this investment approach. (Post-2010, there is some evidence of a reduction in correlation between commodities and developed market equities but the enhanced correlation with emerging market equities remains.)

An integrated view

The contradictory theories and arguments on the two sides of the stabilization/destabilization debate have left many observers confused. One of the aims of this book is to bring some coherence to this issue. Bringing together the disparate insights, this book offers the following conclusions on the link between derivatives trading and prices:

- Theoretically, futures and forward markets may *have either a stabilizing or destabilizing influence* on prices of the underlying, depending on the nature and mix of market participants, the extent of investment interest (as distinct from short-term speculative interest), prevailing interest rates and the prevalence of momentum trading. As regards options, out-of-the-money options have very little stabilizing or destabilizing effects but at-the-money and in-the-money options have effects similar to futures. The stabilizing or destabilizing effects of complex (especially complex financial) derivatives on their underlying would follow these broad principles but generalizations are difficult given the many variations in construction and pay-off structures of complex derivatives.

- Short-term speculation generally has a stabilizing influence on prices. Derivatives markets which are dominated by hedgers and short-term speculators are normally stabilizing (or at least non-destabilizing) in nature. Such markets may exhibit a destabilizing tendency during periods of 'momentum trading'. Momentum trading in the present era appears to be more frequent and more persistent than assumed by classical economists.

- Older empirical evidence had indicated that, historically, in most markets and in most eras, commodity futures trading has been stabilizing or at any rate has not been a source of destabilization. Most of these empirical studies pre-date the twenty-first century. Recent empirical studies using recent market data are not so sanguine and several of them detect a destabilizing tendency.

- The rapid rise and then fall of commodity prices between 2005 and 2012 was primarily attributable to fundamentals – but the amplitude of the fluctuations was increased by derivative-based speculation, which thus became a secondary cause.

- When a futures market attracts long-term speculators ('investors'), who desire to hold a commodity over the long run without intending to use it, it may have a destabilizing effect.

- Long-term speculation (commodity investment), and consequently destabilization, is more likely to occur during periods of low or zero interest rates when the opportunity cost of investing in commodities (which have no yield) is low, and when hedge funds, mutual funds and other such institutions participate in commodity futures.

- Restrictions on short-side speculation[5] (especially when accompanied by direct or indirect regulatory support for higher asset prices) tend to create a destabilizing effect on prices by driving them higher than indicated by fundamentals.

Policy implications

The conventional belief that speculation is generally stabilizing in nature is no longer valid. Momentum trading and herd behaviour are no longer aberrations that can be ignored. There is overwhelming anecdotal (and some empirical) evidence that they do occur frequently and for fairly long periods. It is difficult to be as sanguine as Goss and Yamey (see previous chapter) about the distribution of profits and losses from momentum trading. They argued that it is only one class of traders who profit from destabilizing speculation and not speculators as a whole. This ignores the identity of the different 'speculators' on the market. The reality of the current times is that proprietary trading by banks and institutions is substantial in many markets. These institutions typify Irwin's description of professional speculators who are 'more agile' than the rest, and can get in and out before the rest of the market. As a result, in the current configuration of derivatives markets, one class of traders (say, the investment banks) may be able to initiate or participate in momentum trading and profit from it continuously. Meanwhile others (lay investors and clients) may suffer continuously. The classical theory made the assumption that destabilizing speculators would make losses and hence be wiped out. If, as now appears plausible, one class of speculators (the institutions) is able to profit over the long run through momentum trading, they may be able to keep engaging in that behaviour while an ever-changing group of other speculators keeps making losses[6]. In this scenario, momentum traders remain in the market and are not wiped out. This hypothesis, which at least anecdotally fits the recent facts well, has serious implications for regulatory policy.

First and foremost, it removes the theoretical foundation for the general belief in constructive speculation. It means that no *a priori* conclusion can be reached about the desirability of speculation or of enhanced speculation. Thus, *there is no longer a good theoretical basis for asserting that futures (and by implication other derivatives which have futures and options as building blocks) cannot destabilize prices.* In cricket, there is a rule that when in doubt, the umpire must give the benefit of that doubt to the batsman rather than the bowler. In the past, the default position of economists (though not explicitly so stated) was similar: that when in doubt, regulators should assume that derivatives' effect on prices is benign. That default position is no longer valid. In situations where prices overshoot levels indicated by economic fundamentals and remain at those levels, there are strong grounds for regulators to act to curb speculation. The question for regulators is how to judge whether prices are overshooting levels justified by fundamentals. Another important factor for regulators is the insight, as highlighted by Bhikchandani and Sharma, that herd behaviour and its negative consequences are more likely to occur in emerging markets where transparency may be less and information is thus less likely to be accurate[7].

Secondly, regulators need to keep in mind the increased conflict of interest found in different segments of derivative markets. Benchmark-rigging has become widespread as the examples of LIBOR, the London bullion market fixing and the foreign exchange market have shown (see Chapter 12 for details). This is a new form of negative information externality which is yet to receive much attention from researchers. The extent to which investment banks have become involved in commodity warehousing is a pointer to further risks. Even research is not free of conflict of interest: for instance a frequently cited paper which is highly critical of the report of the US Senate's Permanent Sub-committee on Investigations (see previous chapter) was funded by a commodity investment firm[8].

Thirdly, regulators may need to distinguish between commodities and other risk classes. In the case of purely financial derivatives, the implications remain largely (though not entirely) within the financial sector. But in commodities, especially food and other essentials of common consumption, the implications for inflation and for the impact on the poor are more severe. Given the mixed record of derivatives, it may be wise for regulators to exercise even greater vigilance on these markets.

Finally, regulators should develop good quantitative indicators and norms of excess speculation adapted to specific markets. Working's T ratio is a particularly useful one for futures markets.[9] On the one hand, too little speculation can impede the hedging efficiency of markets but on the other, too much may exacerbate the dangers of momentum trading and negative information effects. Sanders *et al* showed that a T ratio of less than 1.15 was likely to impede proper working of the futures market[10] but it is also evident that many markets greatly exceed this ratio.

Notes and References

1   Jeremy C. Stein, 'Information Externalities and Welfare-Reducing Speculation', *Journal of Political Economy*, Vol. 95, No. 6, 1124, December 1987.

2   Readers should note that this is not the same as short-*term* speculation. Short-side speculation or short speculation is speculation (by selling now and buying later) in anticipation of a falling price, while short-term speculation is speculation for a short *period* of time.

3   Y. Inamura, T. Kimata, T. Kimura and T. Muto, 'Recent Surge in Global Commodity Prices–Impact of Financialisation of Commodities and Globally Accommodative Monetary Conditions', *Bank of Japan Review*, March 2011.

4   M. Lombardi and F. Ravazzolo, *On the Correlation between Commodity and Equity Returns: Implications for Portfolio Allocation*, BIS Working Papers No 420, July 2013.

5   Not to be confused with short-*term* speculation: Short-side speculation or short speculation is speculation (by selling now and buying later) in anticipation of a falling price, while short-term speculation is speculation for a short *period* of time.

6   If the US housing bubble of the first decade of the twenty-first century is used as an analogy, the destabilizing behaviour produced large profits for some and large losses for others – but the second category consisted of average home owners.

7   S. Bhikchandani and S. Sharma, *Herd Behaviour in Financial Markets*, IMF Staff Papers, Vol. 47, No. 3, 2001.

8   H. R. Stoll and R. E. Whaley, 'Commodity Index Investing and Commodity Futures Prices'. Available at: http://www.cftc.gov/ucm/groups/public/@swaps/documents/file/plstudy_45_hsrw.pdf.; it received a grant from Gresham Investment Management LLC which 'pioneered the management of diversified commodity investment portfolios using commodity futures' and 'manages in excess of $16 billion for a variety of clients' (from their website: http://greshamllc.com/en/pages.php?s=1.) Both accessed on 11 July 2014.

9   H. Working, 'Speculation in Hedging Markets', *Food Research Institute Studies*, Stanford University, Vol. 1, Issue 2, 199, May 1960.

10 D. R. Sanders, S. H. Irwin and R. P. Merrin, 'The Adequacy of Speculation in Agricultural Futures Markets: Too Much of a Good Thing?', *Journal of Applied Economic Perspectives and Policy*, Vol. 32, No. 1, 77–94, 2010.

8

Causes of the Rapid Growth in Derivatives Trading: A Historical Perspective

By far the most significant event in finance during the past decade has been the extraordinary development and expansion of financial derivatives.

Alan Greenspan, 19 March 1999[1]

As was seen in Chapter 1, derivatives volumes have expanded stupendously over the last three decades. This chapter provides a broad historical perspective on the reasons for this expansion in the period preceding the global financial crisis of 2008.

Structural changes in financial markets

The period from the late 1960s to the early 1980s witnessed major structural change in world financial markets. It witnessed the rise of the 'eurodollar' market where non-American institutions raised and deposited dollars in Europe and elsewhere. The fixed exchange rate regime that prevailed from 1945 fell apart and most major currencies began to float, creating currency risks that had been absent earlier. In the late 1970s and early 1980s, influenced by 'monetarist' economists like Milton Friedman, several leading central banks (the US and UK for instance) began to target money supply as a means of controlling inflation, using interest rate changes as the main instrument. They thus moved from relatively stable interest rates to frequently changing rates, greatly increasing interest rate volatility.

The Arab–Israeli war and oil embargo of 1973 and the two major oil crises of 1973 and 1979 greatly increased uncertainties in the commodity markets. They also resulted in huge foreign exchange surpluses with major oil producing countries ('petrodollars') which had to find investment avenues in the international markets.

Together, these changes resulted in a quantum leap in the level of uncertainty faced in the financial markets and hence the demand for instruments of risk management such as forwards, futures and options.

While floating exchange and interest rates, commodity price volatility and uncertainties were proximate causes for the growth and use of derivatives, other forces were also at work.

Interventionist capitalism replaced by liberal capitalism

World War II had been preceded by the Great Depression of the 1930s, a time when policies of austerity – anchored in classical economics – had been widespread in the western world. When World War II ended, one personality towered above the rest in the field of economics and that was the Briton, John Maynard Keynes. His approach, which accorded an important place to fiscal policy and government intervention within a market economy, dominated economic policy making at least for a quarter century after the war ended. The combination of high inflation and high unemployment in the Western economies in the 1970s resulted in a mood of introspection and review of the role of governments and their interventionist approaches to economic problems.

Margaret Thatcher became Prime Minister of Britain in 1979 and Ronald Reagan came to office in the 1980 US Presidential election. An intellectual counter-revolution was already brewing in the United States and to a lesser extent in Britain too. Fama published a highly influential paper on the theory of efficient markets in 1970.[2] This held that markets were generally efficient in capturing and reflecting all known information within the market price and so it would generally be futile to try and 'beat' the market. In 1976, Sargent and Wallace published a paper on policy ineffectiveness. They stated that, under the assumption that people were rational and do not make systematic errors, government economic policies would generally be ineffective because people would fully discount the effects of such policies.[3] In other words, if people were rational and could not be fooled by either spending or taxation policies of the government, then it followed that the government should not try to manage the economy actively but simply let people manage their economic affairs in good and bad times. Economic activity would regulate itself and adjust itself to cycles; government intervention was neither necessary nor effective. Thus, the policy of *laissez faire* was given a new lease of life.

Box 8.1: Rationality of economic agents

Interestingly, even at the time they were being proposed, the theories of Fama, Sargent and Wallace and others on market efficiency and rational expectations contradicted the findings of behavioural scientists Kahneman and Tversky. In the early 1970s Tversky handed Kahneman a paper on the psychological assumptions of economic theory. As Kahneman recalled:

"I can still recite its first sentence: 'The agent of economic theory is rational, selfish, and his tastes do not change'. I was astonished. My economic colleagues worked in the building next door, but I had not appreciated the profound difference between our intellectual worlds. To a psychologist, it is self-evident that people are neither fully rational nor completely selfish, and that their tastes are anything but stable."[4]

Once it was concluded that economic activity was self-regulating, the proposition began to be applied more widely. In the US, a wave of de-regulation and liberalization swept the financial sector. Ceilings on interest rates that banks could offer on their deposits were removed. Restrictions on inter-state banking were lifted and the clear separation of commercial and investment banking was slowly chipped away throughout the Eighties, culminating in the repeal of the Glass-Steagall Act in 1999. (From a longer term perspective, the extent of de-regulation first peaked before the Great Depression of the 1930s. De-regulation gave way to re-regulation from the 1940s until the 1970s; from the 1980s, another wave of de-regulation started and continued till 2008,[5] exceeding the previous peak in terms of its scope and depth.)

The process of securitization grew over the same period. A set of individual loans and their associated cash flows was bundled together and aggregated into a marketable security. The creation of such synthetic securities facilitated an increase in credit but it also facilitated the development of new derivatives. Securitization became more and more prevalent and attained new levels of complexity in the first years of the twenty-first century. Minsky, in his very early and far-sighted look at securitization, argued that securitization was partly a lagged response to monetarism.[6]

The mathematical approach to economics

Freedom from regulation unleashed creativity and partly as a result, mathematics was introduced in a big way into economics. Economics used to be part of the humanities. It is said that the oft-cited paper by Harold Hotelling (a pioneer of mathematical economics and statistics) on the economics of exhaustible resources was rejected by the *Economic Journal* because it was too mathematical and he ended up publishing it in the *Journal of Political Economy*. During the twentieth century, economics took a steadily more mathematical turn. Since the 1980s, it is almost as though it aspired to join the hall of natural sciences through its 'dark secret love of mathematical elegance'.[7] The use of mathematics lent an aura of precision and sophistication to finance and economics, further reinforcing the belief in the rational foundations of human choices and decisions.

The extensive inroads that mathematics had made into economics required the deployment of mathematicians and physicists on Wall Street. Their presence and their natural felicity with differential and integral calculus, equations full of Greek letters, and algorithms to solve those equations, convinced Wall Street firms that they could measure and manage risk more easily than they had ever done in the past. The new mathematical methodology enabled the development of derivative pricing models and this enabled previously obscure instruments to become more widely used. (It is another matter that the models were not always accurate or reliable – see Chapter 10.) A key mathematical model that had a revolutionary impact in spurring the growth of options markets in particular and derivatives in general, was the Black–Scholes option pricing model, unveiled in 1971. It made options pricing relatively simple whereas this had earlier required actuarial calculations.

The development of computing power

Initially (until the 1970s), the mathematical approach tended to remain confined to universities (and did not enter the banking and finance industry) because many of the complicated calculations required to translate theoretical models into practice were impossible to do quickly and cheaply. The rapid pace of innovation in computer science, which eventually enabled traders to perform real-time mathematical calculations in split seconds from their desks or even on the trading floor, enabled these models to be put to use in day-to-day trading and this made it possible to create new kinds of complex derivatives.

Secular decline in interest rates

By the early 1980s, the building blocks of the derivatives explosion were falling into place. However, a most important requirement – low interest rates – was yet to fall into place. Derivative products are leverage based (i.e., involve taking debt) because they can be transacted by putting up just a fraction of their value with the rest implicitly borrowed from the market. Leverage, as the word suggests, amplifies gains and losses. Leverage thrives when borrowing is cheap. The seventies and early eighties were marked by high inflation. In 1982, the Federal funds rate was at 16 per cent and the US 10-year Treasury note yielded over 15 per cent. Entering the decade of the eighties, the United States had an inflation rate of 12.4 per cent. Paul Volcker, who became Chairman of the Federal Reserve in 1979, began to squeeze inflation out of the economy, despite the then President Reagan engaging in a massive fiscal expansion. He raised interest rates to astronomical levels and did not mind putting the US economy through two recessions in the space of three years. Both inflation and interest rates peaked then and began a long secular decline, though they remained volatile (with short periods of rising interest rates from time to time).

In 1987, Volcker gave way to Alan Greenspan who was a proclaimed devotee of Ayn Rand, the high priestess of liberalism. He unreservedly extended the logic of self-regulation to the financial industry and was a keen supporter of moves to de-regulate or reduce the regulatory supervision over it. He supported the dismantling of the Glass–Steagall Act (which had imposed restrictions on commercial banks and insurance companies doing investment banking) and encouraged placing as little of the derivatives market activity as possible under the supervision of the Commodity Futures Trading Commission.

His biggest act of support for derivatives was to come later. Though Greenspan himself had warned of 'irrational exuberance' in the stock market in 1996, he later came to believe the boom in share prices was quite rational after all and grounded in productivity improvements from new technology. He raised interest rates briefly in 1999 but when the technology share bubble burst in 2000, he responded with major cuts in interest rates (a classic instance of the 'Greenspan put' – see below). Then the deadly terrorist strike on the World Trade Centre in New York in September 2001 hurt both the stock market and the economy and tipped the economy into a recession. Greenspan unleashed the arrows of massive and successive interest rate cuts from his monetary policy quiver. The Federal funds rate was brought down to 1.75 per cent from 6.5 per cent in 2001, then to 1.25 per cent in 2002 and 1 per cent in 2003. It remained there for the next one year.

The rate cuts by the US forced other countries to follow suit lest their currencies appreciate excessively under the weight of their 'heavier' interest rates compared to the ultra-light US interest rates. Thus, global interest rates – nominal or real – reached historic lows in 2002 and remained there until 2004 before they inched their way back up slowly. Figures 8.1 to 8.4 show how real short rates (nominal 3-month deposit rate adjusted for inflation) were well below their historical averages and how such below-average rates persisted for a few years at the start of the millennium. It should be noted that this covered the major financial centres of the world – the US, the UK, the Eurozone, Switzerland, Australia and Japan (charts for UK and Australia are not shown here, however.)

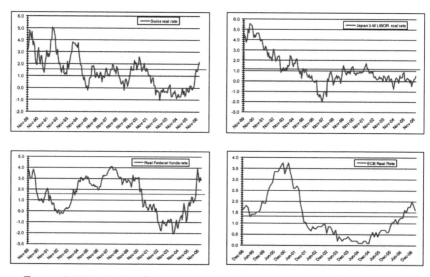

Figures 8.1, 8.2, 8.3, 8.4: Short-term interest rates for Swiss Franc (Swiss real rate), Japanese Yen (three-month real LIBOR), US Dollar (real federal funds rate) and Euro (ECB real rate) respectively, 1989–2007

Source: Bloomberg

Note: Historical average is the horizontal straight line.

Other things being equal, the lower the interest rate, the higher the investment spending. Of course, other things may not be equal. If cheap money signals a less optimistic outlook for the future (as was the case in 2002) it does not necessarily encourage long-term investment. On the other hand low interest rates do facilitate speculative investing and trading (see Box 8.2). There is evidence to support the hypothesis that low interest rates encourage speculative investments even more than real investments.[8] Derivative instruments come in handy for speculative purposes, and the statistics show clearly that speculative use far exceeds use for hedging purposes. This was thus another factor promoting the growth of derivatives trading.

Box 8.2: Low interest rates and speculation

Low interest rates tend to promote speculation for several reasons:

1. Other things being equal, low interest rates are a disincentive for savings through bank deposits. The opportunity cost of not spending is lower. With bank fees sometimes higher than interest rates, keeping money in the bank will even reduce the stock of savings. Hence, it makes sense to take it out and use it to spend or speculate.

2. Low interest rates induce savers to seek higher yielding investments because their targeted returns from savings are unlikely to be attained. They may have a fixed return in mind to supplement their earnings and to provide for their retirement or for bulk expenses. Hence, they seek higher yielding investment options many of which involve speculation.

3. Low interest rates make it easy for foreign exchange speculators to short a currency. When someone (a currency speculator) 'shorts' a currency, they borrow in that currency to sell it in the market. Their hope is that the currency would decline in value so that they can buy it back it at a lower price later and return the currency loan that they had taken. The currency has to drop in value by enough to make it profitable for them to return the loan with interest. Obviously, the lower the rate of interest, the lower the hurdle for a profitable 'short' transaction. That is why central banks, as the first line of defence against a falling currency, raise interest rates. A higher cost of borrowing deters some speculators, and increases the cost for other speculators.

4. Low interest rates facilitate buying on margin. Investors in the stock market buy stocks with a small amount of their own capital, and borrow the rest. This is called leverage. They are using debt as a lever to enhance their returns. Naturally, the lower the interest rate, the greater is the temptation or inducement to engage in buying on the margin.

The role of foreign exchange reserve accumulation

The historical low in interest rates ushered in at the start of the millennium had coincided with another phenomenon: the accumulation of foreign exchange reserves by central banks in developing countries, principally China and oil exporting nations. This was in response to the Asian crisis when Asian nations felt the absence of adequate foreign exchange reserves to defend their currencies. When they ran out of reserves, they had to go to the International Monetary Fund (IMF) for assistance and accept onerous conditions. They swore never again to find themselves in such a situation. So, they began to accumulate foreign exchange reserves and keep their currencies undervalued relative to what was seen as the fundamental equilibrium.

On its part, having devalued its currency in 1993 and thus having set in motion the train of events that culminated eventually in the Asian crisis in 1997–98, China entered the new millennium facing a massive currency disadvantage. The super-normal depreciation of other Asian currencies and a rapidly depreciating US dollar due to abysmally low interest rates in the US had made the Chinese fear substantial erosion of their export competitiveness. China, having set its sights on becoming a major global economic force powered by exports – a strategy that Japan deployed to great effect in the Sixties and Seventies – decided to intervene substantially in foreign exchange markets to keep its currency competitive. China began to accumulate foreign exchange reserves with a zeal that left others far behind, reaching $3.95 trillion in March 2014 (see Figure 8.1).

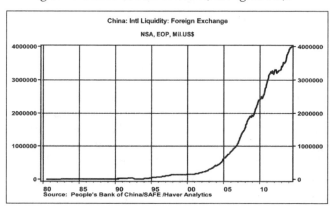

Figure 8.5: Total Foreign Exchange Reserves of China (incl. gold) as of end-March 2014 (in millions of U.S. dollars)
Note: NSA/EOP denote Non-Seasonally Adjusted/End of Period.

Then, the question was what to do with the foreign exchange reserves. They had to be invested in the countries in whose currencies they were held. Most of the reserves were held in US dollars since it is the global transaction and numeraire currency. Reserves cannot be held in illiquid, long gestation or long duration investments. They are needed in a crisis. Moreover, central banks are not investment managers.[9] Hence, the bulk of the reserves went into liquid Treasury securities. The investment in Treasury securities had the effect of helping to keep interest rates low by lowering borrowing costs for the US government and thereby for all other debt instruments.

That was the direct contribution of foreign exchange reserve accumulation of emerging central banks to the boom in derivatives. The indirect contribution is a little more complex.

Flat yield curve and behavioural impact of resulting profit squeeze

The bond markets normally display a 'yield curve' whereby the interest rate on longer term bonds is higher than on shorter term bonds. For instance, if the interest rate on a 1-year bond is 5 per cent, the interest rate on a 10-year bond might be 7 per cent and on a 30-year bond, 8 per cent. Most of the investment of foreign exchange reserves was at the longer end of the maturity distribution and this made the yield curve (the differential between short-term and long-term interest rates) flatter than it would normally be. Banks typically borrow short term and lend long term. The duration gap also affords them the interest rate margin and generates their profits. When long-term interest rates are squeezed lower because of foreign central banks parking their reserves in Treasuries, the banks find themselves with a lower profit margin. Thus the flatter yield curve in recent years meant that bankers' profits were squeezed.

The flatness of the yield curve came on top of pressure on profits due to international competition, since most Western markets are open to banks from all countries. Bankers had to take higher risks to generate profits.

Why were profits important? Were they important to shareholders? In theory, the answer is 'yes'. In reality, shareholder wealth maximization seems to have provided an acceptable ruse for managers to boost their own compensation since the bulk of their contingent compensation was tied to short-term profitability. Chart 8.6 below shows how wages in the financial industry grew disproportionately to benchmark wages between 1990 and 2008. (The benchmark wage represents the average wage in the private sector adjusted for changes in skill levels in the financial sector.)

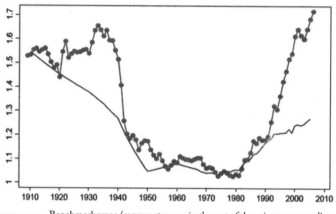

Benchmark wage (represents wage in the rest of the private sector adjusted for changing skill levels in the financial sector)

Actual financial sector wage

Figure 8.6: Actual wages in the financial industry vis-à-vis benchmark

Source: Wages and Human Capital in the U.S. Financial Industry: 1909–2006, Thomas Philippon and Ariell Reshef, New York University and University of Virginia respectively, December 2008

One way to boost returns is to trade more derivatives. The chain of causation went thus:

- a large part of the remuneration for managers and traders was based on profits in a given year;
- therefore they had an incentive to increase profits;
- normal margins were squeezed by increased competition and a flattened yield curve;
- therefore higher profits had to come from taking more risks;
- derivatives offered a convenient way to take more risks; and
- therefore, derivatives trading expanded.

From the point of view of individuals working in the banks, the more these derivatives were OTC types, the better since they were less under regulatory scrutiny and were outside the ambit of restrictions and margin requirements imposed by exchanges.

The 'Greenspan Put' and 'Too Big To Fail'

A strategy of higher returns through higher risk carried an enhanced probability of insolvency – which in economic theory is supposed to restrain rational market participants from taking excessive risk. In practice, this did not happen, partly because of the actions of the US Federal Reserve under Greenspan. In one respect, Greenspan's interventionist instincts were at odds with his philosophical guru: whenever financial asset prices declined substantially, he rode to the rescue of financial markets with cuts in interest rates and liquidity support. This happened time and again, and the measure earned the sobriquet of the 'Greenspan put' – a put option available to all equity investors in the event of a fall in the market. Another interventionist action of the Federal Reserve under Greenspan was the rescue of the hedge fund Long Term Capital Management in 1998 when, rather than let the investors face the full consequences of their actions, the Federal Reserve coordinated a bailout by banks. This sent a signal that if an institution was 'too big to fail' it could expect intervention. It attenuated the risk of bankruptcy that, in financial theory at least, acts as a restraint against the taking of excessive risk and further encouraged the tendency of big investment banks to develop and invest in derivatives.

Conclusion

The extraordinary growth in derivatives markets between the 1970s and 2008 was a result of many factors:

- long-term structural trends in the global economy (increased volatility in an era of larger capital flows and floating exchange and interest rates, new technology and knowledge enabling use of complex models, etc.)
- specific economic policies of large economies like the USA (low interest rates inducing enhanced speculation) and China (low exchange rate and reserve accumulation requiring investment avenues);
- policy attitudes (laissez faire and deregulation); and
- behavioural responses of the financial services industry to policies.

Notes and References

[1] A. Greenspan, *Financial Derivatives,* speech before the Futures Industry Association, Boca Raton, Florida, 19 March 1999. Available at: http://www.federalreserve.gov/boarddocs/speeches/1999/19990319.htm. Accessed on 11 July 2014.

2   E. Fama, 'Efficient Capital Markets: A Review of Theory and Empirical Work', *Journal of Finance*, Vol. 25, No. 2, 383–417, May 1970.

3   T. Sargent and N. Wallace, 'Rational Expectations and the Theory of Economic Policy', *Journal of Monetary Economics*, Vol. 2, No. 2, 169–83, April 1976.

4   Michael Lewis, 'The King of Human Error', *Vanity Fair*, December 2011.

5   T. Philippon and A. Reshef, 'Wages and Human Capital in the U.S. Financial Industry: 1909–2006', New York University and University of Virginia respectively, December 2008. Available at: http://pages.stern.nyu.edu/~tphilipp/papers/pr_rev15.pdf. Accessed on 14 July 2014.

6   H. P. Minsky, *Securitization*, Hyman Minsky Archive, Paper 15, 1987. Available at: http://digitalcommons.bard.edu/ hm_archive/15. Accessed on 14 July 2014.

7   E. Derman and P. Wilmott, *The Financial Modellers' Manifesto*, 7 January 2009. Available at: http://papers.ssrn.com/sol3/papers.cfm?abstract_id=1324878. Accessed on 14 July 2014.

8   See, for instance, 'The Fed Discovers Hyman Minsky', Free Exchange, *The Economist*, 7 January 2010.

9   It is a different matter that many governments in Asia, including China, Qatar, Abu Dhabi and Singapore, set up sovereign wealth funds to invest their foreign exchange reserves. From an economist's point of view, this is a controversial move with potential undesirable consequences for the integrity of the marketplace.

9

The Role of Derivatives in the Global Financial Crisis of 2008

In 2008, the financial system failed. The financial regulatory system failed. Though there were many causes of the 2008 financial crisis, derivatives played a central role.

Gary Gensler[1]

The global financial crisis of 2008 was one of the most important economic events of recent decades, with long-lasting consequences. The causes of the crisis were several but there is little doubt that derivatives were one of the factors. This chapter begins with a very brief and simplified description of the crisis and its origins, and then examines the specific role that derivatives played.

The background and origin of the crisis

At the beginning of the twenty-first century a series of events prompted the US Federal Reserve to follow a loose monetary policy. In 1996, the then Federal Reserve Chairman, Alan Greenspan, had expressed concerns over 'irrational exuberance' in the stock market, but in the following three years share prices rose even higher. Greenspan became convinced that these increases were not irrational and reflected the productivity increases arising from the new internet-based technologies and, therefore, chose not to tighten monetary policy. There was an unexpectedly steep fall in the US stock market in 2000, when the earlier 'dotcom boom' ended and the prices of technology stocks, in particular, collapsed. It appeared that the Federal Reserve felt that the stock market crash might put this growth in jeopardy through a negative 'wealth effect' (i.e., if people feel less wealthy, they may spend less and thus reduce aggregate demand in the economy). In order to avoid or minimize a recession, the Federal Reserve felt obliged to provide a monetary stimulus. The terrorist attack of 11 September 2011 led to further interest rate cuts (another instance of the 'Greenspan put' mentioned in Chapter 8). With the benefit of hindsight, one can argue that *Al Qaeda* had some role to play in the global financial crisis of 2008.

The Federal funds rate in America was slashed to a low of 1.0 per cent by 2003. It was held there for another year after that. The US dollar weakened as a result. Other countries lowered their interest rates partly in response to the aggressive reduction in interest rates by and in the US overall, easy credit conditions were the norm in the US and most of the world for the early years of this century.

Fuelled by low interest rates and easy credit, there was rapid growth in mortgage lending by US banks for the purpose of purchasing house property between 2000 and 2006. The increase in demand for houses naturally led to a rise in real estate prices.

All mortgage borrowers are expected to ensure that the value of their loan is less than the value of the collateral (house property). The difference between the value of a house and the amount of the loan given to acquire it is the 'equity' which the owner of the house has to provide and then maintain. If a house is worth a million dollars, a bank may be willing to lend, say, 70 per cent of the value or $700,000 to acquire it with the balance of $300,000 being the equity that the buyer has to put up. If the price of the house were to fall beyond a certain tolerance level, the bank would require an infusion of equity by the owner to bring back the loan-to-value ratio to 70 per cent. For instance, if the price of the house falls to $800,000, the bank would only provide 70 per cent of 800,000 or $560,000. To reduce the loan from the original value of $700,000 to $560,000 the owner of the house would have to bring in about $140,000. If this were not done, the bank would have the right to repossess the property and then 'foreclose' and sell it. The owner might lose a large part, or all, of the equity in such distress sales.

On the other hand, when the price of houses rises, the loan-to-value ratio will fall. In most countries, it is not normal or conventional for lenders to allow the owner to readily reduce the amount of equity taking advantage of a rise in house prices. However, in the highly de-regulated US market, this was common and mortgage lenders competed with each other to allow owners to get back part of their equity by re-negotiating the mortgage. Re-negotiations would involve a fee, which was a seemingly risk-free income for the lender and this was the driving force for the sales staff of the banks. Thus, when house prices rose, owners were able to withdraw some of the equity they had put in earlier. The disadvantage from an economic point of view was that any subsequent fall in house prices would now require a re-infusion of equity, which the owner might not be able to do because they might have spent the money received.

Over a period of time, mortgage lending was extended even to 'sub-prime' borrowers, those whose creditworthiness was below the 'prime' quality normally expected for bank lending. The lending was on very liberal terms with small levels of equity, and based on optimism that house prices would continuously rise and therefore the borrowers' lack of creditworthiness or inadequacy of equity would not be a problem in recovering the loan. On this optimistic basis, sub–prime borrowers were often allowed to start with very low payments using a low 'introductory rate' initially, with the interest rate and monthly payments increasing after a year or two. For instance the rate of interest might be only 3 per cent in the first year but rise to 5 per cent in the next year. These were also called 'teaser rates' in the sense that they would tease the borrower into taking the loan based on easy initial affordability.

Another feature of the US housing market was that these individual mortgages were 'securitized' or 'packaged' into 'mortgage backed securities' (MBS), consisting of a group of mortgages. (The term 'asset backed securities' is similar and refers to a wider class of assets.) These were then further securitized into 'collateralized debt obligations' (CDOs) by segregating the interest payments into tranches. The over-simplified example below illustrates the working of CDOs.

Example 9.1: CDO tranches

Bank A has made loans to 100 borrowers. It converts these individual loans into an MBS comprising the same 100 mortgages. It sells this MBS to Finance Company B and the default risk is also passed on from A to B.

The payment expected on each mortgage is $1000 per month. Thus, if all borrowers pay without defaulting, the monthly cash inflow would be $100,000. A credit rating agency scrutinizes the loans comprised in the MBS and estimates the probability of recovering various amounts as follows:

Recovery level	Probability
At least $ 5,000	99.999 per cent
At least $ 25,000	98 per cent
At least $ 50,000	95 per cent

Company B now repackages the MBS into various tranches of CDOs — one with a monthly cash flow of $5, another with a cash flow of $(25-5) = $20 and so on. Based on the probability estimates, the first tranche is rated as 'AAA', and is purchased by another Bank C. Though the overall MBS may consist of sub–prime mortgages, the first tranche is now considered a highly creditworthy security with AAA rating. Bank C may later sell the AAA-rated CDO to Insurance company D or to Bank E in another country.

The default risk on the CDOs was often covered by purchasing CDSs, which, as seen earlier, are derivative instruments. The sellers of the CDS were financial institutions and insurance companies. They priced the CDS based on credit ratings issued by rating agencies. This is the mechanism through which derivatives played a role in both the housing boom and the subsequent bust and crisis.

Till 2000, there were regulatory restrictions, which required reporting of OTC CDS and other swap transactions in the US. The law was amended in 2000 (through the Commodity Futures Modernisation Act 2000) exempting such OTC transactions completely from regulation. In the absence of regulation, the market in such instruments exploded and because it was an unregulated market, the volumes were not apparent to outside observers and data was not published. Credit default swaps are not really 'swaps' in the conventional sense of the term, which denotes an exchange of cash flow streams, and are in fact credit insurance contracts; yet because they were called swaps and not treated as insurance, they escaped the regulatory requirements of insurance. (The use of the term 'swap' was, as will be seen later, for this very purpose.) So, even when they were issued by insurance companies like American Insurers Group (AIG), the issuers were not required to hold reserves to cover any potential losses. Many of the issuers thought these instruments were very safe because they carried AAA or AA ratings from rating agencies and this promoted rapid growth in CDS issuance.

After 2006, housing prices in the US began falling to the surprise of those in the financial services industry. One important reason was that the low introductory rate periods came to an end for many borrowers and the monthly payments required from many of the sub-prime borrowers went up. When they were unable to pay these higher monthly instalments, their properties were foreclosed and repossessed by the banks. Another was a gradual saturation of the sub-prime market. Thus commenced a declining trend in house prices. When house prices fell, many loans began to have inadequate or even negative equity, i.e., the house value became less than the value of the loan. Being sub-prime borrowers, the owners were unable to make up the difference by injecting more money and the loans went into default. Soon, the rate of default on such loans turned out to be much higher than had been anticipated by the credit rating agencies. As a result, many of the CDOs also began to suffer default on the payments. Those who had insured against such defaults by purchasing CDS, began to invoke the CDS and this created an unexpected liability for the sellers of the CDS.

Another trigger for the crisis was the choking off of global economic growth by a rise in oil prices. The price of crude oil rose steadily from around 10 dollars per barrel in 1998 to around 70 dollars per barrel by summer 2007 but then doubled in the next 12 months to reach a level of 147 dollars per barrel. Global growth caved in. Once growth collapsed, the financial edifice built on leverage quickly imploded.

As loans began to go bad and CDSs began to be invoked, a number of institutions were unable to meet their obligations. The absence of clear and verifiable information on value and ownership of CDO and CDS assets and liabilities created great uncertainty in the financial system. In 2008, the CDS/ CDO market crashed and many 'venerable' financial institutions collapsed. Bear Stearns, Northern Rock, American Insurance Group and Lehman Brothers are among those that either collapsed or were nationalized on the verge of collapse, while many others suffered catastrophic losses. The effects touched developing countries too affecting, for instance, the Indian private sector bank ICICI. The failure of so many banks unnerved the financial system and a credit squeeze ensued as banks began to distrust the creditworthiness of one another. This created a global economic recession now termed the 'Great Recession'.

The vast amounts involved were such that governments in the US, UK and several European countries had to directly provide financial support to banks with public funds (usually characterized as 'bail-outs') to prevent a complete collapse of the banking system and loss of deposits by the common depositors. In the aftermath of the crisis, some western capitalist economies ended up with more nationalized banks than formerly socialist India. The global economy has not fully recovered from the consequences of the crisis even at the time of writing.

The global dimension

If the origins of the problem were in the US, how did it become a worldwide crisis?

Firstly, global financial markets are now integrated to a much larger degree than often recognized. This is partly due to the relatively unrestricted capital flows that are now allowed by most countries. Many banks and finance companies outside the US (including some developing country banks) purchased CDOs as an investment. The CDO/CDS market acquired an enormous size and vast geographical sweep.

Secondly, as mentioned in Chapter 6, herd behaviour is common among investors. The modern tendency in investment services, albeit somewhat self-serving, is to measure investment performance against a benchmark of similar investors rather than in absolute terms. Because they would like to be sure they are doing better, or at least not worse, than the benchmark, institutional investors like pension funds and mutual funds — and their consultants and investment advisors – would rather be part of the crowd than stand out and expose themselves for being wrong. This herd mentality gives rise to correlated trends in global financial markets as it accentuates both buying and selling frenzies.

The third reason for the global nature of the crisis was that the intellectual framework of the financial system in most countries was fully or partially imported from the United States. In earlier eras, many countries had ideological positions which were opposed to market capitalism. For better or for worse, this reduced the extent to which prevailing western economic ideas affected the world as a whole. After the fall of the Soviet Union, and the spread of the free market ideology, US intellectual ideas have had much larger influence.

Fourthly, most countries operate on a formal or informal dollar standard, i.e., target a certain level for the exchange rate of their currency vis-à-vis the dollar. When the US dollar strengthens due to restrictive monetary policies in the US, these countries too tighten policies to avoid excessive currency weakness. They accentuate US tightening. When the US has a loose monetary policy, the US dollar weakens and their currencies appreciate. They counter it by following loose policies of their own. Thus, they accentuate US easing. This is what happened between 2002 and 2007. As the US adopted looser policies in this period, most countries followed suit, in what Raghuram Rajan (governor of the Reserve Bank of India) termed 'competitive monetary easing'.[2]

For all these reasons, the US housing bubble became a global credit bubble. When that bubble burst, it created a global crisis.

What went wrong?

The main causes of, and issues relating to, the crisis can be divided into two parts: broader economic factors (unrelated to derivatives) and the more specific contribution of financial innovation and derivatives. These are examined further below, starting with factors not related to derivatives.

Excessive credit

As was seen above, the 'housing bubble' (excessive house prices) was a cause of the crisis. Not all bubbles burst and not all bursts turn into global crises. The enormity of the problem from a 'burst bubble' is influenced by the amount of leverage that went into the bubble. An asset price bubble, when it ends, does not create a crisis unless it was also accompanied by a credit bubble. The period after the collapse of share prices in America in 2000 (known as the dotcom bust) witnessed (as was mentioned above) a very loose monetary policy from the US Federal Reserve and this excessive credit was the helium that inflated the bubble beyond danger level.

Credit rating failures

Going by economic theory, as more and more credit is issued, the riskiness of credit should come into sharper focus and debt should be priced correctly and appropriately, for the growing risk entailed as more of it is issued. That is where things went very wrong. Credit rating agencies did not identify the growing risk and the rating agencies thus had a very big role in the crisis. The business model of credit raters — where the issuer pays the agency — has much to with this.

Loose monetary policy leading to rising commodity prices

The only way the increase in prosperity created by the housing-cum-credit bubble could last was through ever-rising home prices. Financial market participants genuinely thought that was not outlandish. The Federal Reserve was raising interest rates only gradually, if at all. The unemployment rate was low and incomes were growing. There was a belief that the major economies, and the USA in particular, were in a 'Great Moderation'. This was based on evidence that the volatility of consumption, investment and output had 'moderated' and remained low for many years since 1984. Ben Bernanke, before he became Federal Reserve Chairman, offered three possible explanations for the decline in volatility: structural change, improved macroeconomic policies and 'good luck'.[3] Suffice it to say that it was felt that the Great Moderation was here to stay and major recessions were unlikely to occur. So, the foundations of an everlasting housing boom were in place — or so many thought.

Then, unexpected 'one-off' factors came into play: food and energy prices began to rise and they rose relentlessly, contributing to the halting of the hoped for virtuous cycle. Commodities were always in excess supply in the 1980s and 1990s. That changed in the new millennium. Synchronized global growth, facilitated by the loose monetary policy followed in many countries, raised demand for commodities.

The role of financial 'innovation' in general and derivatives in particular

The causative factors of the crisis mentioned above were independent of financial 'innovation' and thus it is likely that serious problems would have arisen anyway. However, financial 'innovations' and derivatives did end up contributing in a large way, making the problems much larger than they would otherwise have been.

The term 'financial innovation' became common after the late 1990s as a way of referring to the plethora of new instruments, markets and complex tailored transactions, many of which involved creating new derivative instruments or using existing ones in new ways. (The term has been put in inverted commas here because 'innovation' conveys a positive sense of improvement but many new instruments were not necessarily 'improvements' and may have had negative effects. Further, systemic considerations, i.e., the wider effects, were rarely applied when judging innovations to be good or bad.)

Securitization and new instruments

Securitization (converting individual one-on-one liabilities and assets into securities that can be bought and sold) itself was a major financial innovation. It helped in risk management and in freeing up balance sheets. If a bank can sell its loans to another entity and if those loans can then be sliced into securities of different risk categories and resold by that entity based on the usual payment and failure patterns of interest and principal, then banks' balance sheets are freed up and the risk of the loan portfolio is shared by many market participants.

Unfortunately, however, financial market participants have a knack of taking a good thing and using so much of it that it turns toxic. While securitization itself was a legitimate innovation, further securitization of securitized loans (through CDOs) was probably not. When securitized mortgage loans were further securitized and sliced into CDOs with different risk categories, it resulted in the creation of a massive secondary market in these complex derivative securities. In some cases there were CDOs, which consisted of parcels of other CDOs (known as 'CDO squared'.) This led to a situation where the ultimate risk-bearer could often not be identified. In reality, there was no safe category anymore in these instruments that were securitized multiple times over. Further, in effect, a mountain of leverage had been built on the original home mortgage; a progressively smaller and weaker foundation of equity supported a huge securitization (debt) superstructure.

It is one thing to securitize the loans that banks made – whether they are loans made for homes (mortgages), automobile purchases (car loans) or for education (student loans) and consumer credit (credit card) - but it is another thing for securitization to *drive the supply of loans*, which began to happen[4]. Securitization was a source of lucrative fees to banks, brokers and rating agencies. Mortgage banks and brokers chased potential borrowers to make loans so that these mortgage loans could be securitized. Unsurprisingly, the quality of loans deteriorated as the marginal borrower had no income, no job or assets (the so-called NINJA) and yet was 'made' eligible to receive loans. Considerable fraud and deception were features of this mortgage loan and securitization binge. It is not only the case that the tail (financial sector) wagged the dog (the real economy) but also within the financial sector, many other tails wagged their respective dogs. Securitization of mortgage loans, especially between 2005 and 2007, was a classic example.

Overall, the combination of the somewhat older innovation of securitization

(ABS or asset-backed securities/MBS) with the relatively new innovations of CDOs and CDS played a major role in creating a false sense of security. The general impression, shared by many experts including those in central banks, was that risks had been properly 'priced, sliced and diced' - i.e., the extent of risk had been quantified precisely, parcelled into tranches, priced accurately in accordance with risk, and sold to institutions most capable of bearing it. (This was assumed to be part of the reason for the 'Great Moderation'.) Therefore, it was assumed, risk was now spread in a more efficient manner, an assumption that went spectacularly wrong.

Excessive de-regulation of OTC derivatives

Prior to 2000, derivatives traded outside regulated exchanges suffered from legal infirmities that made them difficult to enforce because they ran the risk of being treated as gambling contracts. In the US, restrictions on OTC derivatives were removed by the Commodity Futures Modernisation Act of 2000 leaving them completely unregulated. The Glass–Steagall Act (Banking Act 1933) of the US was gradually relaxed and finally repealed in 1999 and this made it possible for investment banking to be combined with commercial banking. These changes facilitated the growth of the CDS industry whereby banks and financial institutions offered credit insurance, albeit named credit default 'swap'. As mentioned earlier, unlike a true swap, a CDS does not involve the swapping of streams of cash flows. In essence, it is nothing but an insurance contract – an agreement to pay a sum in the event of a particular uncertain event occurring in return for a fixed premium paid in advance. (However, normal insurance contracts require an insurable interest, i.e., the person taking out the insurance must have an interest in the preservation of the asset. For instance, a person cannot take out insurance on an asset owned by a stranger or on a stranger's life). The use of the term credit default swap instead of credit default insurance was to avoid the industry being regulated by insurance regulators.

Self-regulation and non-transparency of derivatives

CDSs were not traded in recognized exchanges where the exchange becomes the 'buyer to every seller' and the 'seller to every buyer'. They were traded bilaterally between counterparties. Therefore, they were subject only to the regulations of the International Swaps and Derivatives Association (ISDA) and this is an industry body. It is not a regulator.

The severe weaknesses of self-regulation in this area were illustrated in 2012 by the debt restructuring that Greece announced, which was tantamount to a sovereign default. The ISDA initially ruled that they would not treat this as a default event and credit default swaps would not be paid (on grounds that the original proposal supposedly only invoked voluntary participation on part of the debt-holders), nullifying the very purpose of buying credit default protection. Subsequently, when the Hellenic Republic invoked collective action clauses to force all debt–holders to participate in the debt restricting, ISDA ruled that a credit event had occurred triggering payments under the credit default swaps that had been bought (either by bond-holders to protect from losses or by speculators to profit from a Greek default or debt restructuring.[5]) The episode illustrated that credit default swaps carried an element of 'discretion' to be exercised by the self-regulatory body, possibly in its own interest, and could not necessarily be relied upon when they were most needed.

The bigger problem with the OTC market was that (because it was not exchange–traded) there were no real-time statistics on gross and net exposures for the market as a whole or for individual participants. The gross figure becomes misleading because some of the positions will cancel out. Yet, at the time of the crisis, it was unclear to participants and regulators what the net exposure was vis-à-vis the gross and hence the worst was assumed by all.

Moral hazard and perverse incentives resulting from certain 'innovations'

A credit default swap is an insurance against credit default risk. Hence, logically it should be bought by the holders of bonds that face a credit risk. However, it was noted above that CDS – not being classified as insurance – does not require an insurable interest. Because of this, the amount of the CDSs outstanding in the world dwarfs the amount of outstanding bonds (and in 2007 was greater than global GDP). Many institutions acquired CDS on the secondary market as *investments* without any interest in the original credit. If so much money is at stake on a disaster happening (credit default), then perhaps, there is a perverse incentive to make the risk materialize rather than take measures to prevent it from happening. Thus, there is moral hazard written all over the credit default swap industry. The SEC did bring a suit against some participants in the industry alleging that some of the mortgage securitizations had underlying mortgages that were handpicked to fail and then the investor bought credit default swaps on them![6]

Even if such behaviour was more the exception than the norm, the moral hazard was that *the ability to get rid of the credit risks after a loan was made reduced the attention paid by lenders to assessing credit quality at the time of making the loan.* As Keys *et al* pointed out, '[t]here is now substantial evidence which suggests that securitization, the act of converting illiquid loans into liquid securities, contributed to bad lending by reducing the incentives of lenders to carefully screen borrowers'.[7]

Yet another moral hazard was that many complex derivatives involved large fees for the institutions structuring them. This created an incentive for complicated structured transactions to be peddled by investment advisers, but the resulting complexity reduced the level of information and transparency in the market.

CDSs were issued by insurance companies (e.g., AIG, MBIA or Municipal Bond Insurance Association and AMBAC or American Municipal Bond Assurance Corporation) in such large volumes that they were bound to run into payment difficulties once home prices started to decline and borrowers fell behind on mortgages. Defaults rose and so did non-performing mortgages. Securitized instruments quickly unravelled triggering payments on the CDS. That proved too much for these three 'insurance' companies. AIG had to be bailed out by the US Treasury so that they could make good on their CDS payments to Wall Street institutions that had bought them as protection against the failure of mortgage backed securities (which they sold to their clients and retained in their portfolios too).

Ideological complacency

If there was one underlying thread, it was the failure to grasp the overall systemic risk of the various market practices that were simultaneously at play in that period. There was a widespread and deeply held belief that risk did not matter as it had been diversified away and hence tamed. This fitted well with a view that markets know best and that governmental regulation should be avoided or minimized. Conventional wisdom was that the financial sector had acquired the tools (through securitization, derivatives and other forms of financial innovation) to diversify risk and even eliminate it. Monetary policy makers felt they had learned to handle business cycles. They had convinced themselves and the rest of the world, by sheer dint of repetition, that it was their skillful handling of monetary policy in the 1980s and 1990s that had ushered in the Great Moderation and the lengthy period of non-inflationary growth. They had dismissed occasional aberrations like the LTCM incident as one-off factors. Hence, policymakers and financial market participants had become confident that there was no crisis that could not be handled by fine tuning policy. Even better, policymakers had the tools and experience to prevent crises from arising in the first place.

There was also a feeling that financial innovation had produced major economic benefits and the very size of the GDP contribution from the financial sector was cited as clear evidence of this. Before the crisis, total factor productivity growth in the financial sector exceeded that in the rest of the economy. It was thought that financial innovation had enabled the banking system to better manage risk and more efficiently allocate capital and these efficiency gains legitimately allowed the 'factors of banking production (labour and capital) to reap the benefits through high returns (wages and dividends)'.[8] In retrospect, it is clear that the economic gains from the financial sector were overestimated. Haldane and Madouros noted that the high pre-crisis returns to banking had a much more mundane explanation: 'they reflected simply increased risk-taking across the sector. This was not an outward shift in the portfolio possibility set of finance. Instead, it was a traverse up the high-wire of risk and return.'[9]

Indeed, Turner went so far as to say that some of the 'output' of the financial sector may in fact have been rents extracted from the real economy and thus some of the contribution might have been negative:

> There is no clear evidence that the growth in the scale and complexity of the financial system in the rich developed world over the last 20 to 30 years has driven increased growth or stability, and it is possible for financial activity to extract rents from the real economy rather than to deliver economic value. Financial innovation and deepening may in some ways and under some circumstances foster economic value creation, but that needs to be illustrated at the level of specific effects: it cannot be asserted a priori or on the basis of top level analysis.[10]

If an unduly benign and favourable perception of the role of finance had not taken hold, regulators may not have taken their obligations as lightly as they did.[11] They might have prescribed higher capital requirements for investment banks and might not have let credit default swaps stay outside the regulatory purview.

Conclusion

The global financial crisis had many causes, not all of which relate to derivatives. However, the complexity of some important derivative instruments and an exaggerated belief in the effectiveness of market forces and of self-regulation by the derivatives industry were important contributing factors.

At the time of writing, it is not clear that the mistakes have been so well understood that they would never be repeated. Financial institutions continue to resist legitimate regulatory restrictions and regulators and governments do not always appear to be standing firm against them.[12] Capital continues to be priced so cheaply as to encourage reckless speculation rather than providing the right incentive for saving and investment activities. There is talk again of the resumption of the 'Great Moderation'.[13] Many investors too seem to think that low interest rates and monetary liquidity would bail them all out, whereas the evidence of history is that such policies were the ones that precipitated the crisis.

Notes and References

[1]   Gary Gensler, Chairman, U.S. Commodity Futures Trading Commission in his testimony before the Financial Crisis Inquiry Commission, July 2010.

[2]   R. Rajan, 'Competitive Monetary Easing: Is It Yesterday Once More?', Remarks at the Brookings Institution, 10 April, 2014. Available at: http://rbi.org.in/scripts/BS_SpeechesView.aspx?Id=886. Accessed on 14 July 2014.

[3]   B. Bernanke, 'The Great Moderation', Speech at the meetings of the Eastern Economic Association, Washington, D.C., 20 February 2004. Available at: http://www.federalreserve.gov/boarddocs/ speeches/2004/20040220/default.htm. Accessed on 14 July 2014.

[4]   B. Keys, T. Mukherjee, A. Seru and V. Vig, 'Did Securitization Lead to Lax Screening? Evidence from Sub-prime Loans', EFA Meetings Paper. Available at http://papers.ssrn.com/sol3/papers.cfm?abstract_id=1093137. Accessed on 14 July 2014.

[5]   'Frequently Asked Questions' (FAQ) released by ISDA on 9 March 2012. Available at: http://www2.isda.org/attachment/NDEyNQ==/Greek_Sov_Debt_FAQ_Update_03-19-2012_FINAL.pdf. Accessed on 14 July 2014.

[6]   Reuters, 'Factbox: How Goldman's ABACUS deal worked'. Available at: http://www.reuters.com/article/2010/04/16/us-goldmansachs-abacus-factbox-idUSTRE63F5CZ20100416. Accessed on 14 July 2014.

[7] B. Keys, T. Mukherjee, A. Seru and V. Vig, 'Financial Regulation and Securitization: Evidence from Subprime loans', paper presented at the Carnegie-Rochester Conference on Public Policy, November 2008.

[8] A. G. Haldane and V. Madouros, 'What is the Contribution of the Financial Sector?', 22 November 2011. Available at: http://www.voxeu.org/article/what-contribution-financial-sector. Accessed on 6 November 2014.

[9] *Ibid.*

[10] Adair Turner, 'What Do Banks Do? Why Do Credit Booms and Busts Occur and What Can Public Policy Do About It?', Chapter 1 of *The Future of Finance – The LSE Report*. London School of Economics and Political Science, 2010.

[11] Edmund L. Andrews, 'Greenspan Concedes Error on Regulation', *The New York Times*, 24 October 2008.

[12] Roger Lowenstein, 'Derivatives Lobby has U.S. Regulators on the Run'. Available at: http://www.bloomberg.com/news/2012-04-17/derivatives-lobby-has-u-s-regulators-on-the-run.html. Accessed on 14 July 2014.

[13] M. D. Gadea, A. Gomez-Loscos and G. Perez-Quiros, 'Has the Great Recession ousted the Great Moderation?', Bank of Spain, February 2013.

10

Models and their Effects on Markets

Whenever we make a model of something involving human beings, we are trying to force the ugly stepsister's foot into Cinderella's pretty glass slipper. It doesn't fit without cutting off some essential parts.

Emanuel Derman and Paul Wilmott[1]

Derivatives traders and institutions today rely extensively on the use of mathematical models in deciding when, how, and how much to trade. Some of these models are public knowledge and near-universal in their application, the best example being the Black–Scholes options pricing model which is used to determine the 'right' premium to be charged for an option. Others are proprietary and used within individual institutions to help them decide on the kinds of trades they will undertake. This chapter examines some of the effects that the use of models has on the derivatives markets.

Quantitative modelling in economics is by no means a special feature of derivatives markets. Macro-econometric models and growth models (among others) have been around for many years. The Feldman–Mahalanobis growth model was the basis of India's early efforts at planned economic growth during the Second Five Year plan (1952). However, because of the unrealism of their assumptions, 'analysis based on traditional macro-econometric models has disappeared from the peer-reviewed academic literature of the past thirty years.'[2] Kling considered macro-econometric models to be inherently unscientific because 'unlike the objects of controlled experimentation, real-world events are often unique and non-repeatable' and dubbed macro-econometrics 'the science of hubris'.[3]

Models are however extremely important in derivatives markets. Apart from their use in decision-taking for traders, models are also used to determine the market values of financial instruments and to estimate unrealized gains and losses for the purpose of periodic financial statements, published as well as internal. The general accounting principle followed for financial instruments for balance sheets is that of 'fair value' which usually approximates to the common sense understanding of 'market value'. However, not all derivatives have liquid markets where the fair value can be directly determined by reference to market prices. In such cases, models are often used to determine fair value and this practice is known as 'mark-to-model' (cf. 'mark-to-market').

The orthodox view of economists is that models and theories are methods of observing and describing reality and getting a better understanding of it, just as, say, Newton's laws of motion enable a better understanding of gravity and mechanics. The formulation of a new theory or insight does not change the world any more than Newton's discovery altered the behaviour of falling apples. In short, economists provide description or analysis, not invention just as Newton's laws are descriptions not inventions. However, things are not so simple. In the case of economics, one is dealing with human beings who, unlike celestial bodies, are not impervious to what other human beings do or think. An important insight into the effect of economics on the behaviour of economies is the concept of 'performativity', and in particular its implications for models and their impacts on the functioning of derivatives markets.

The concept of performativity

Austin, writing in the context of linguistics and not economics, had propounded that utterances are of two kinds which he called 'constative' and 'performative'.[4] Constative utterances are those that describe a state of things and do no more: 'the glass is on the table', or 'it is raining'. Performative utterances are those where the *statement itself* does something or 'performs' an act.[5] The statement 'I apologise' is, in and of itself, the performance of the apology; the statements 'I bless you' or 'I sentence you to life imprisonment' are similar. Callon and others have argued that economics is performative in the sense that 'it contributes to the construction of the reality it describes'.[6] Thus they argue that economics may alter the economy rather than merely describe or observe how the economy or an economic process functions.(It should be noted, though this is often not made clear in the literature, that adoption of theories by means of government policy or legislation is not performativity – here behaviour is changed by policy, with policy influenced by theory.)

Performativity can occur to differing degrees. The weakest form occurs when some aspect of economics (a tool, a model) is simply *used* in the real economy. It may not affect the economy itself. A slightly stronger form of performativity is where the theory acts to influence and *have an effect on real economic processes and the way they are carried out.* The strong form is when the reality *shapes itself along the lines of the theory* or model. Mackenzie (see Figure 10.1) calls these 'generic', 'effective' and 'Barnesian' performativity respectively (the last term being derived from the work of the sociologist Barnes).[7] In certain circumstances, the theory may actually move economic processes away from the direction implied by the theory and this can be called 'counter-performativity'.

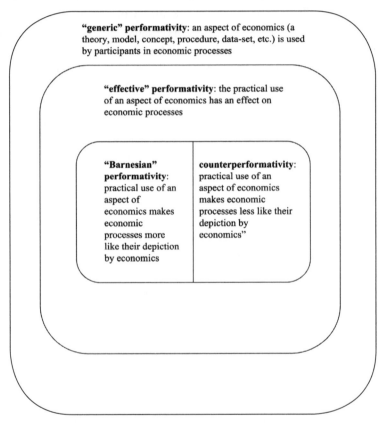

Figure 10.1: Different degrees of performativity

Source: Donald Mackenzie, Is Economics Performative? Option Theory and the Construction of Derivatives Markets, Annual meeting of the History of Economics Society, Tacoma, WA, June 25, 2005.

Performativity is similar to but not the same as a 'self-fulfilling prophecy' for two reasons. Firstly, performativity carries no implication that the theory is false whereas self-fulfilling prophecies are generally those which, though false to start with, become true by dint of repetition. Secondly, performativity can sometimes run in the reverse direction with the existence of the model or theory producing the opposite result (i.e., self-negation), as in the opinion poll illustration in Box 10.1.

Box 10.1: Performativity of opinion polls vis-à-vis election results

A simple but easily understandable example of performativity comes from a very different sphere – electoral politics. Opinion polls are, in theory, merely a way to gauge the current state of the election campaign and are in a sense a 'descriptive model'. India, like Great Britain, follows a 'first-past-the-post' electoral system; most parliamentary seats have three or more serious candidates contesting, so many winners secure less than 50 per cent of the popular vote. India has witnessed major disputes between political parties, the Election Commission and the news media about the effects of opinion polls and exit polls on actual voting in elections. On the one hand, protagonists of opinion polls (usually the media which benefits financially from enhanced circulation and viewership through polls) argue that they merely reflect public opinion. Opponents argue that poll results actually change voter behaviour, particularly through tactical voting when voters discover (through the opinion poll) that their first choice candidate is unlikely to win and shift their votes to another candidate.

It is not inconceivable that the publication of an opinion poll may itself change the actual votes polled by various candidates, because of tactical voting, and even lead (counter-performatively) to the victory of a different candidate from the one predicted in the poll. For instance, assume there are 3 candidates and the opinion poll (which is done properly) reflects that Candidates A, B and C have 40 per cent, 35 per cent and 25 per cent support respectively. The publication of the poll will make it clear to the supporters of C that their candidate is unlikely to win. They now assess whether they prefer A or B. If a sufficient number of them prefer B (in this case, 5 per cent out of the 25 per cent initially supporting C), then A may end up losing the election because of the publication of the opinion poll; instead of being a descriptive model, the opinion poll has changed the result. Thus the *process of anticipating voter behaviour may itself alter voter behaviour*. (The point here is not on the pros and cons of different electoral systems but to illustrate performativity.)

Callon and Mackenzie are both sociologists, not economists and their view of performativity has been criticized by several economists (and some critics have gone as far as to suggest that this may be an attempt by sociologists to enter the lucrative area of economic consultancy[8]). The weaker forms of performativity are the most difficult to accept. Didier, also a sociologist, expressed scepticism at the use of the term performative for a situation where statistics merely 'influence' or 'have effects' on the economy.[9]

Quite apart from conceptual criticisms, a problem with the concept is that it is not useful from a practical policy-making perspective when defined (à la Mackenzie) to include the weaker forms such as 'generic' and 'effective' performativity. Even the publication of economic statistics would be 'performative' in that sense. When so widely defined, it is close to saying that almost everything that is done has some effect on something else – true, but not of practical use. Thus at the level of economic policy in general, the usefulness of the concept appears limited, except perhaps in suggesting that bad economic theories (and not just bad economic policies) can have costs for the real economy if they influence the real economy.

Practical implications for models

To the extent that a theory or model has a *strong* performative effect, i.e., the theory is so strong or widespread that it ends up *shaping reality in its own image*, it warrants more attention. The evidence is that financial models tend to have a stronger performative effect within their spheres than broader economic theories. Thus performativity has greater significance for derivatives markets than for economics in general.

Mackenzie has established with meticulous detail that the Black–Scholes option pricing model played a strong performative role in the markets.[10] The model in effect 'became' the market for a considerable period of time until the 1987 stock market crash. This effect stemmed partly from the intrinsic conceptual strengths and elegance of the model but also from active efforts by academics, including those who propounded the model, to 'sell it'. For instance, Fischer Black (of the eponymous model) used to sell sheets containing the deltas etc. corresponding to various price levels, in the days before ubiquitous availability of computers. The ability to 'precisely' price options played a role in changing the views of regulators on whether these instruments were 'gambles'. Terms like volatility and 'beta' and 'delta' are in common use in the markets and part of the thought process of participants. In essence, the model became not a 'camera' to view and understand the market, but an 'engine' which drove it.[11]

The Black–Scholes formula is not the only example of strong performativity. It can be argued that the efficient market hypothesis has also had fairly strong performative effects: many market participants operate on the assumption that the hypothesis is true, and base their trades on algorithms which are designed to identify and exploit what they see as 'anomalies'. This has continued even when there is strong evidence that markets are not necessarily, or always, efficient.(The spectacular collapse of the model-driven LTCM hedge fund came more than a decade after the crash of 1987 had already exposed gaps in the efficient market hypothesis.) Thus, behaviour may be conforming to the theory, not because the theory is right but because the theory exists and is sufficiently widely believed for it to be an effective guide to the behaviour of others – the kind of second or third degree anticipation referred to by Keynes (see Chapter 6).

Over-confidence in models

One of the findings that arose from the 2008 financial crisis was that institutions and their staff had placed implicit reliance on mathematical models even when the models were either inaccurate or simplistic. Many had done so without a full understanding of their limitations or weaknesses. Derman and Wilmott, both well known for their skills in quantitative finance and modelling, produced the 'Financial Modeller's Manifesto', which eloquently set out the flaws and came up with a simple practical credo for the use of models. The manifesto is reproduced in full in Appendix 10.1.

Modelling and its effect on netting

In theory, derivatives contracts are zero sum transactions. The economic gains to one party are equal and opposite to the economic losses to the counterparty. In the case of exchange-traded derivatives, this holds good in accounting practice as well as economic theory, because the market price or value at any given time is 'discovered' and published. The seller and buyer must both use the same reference price (give or take the bid/ ask spread reflecting dealers' margins).

In respect of OTC derivatives, especially the more complex ones, the current value is calculated using models. But there is no certainty that the two parties to a transaction are using the same model or even the same assumptions. Part of the problem in valuing CDOs during the debt crisis was the difference in valuation approaches between the institutions that created ABS and the institutions that then created synthetic CDOs on them.[12] It is thus possible that in terms of reported accounting profits or losses, a single transaction may produce either a positive or negative sum when the sum total of the gains and losses of the two parties are added up. This can lead to difficulties for regulators and for market participants in gauging net exposures. Indeed it is possible for non-existent or illusory 'wealth' to be created or destroyed simply through accounting entries when derivatives are valued using 'mark-to-model' methods. As Warren Buffett put it, in extreme cases, mark-to-model degenerates into mark-to-myth.[13]

Overall it is crucial for market participants, accountants and regulators alike to remember that derivatives models are models – not reality.

Appendix 10.1:

The Financial Modellers' Manifesto
by
Emanuel Derman and Paul Wilmott

A spectre is haunting Markets – the spectre of illiquidity, frozen credit, and the failure of financial models.

Beginning with the 2007 collapse in subprime mortgages, financial markets have shifted to new regimes characterized by violent movements, epidemics of contagion from market to market, and almost unimaginable anomalies (who would have ever thought that swap spreads to Treasuries could go negative?). Familiar valuation models have become increasingly unreliable. Where is the risk manager that has not ascribed his losses to a once-in-a-century tsunami?

To this end, we have assembled in New York City and written the following manifesto.

Manifesto

In finance we study how to manage funds – from simple securities like dollars and yen, stocks and bonds to complex ones like futures and options, sub-prime CDOs and credit default swaps. We build financial models to estimate the fair value of securities, to estimate their risks and to show how those risks can be controlled. How can a model tell you the value of a security? And how did these models fail so badly in the case of the sub-prime CDO market?

Physics, because of its astonishing success at predicting the future behaviour of material objects from their present state, has inspired most financial modelling. Physicists study the world by repeating the same experiments over and over again to discover forces and their almost magical mathematical laws. Galileo dropped balls off the leaning tower, giant teams in Geneva collide protons on protons, over and over again. If a law is proposed and its predictions contradict experiments, it's back to the drawing board. The method works. The laws of atomic physics are accurate to more than ten decimal places.

It's a different story with finance and economics, which are concerned with the mental world of monetary value. Financial theory has tried hard to emulate the style and elegance of physics in order to discover its own laws. But markets are made of people, who are influenced by events, by their ephemeral feelings about events and by their expectations of other people's feelings. The truth is that there are no fundamental laws in finance. And even if there were, there is no way to run repeatable experiments to verify them.

You can hardly find a better example of confusedly elegant modelling than models of CDOs. The CDO research papers apply abstract probability theory to the price co-movements of thousands of mortgages. The relationships between so many mortgages can be vastly complex. The modellers, having built up their fantastical theory, need to make it useable; they resort to sweeping under the model's rug all unknown dynamics; with the dirt ignored, all that's left is a single number, called the default correlation. From the sublime to the elegantly ridiculous: all uncertainty is reduced to a single parameter that, when entered into the model by a trader, produces a CDO value. This over-reliance on probability and statistics is a severe limitation. Statistics is shallow description, quite unlike the deeper cause and effect of physics, and can't easily capture the complex dynamics of default.

Models are at bottom tools for approximate thinking; they serve to transform your intuition about the future into a price for a security today. It's easier to think intuitively about future housing prices, default rates and default correlations than it is about CDO prices. CDO models turn your guess about future housing prices, mortgage default rates and a simplistic default correlation into the model's output: a current CDO price.

Our experience in the financial arena has taught us to be very humble in applying mathematics to markets, and to be extremely wary of ambitious theories, which are in the end trying to model human behaviour. We like simplicity, but we like to remember that it is our models that are simple, not the world.

Unfortunately, the teachers of finance haven't learned these lessons. You have only to glance at business school textbooks on finance to discover stilts of mathematical axioms supporting a house of numbered theorems, lemmas and results. Who would think that the textbook is at bottom dealing with people and money? It should be obvious to anyone with common sense that every financial axiom is wrong, and that finance can never in its wildest dreams be Euclid. Different endeavours, as Aristotle wrote, require different degrees of precision. Finance is not one of the natural sciences, and its invisible worm is its dark secret love of mathematical elegance and too much exactitude.

We do need models and mathematics – you cannot think about finance and economics without them – but one must never forget that models are not the world. Whenever we make a model of something involving human beings, we are trying to force the ugly stepsister's foot into Cinderella's pretty glass slipper. It doesn't fit without cutting off some essential parts. And in cutting off parts for the sake of beauty and precision, models inevitably mask the true risk rather than exposing it. The most important question about any financial model is how wrong it is likely to be, and how useful it is despite its assumptions. You must start with models and then overlay them with common sense and experience.

Many academics imagine that one beautiful day we will find the 'right' model. But there is no right model, because the world changes in response to the ones we use. Progress in financial modelling is fleeting and temporary. Markets change and newer models become necessary. Simple clear models with explicit assumptions about small numbers of variables are therefore the best way to leverage your intuition without deluding yourself.

All models sweep dirt under the rug. A good model makes the absence of the dirt visible. In this regard, we believe that the Black–Scholes model of options valuation, now often unjustly maligned, is a model for models; it is clear and robust. Clear, because it is based on true engineering; it tells you how to manufacture an option out of stocks and bonds and what that will cost you, under ideal dirt-free circumstances that it defines. Its method of valuation is analogous to figuring out the price of a can of fruit salad from the cost of fruit, sugar, labour and transportation. The world of markets doesn't exactly match the ideal circumstances Black-Scholes requires, but the model is robust because it allows an intelligent trader to qualitatively adjust for those mismatches. You know what you are assuming when you use the model, and you know exactly what has been swept out of view.

Building financial models is challenging and worthwhile: you need to combine the qualitative and the quantitative, imagination and observation, art and science, all in the service of finding approximate patterns in the behaviour of markets and securities. The greatest danger is the age-old sin of idolatry. Financial markets are alive but a model, however beautiful, is an artifice. No matter how hard you try, you will not be able to breathe life into it. To confuse the model with the world is to embrace a future disaster driven by the belief that humans obey mathematical rules.

MODELERS OF ALL MARKETS, UNITE! You have nothing to lose but your illusions.

The Modelers' Hippocratic Oath

~ I will remember that I didn't make the world, and it doesn't satisfy my equations.

~ Though I will use models boldly to estimate value, I will not be overly impressed by mathematics.

~ I will never sacrifice reality for elegance without explaining why I have done so.

~ Nor will I give the people who use my model false comfort about its accuracy. Instead, I will make explicit its assumptions and oversights.

~ I understand that my work may have enormous effects on society and the economy, many of them beyond my comprehension.

Emanuel Derman and Paul Wilmott, January 7, 2009[14]

Notes and References

1 E. Derman and P. Wilmott, *The Financial Modellers' Manifesto*, 7 January 2009. Available at: http://papers.ssrn.com/sol3/papers.cfm?abstract_id=1324878. Accessed on 14 July 2014.

2 A. Kling, 'Macroeconometrics: The Science Of Hubris', *Critical Review*, Vol. 23, 123–33, 2011.

   Available at: http://dx.doi.org/10.1080/08913811.2011.574475.

3 *Ibid.* Accessed on 14 July 2014.

4 J. L. Austin, *How to Do Things With Words*. Clarendon Press, Oxford, 1962.

5 Economists will note the similarity and difference between the 'constative vs. performative' distinction and the 'positive (descriptive) vs. normative (prescriptive)' distinction which is common in economics. Constative statements correspond to positive statements; however performative statements are not the same as 'normative' statements because they *perform* rather than merely prescribe or assert.

6 M. Callon, 'What Does It Mean To Say That Economics Is Performative', CSI Working Paper series No. 5, Centre de Sociologie de l'innovation, Paris, 2006.

7 D. MacKenzie, *Is Economics Performative? Option Theory and the Construction of Derivatives Markets*. Annual meeting of the History of Economics Society, Tacoma, WA, 25 June 2005. Available at: http://www.espanet2012.info/__data/assets/pdf_file/0017/3419/is_economics_performative.pdf. Accessed on 14 July 2014.

8   P. Mirowski and E. Nik-Kah, 'Markets Made Flesh: Performativity and Problems in Science Studies Augmented with consideration of the FCC auctions', 192, Chapter 7 in D. MacKenzie, F. Muniesa and L. Siu (Eds.), *Do Economists Make Markets? On the Performativity of Economics.* Princeton University Press, 2007.

9   E. Didier, 'Do Statistics "Perform" the Economy', Chapter 10 in D. MacKenzie, F. Muniesa and L. Siu, *op. cit.*

10 D. MacKenzie, F. Muniesa and L. Siu (Eds.), *op. cit.*

11 J. Daemen. 'Review of Donald Mackenzie's An Engine not a Camera: How Financial Models Shape the Markets', *Erasmus Journal for Philosophy & Economics*, Vol. 1, No. 1, 147–53, Autumn 2008.

12 D. Mackenzie, 'Beneath All the Toxic Acronyms Lies a Basic Cultural Issue', *Financial Times*, 26 November 2009.

13 Edited excerpts from the Berkshire Hathaway Annual Report for 2002. Available at: http://www.fintools.com/docs/Warren%20Buffet%20on%20Derivatives.pdf. Accessed on 11 July 2014.

14 E. Derman and P. Wilmott, *op.cit.*

11

Derivatives and Emerging Markets – Part I

Futures and options exchanges are one of the main institutions of liberal economic systems...
Turkish companies are constantly influenced by global financial developments. Thus, the
need for the use of risk management tools and for the establishment and unfettered operation
of derivatives exchanges in Turkey is clear.

Cem Saatsioglu, Iskender Karagul, and Ara G. Volkan (2005)[1]

Widespread use of derivatives is a recent phenomenon and it is no surprise, therefore, that the use of derivatives in emerging markets is still evolving. The literature on the availability, use and trading of derivatives by emerging economies shows an interesting pattern. Prior to the global financial crisis, the literature is enthusiastic about the introduction of derivatives (for example, see quotation above).

However, much caution enters into the debate post-2008. While the relative underdevelopment of financial markets in developing countries is generally considered a handicap, in respect of derivatives it may have some advantages. Insofar as the global financial crisis of 2008 enables emerging markets to learn from, and avoid, the mistakes that developed countries made and improve their regulatory framework, the crisis should be deemed a blessing in disguise for them.

This chapter looks at the role of derivatives in emerging markets. In this chapter, the term 'emerging markets' is usually used in the generally recognized sense of a subset of countries that are relatively advanced among the wider group of developing countries, but is sometimes (when the context requires) used to connote that wider universe.

Derivatives *in* emerging economies, used *by* emerging economies and *on* emerging economies

Derivatives impinge on emerging market economies in several ways. Firstly, there are those countries which have built their own derivatives markets, both exchange-traded and OTC. Here, the interesting issues relate to the wider economic impact of, and regulatory framework for, these markets.

Secondly, economic entities in developing countries and emerging economies make use of derivatives markets; these markets need not necessarily be situated in emerging economies. After, all economic entities in these countries would want to use derivatives for exactly the same reasons as those in developed economies – for hedging, for speculation etc. In that sense it may seem that there is nothing 'special' about derivatives usage in developing countries. However, developing countries do have some special features:

- Many of them derive a large share of their national income from the primary sector (agriculture or mining) where prices are more volatile, rather than from the secondary or tertiary sectors; indeed this is a clear marker of underdevelopment.

- They are both physically (because of poorer infrastructure) and financially (because of lower incomes) more vulnerable to natural calamities, which may affect people or production.

- They have, as a result of lower incomes, less risk-bearing capacity.

Thus risk management is actually more important for developing countries than for the developed countries. Derivatives hold a lot of promise in terms of helping developing countries deal with some of their special economic problems.

Finally, derivative securities based on emerging market risks (even if issued in, by, and for developed economy entities) may, indirectly, impinge on the emerging markets themselves. Governments and regulators in developing countries need to be aware of, and prepared for, these effects.

This chapter touches largely upon the first of these aspects (derivatives markets in emerging economies) while the next chapter mainly covers the remaining two. Both chapters use a case study approach, looking at specific examples that illustrate the wider issues.

Size of derivatives markets in emerging economies

Before looking at case studies, it is useful to get some understanding of the size of the derivatives markets in emerging economies. Data on these markets are not as plentiful, consistent or well collated as one would like for this purpose.

OTC derivatives

The average daily foreign exchange turnover in select emerging markets is presented in Table 11.1 below. Foreign exchange turnover in emerging markets (somewhat arbitrarily including Hong Kong SAR, Singapore and Korea in the 'emerging' markets category) constituted around 16 per cent of the overall foreign exchange market average daily turnover observed in April 2013, up from 13.7 per cent in 1998. While the global daily turnover has gone up by just over three times in the last 15 years, foreign exchange turnover in emerging markets has gone up by a little under four times. Hong Kong and Singapore alone contributed 80 per cent of the turnover in these select emerging markets in 1998 but their share has dropped to 64 per cent in the most recent survey as others such as Russia, China, India, Korea and Mexico have caught up. Russia, despite being a much smaller economy than China, India or Korea, contributed $61 billion to the daily foreign exchange turnover. While some of this turnover may be spot transactions, the bulk of it is forward contracts and hence derivative transactions.

Table 11.1: Foreign exchange derivatives turnover in emerging markets

Geographical distribution of global foreign exchange market turnover[1]. Net-gross basis[2] daily averages in April, in billions of US dollars and percentages.

Country	1998 Amount	%	2001 Amount	%	2004 Amount	%	2007 Amount	%	2010 Amount	%	2013 Amount	%
Argentina	2	0.1	...	...	1	0.0	1	0.0	2	0.0	1	0.0
Brazil	5	0.2	6	0.3	4	0.1	6	0.1	14	0.3	17	0.3
Chile	1	0.1	2	0.1	2	0.1	4	0.1	6	0.1	12	0.2
Colombia	...	...	0	0.0	1	0.0	2	0.0	3	0.1	3	0.1
Mexico	9	0.4	9	0.5	15	0.6	15	0.4	17	0.3	32	0.5
Peru	...	...	0	0.0	0	0.0	1	0.0	1	0.0	2	0.0
China	0	0.0	...	...	1	0.0	9	0.2	20	0.4	44	0.7
Hong Kong SAR	80	3.8	68	4.0	106	4.1	181	4.2	238	4.7	275	4.1
India	2	0.1	3	0.2	7	0.3	38	0.9	27	0.5	31	0.5
Indonesia	2	0.1	4	0.2	2	0.1	3	0.1	3	0.1	5	0.1
Korea	4	0.2	10	0.6	21	0.8	35	0.8	44	0.9	48	0.7
Malaysia	1	0.1	1	0.1	2	0.1	3	0.1	7	0.1	11	0.2
Philippines	1	0.0	1	0.1	1	0.0	2	0.1	5	0.1	4	0.1
Singapore	145	6.9	104	6.1	134	5.1	242	5.6	266	5.3	383	5.7
Taiwan (China)	5	0.2	5	0.3	9	0.4	16	0.4	18	0.4	26	0.4
Thailand	3	0.1	2	0.1	3	0.1	6	0.1	7	0.1	13	0.2
Czech Republic	5	0.2	2	0.1	2	0.1	5	0.1	5	0.1	5	0.1

Country	1998		2001		2004		2007		2010		2013	
	Amount	%	Amount	%	Amount	%	Amount	%	Amount	%	Amount	%
Hungary	1	0.1	1	0.0	3	0.1	7	0.2	4	0.1	4	0.1
Poland	3	0.1	5	0.3	7	0.3	9	0.2	8	0.2	8	0.1
Israel	...	...	1	0.1	5	0.2	8	0.2	10	0.2	8	0.1
Russia	7	0.3	10	0.6	30	1.1	50	1.2	42	0.8	61	0.9
Saudi Arabia	2	0.1	2	0.1	2	0.1	4	0.1	5	0.1	5	0.1
South Africa	9	0.4	10	0.6	10	0.3	14	0.3	14	0.3	21	0.3
Turkey	...	...	1	0.1	3	0.1	4	0.1	17	0.3	27	0.4
Total (countries above)	287.5	13.7	247.4	14.5	370.1	14.2	667.4	15.6	783.2	14.5	1,045.7	15.7
Total	2,099.4	100.0	1,704.7	100.0	2,608.1	100.0	4,281.1	100	5,043.0	100.0	6,671.5	100.0

Source: *Table 6, Bank for International Settlements Triennial Central Bank Survey, Foreign exchange turnover in April 2013: preliminary global results.*

Notes provided by BIS: (1) Data may differ slightly from national survey data owing to differences in aggregation procedures and rounding. (2) Adjusted for local inter-dealer double-counting (ie 'net-gross' basis).

The story of interest rate derivatives in key emerging markets is far more modest (see Table 11.2). The total daily turnover globally is around $2.8 trillion. Emerging markets account for only $111.6 billion and that is 4 per cent of the global turnover. Just two centres – Singapore and Hong Kong – account for nearly 60 per cent of the total emerging market turnover. Between 2004 and 2007, there was a big jump in the average daily turnover of interest rate derivatives in emerging markets, rising from around $30 billion to around $98 billion. That is more than a three-fold jump in just three years. However, the global crisis slowed the juggernaut. Between the 2007 and 2010 surveys, there was actually a decline in the daily turnover, though it picked up again thereafter.

Table 11.2: Interest rate derivatives turnover in emerging markets

Geographical distribution of global OTC interest rate derivatives market turnover[1]. Net-gross basis[2] daily averages in April, in billions of US dollars and percentages.

Country	1998		2001		2004		2007		2010		2013	
	Amount	%	Amount	%	Amount	%	Amount	%	Amount	%	Amount	%
Argentina	...	...	...	...	...	...	...	...	...	...	0	0.0
Brazil	...	...	0	0.0	1	0.1	0	0.0	7	0.3	4	0.1
Chile	...	...	...	...	0	0.0	0	0.0	0	0.0	0	0.0
Colombia	...	...	...	...	...	...	0	0.0	0	0.0		0.0
Mexico	0	0.1	0	0.1	1	0.1	3	0.1	1	0.1	2	0.1
Peru	...	...	...	...	...	...	0	0.0	0	0.0	0	0.0
China	...	...	...	...	...	...	...	...	2	0.1	13	0.5
Hong Kong SAR	2	0.7	3	0.4	11	0.8	17	0.8	18	0.7	28	1.0
India	...	...	0	0.0	1	0.1	3	0.2	3	0.1	3	0.1
Indonesia	...	...	0	0.0	0	0.0	0	0.0	0	0.0	0	0.0
Korea	0	0.0	0	0.0	1	0.1	5	0.2	11	0.4	8	0.3
Malaysia	0	0.0	0	0.0	0	0.0	0	0.0	0	0.0	0	0.0
Philippines	...	...	...	...	0	0.0	0	0.0	1	0.0	0	0.0
Singapore	5	1.6	3	0.5	9	0.6	57	2.6	35	1.3	37	1.3
Taiwan	0	0.0	0	0.0	2	0.1	1	0.1	2	0.1	1	0.0
Thailand	...	...	0	0.0	0	0.0	0	0.0	1	0.0	1	0.0
Czech Republic	...	...	0	0.0	1	0.0	1	0.0	0	0.0	0	0.0
Hungary	0	0.0	0	0.0	1	0.0	1	0.0	0	0.0	0	0.0
Poland	...	...	0	0.1	3	0.1	3	0.1	2	0.1	3	0.1
Israel	...	...	...	...	...	...	...	...	...	...	0	0.0
Russia	...	...	...	...	...	...	...	...	...	...	0	0.0
Saudi Arabia	0	0.1	0	0.0	0	0.0	0	0.0	0	0.0	0	0.0
South Africa	1	0.2	1	0.1	3	0.2	4	0.2	6	0.2	11	0.4
Turkey	...	...	...	...	0	0.0	00.0		0	0.0	0	0.0
Total (countries above)	9.1	2.6	8.1	1.2	30.4	2.3	97.7	4.5	89.0	3.4	111.6	4.0
Total	343.6	100.0	676.1	100.0	1,330.5	100.0	2,173.2	100.0	2,648.8	100.0	2,758.6	100.0

Source: Table 5, Bank for International Settlements Triennial Central Bank Survey OTC interest rate derivatives turnover in April 2013: preliminary global results.

Notes provided by BIS: (1) Single currency interest rate contracts only. Data may differ from national survey data owing to differences in aggregation procedures and rounding. Data for the Netherlands are not fully comparable over time due to reporting improvements in 2013. (2) Adjusted for local inter-dealer double-counting (i.e., 'net-gross' basis).

The notional amount of OTC equity derivatives globally was $6.25 trillion, as of December 2012. Even with the most liberal interpretation of the data, the tally for emerging markets was just a little more than $1 trillion, (see Table 11.3).[2]

Table 11.3: Regional distribution of equity derivatives

By instrument and market
In billions of US dollars

Instruments / market	Notional amounts outstanding					Gross market values				
	Dec 2010	Jun 2011	Dec 2011	Jun 2012	Dec 2012	Dec 2010	Jun 2011	Dec 2011	Jun 2012	Dec 2012
Total contracts	**5,635**	**6,841**	**5,982**	**6,313**	**6,251**	**648**	**708**	**679**	**645**	**605**
US equities	1,565	1,739	1,700	1,903	1,936	191	202	220	314	216
European equities	2,793	3,414	2,675	2,646	2,829	311	342	295	276	242
Japanese equities	595	712	644	641	460	72	79	73	71	59
Other Asian equities	252	346	387	438	322	24	24	29	24	24
Latin American equities	58	77	68	76	132	5	7	8	10	11
Other equities	372	554	509	610	573	39	55	55	49	53
Forwards and swaps	**1,828**	**2,029**	**1,738**	**1,880**	**2,045**	**167**	**176**	**156**	**147**	**157**
US equities	544	551	563	630	669	51	48	43	42	49
European equities	941	1,016	798	841	915	91	92	76	67	68
Japanese equities	79	101	78	85	88	7	7	6	8	8
Other Asian equities	52	62	53	64	75	4	5	5	5	6
Latin American equities	20	42	31	31	73	2	4	4	4	6
Other equities	192	257	214	229	224	13	20	21	21	20
Options	**3,807**	**4,813**	**4,244**	**4,434**	**4,207**	**480**	**532**	**523**	**497**	**448**
US equities	1,022	1,188	1,137	1,273	1,267	140	155	177	171	168
European equities	1,852	1,398	1,876	1,805	1,914	220	249	219	210	174
Japanese equities	516	611	566	555	172	71	72	67	63	51
Other Asian equities	200	284	333	374	247	20	18	22	20	18
Latin American equities	37	35	37	45	59	3	3	4	6	5
Other equities	180	296	294	381	349	27	34	34	28	33

Source: Statistical Annex, BIS Quarterly Review, *September 2013*

Exchange-traded derivatives

According to BIS data, the notional amount outstanding on exchange-traded financial derivatives was $68.2 trillion as of June 2013. Even if one is liberal in classifying all ETD traded in Asia-Pacific and 'other' markets as belonging to 'emerging' markets, the total size is about $5.2 trillion which provides an upper limit to the 'emerging market' share. So, in terms of BIS data, emerging economies amount to less than 8 per cent of the overall notional amount outstanding in ETDs.

However, it is important to note that these figures relate only to those financial derivatives reported by the BIS. They exclude single-stock futures and commodity futures which do have large volumes in countries like India and China. Unfortunately, consistent data for these is not readily available. Data from the World Federation of Exchanges are based on turnover, not on outstanding amounts of open positions, and thus cannot be directly compared. Turnover data include 'rollovers' and thus some double counting and so is also less useful in terms of gauging size.

Table 11.4 presents turnover data for the main derivatives exchanges in emerging markets.

Table 11.4: Exchange traded equity and commodity derivatives; major emerging markets

Country [1]	Notional turnover in $ million (2013)		
	Equities	Commodities	Equities + commodities
Colombia	499.8	6.6	506.3
Hungary	3,026.6	138.5	3,165.0
Mexico	32,762.7	0	32,762.7
Turkey	63,692.8	807.7	64,500.5
Malaysia	71,426.2	151,944.0	223,370.2
South Africa	507,395.0	50,474.2	557,869.1
Russia	979,865.0	46,600.9	1,026,465.8
Israel	646,561.3	409,237.0[2]	1,055,798.3[2]
Brazil	1,737,097.7	10,286.9	1,747,384.5
India	7,585,272.8	2,841,133.0	10,426,405.8
China	22,909,400.0	20,603,720.0	43,513,120.0
Total	34,536,999.6	24,114,348.7	58,651,348.2

Source: World Federation of Exchanges except for Indian commodities for which data is based on Forward Markets Commission Annual Report 2012–13 converted at Rs. 60 per dollar.

Notes: [1] Exchanges: Colombia: Colombia SE; Hungary: Budapest SE; Mexico: MexDer; Turkey: Borsa Istanbul; Malaysia: Bursa Malaysia Derivatives; South Africa: Johannesburg SE; Russia: Moscow Interbank Currency Exchange (MICEX)/Russian Trading System (RTS); Israel: Tel Aviv SE; Brazil: BM&F (Bolsa de Valores, Mercedorias & Futuros) Bovespa; India: Equities Bombay Stock Exchange (BSE) and National Stock Exchange (NSE), Commodities – Multi Commodity Exchange of India (MCX), National Commodity and Derivatives Exchange (NCDEX), National

Multi-Commodity Exchange (NMCE), ACE and, Indian Commodity Exchange (ICEX) + regional exchanges ; China: Equities China Financial Futures Exchange, Commodities - Dalian CE, Shanghai Futures Exchange, Zhengzhou CE. (SE= Stock Exchange, CE= Commodities Exchange. [2]Israel commodities data is for 2012; Equities + Commodities figure is the sum of Equity data for 2013 and commodities data for 2012.

Regulatory framework leap-frogging developed markets: The case of Brazil

Notwithstanding their small role in global OTC and ETD markets, some emerging economies have done well to put in a regulatory framework for derivatives trading that is arguably more robust than developed markets. At the top of the list is Brazil.

Unlike the US or Europe, or indeed the rest of the world, Brazil's domestic derivatives market is dominated by products cleared through a central counterparty. 80 per cent of Brazilian derivatives are traded on an exchange, with BM&F Bovespa – the country's only securities, commodities and futures exchange – taking on counterparty risk. All details of trades are stored in its central securities repository.

An important feature of the Brazilian framework is that clearing houses in Brazil *also register OTC derivatives* and thus greatly improve market surveillance of OTC derivatives. Domestic OTC trades, which account for 20 per cent of the overall market, are required to be reported to one of two data repositories. Some OTC contracts are cleared and reported on BM&F, but the majority are registered with Central de Custodia e de Liquidacao Financeira de Titulos or CETIP, one of Latin America's largest custody and settlement houses. This information is then monitored by CETIP throughout the day for the build-up of systemic risk. Clearing houses serve several important functions. One is that they raise the credit quality of market participants. All must trade with collateral. Second, clearing houses facilitate the post-trading process.

Brazil also has sophisticated middle and back office processes, which include a settlement cycle of 'T+0' – i.e., the trade is settled on the same day it is initiated. This has resulted in high levels of transparency for all participants as well as regulatory access to information and supervision. Overall, Brazil's regulators have complete oversight of all segments of the derivatives markets.

It is sometimes felt that tight regulation may impede the development of markets, especially when markets are in their infancy as may be the case in emerging economies. The Brazilian experience does not corroborate this. BM&F Bovespa became the world's sixth largest derivatives exchange by contract volume in 2010 and the number of futures and options traded on the exchange increased by 54.5 per cent from the previous year, to over 1.42 billion contracts, according to the Futures Industry Association's survey of the world's leading derivatives exchanges published in March 2011. As the *Financial Times* put it, 'in terms of transparency and systemic risk management, Brazil is topping the league table.'[3]

Another interesting message from Brazil's experience is that it contradicts the standard self-interest driven complaint of market participants that moving OTC trades to exchange-traded platforms would shrink volumes and crimp market liquidity. Regulators need to take note.

Commodity- and capital flow-based currency risks: the case of Chile

Chile is rightly regarded as a role model in many areas for developing economies. Early in its economic reform process, it developed deep pensions markets with defined contributions. It has an independent central bank backed up by very clear fiscal rules for the government to follow. The central bank targets inflation. The inflation rate in Chile has not gone above 4 per cent since 1998. It had adopted capital controls against short-term capital flows through the use of unremunerated reserve requirements. Frankel provided a brief glimpse of Chilean fiscal rules:

> Chile ran large surpluses during the copper boom of 2003–08, and subsequently was able to ease its fiscal policy substantially in the recession of 2009. This achievement was not solely the result of wise policy-makers choosing the right policies. They were helped by an institutional framework that was put into place in 2000, and that can offer useful lessons for others. Chile's fiscal institutions consist essentially of three rules. First, each government must set a budget target. Second, as in Switzerland, the target is phrased in structural terms: deficits are allowed only to the extent that (i) output falls short of trend, in a recession, or (ii) the price of copper is below its trend. The target for the structural budget surplus was set at zero in 2008 under President Michelle Bachelet, which implied a substantial actual surplus because the oil price was high and the economy was booming.

Third, the determination of what is structural and what is cyclical is made by two panels of independent experts who project ten-year trends, outside the political process. The result is that Chile avoids the pattern of 32 other governments, where forecasts in booms are biased toward over-optimism. Chile's institutions explain why it was able to run surpluses in the 2003–07 boom. The United States and Europe failed to do so in part because their fiscal authorities made systematically over-optimistic forecasts during this period of expansion.[4]

In contrast, French-Davis regrets that Chile's nuanced approach to economic liberalization gave way to a more finance-centric model of development in the late nineties.[5] On top of his future reform list is the regulation of speculative capital inflows.[6]

Chile is a country rich in natural resources and a major exporter of copper. Its export of copper obviously involves foreign exchange risk. With its liberal foreign investment rules both for portfolio and direct investment, Chile attracted large capital inflows. Foreign investors needed to hedge their Chilean peso risk. In the absence of derivatives markets, banks could create a synthetic short position in Chilean pesos i.e., borrow pesos, convert them into hard currencies in the spot market and invest the hard currency overseas, matching the tenor of the loan. This would create a capital outflow (borrowing in the local currency and lending or investing in hard currency). To that extent, a synthetic hedge *would neutralize the beneficial impact of capital inflows in augmenting domestic savings.*

Availability of foreign exchange derivatives mitigates the offsetting capital outflow that is inevitable in synthetic hedges as described above. It was therefore quite natural that Chile should develop an active domestic derivatives market in foreign exchange (see Figure 11.1).

The market for derivatives in Chile too is dominated by foreign exchange. Indeed, based on turnover, the current composition of the derivatives market is 74 per cent for currency derivatives, 22 per cent for interest rate derivatives and only 4 per cent for commodity derivatives. Information on foreign exchange derivatives is highly abundant relative to other derivatives. Information on interest rate derivatives reported to the Central Bank is quite limited and corresponds to the price of interest rate swaps obtained through a daily survey to two traders.[7]

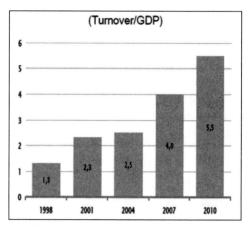

Figure 11.1: Foreign exchange derivative market turnover in Chile

Source: 'Derivative market: the experience of Chile', Luis A.Opazo R, Irving Fisher Committee (IFC) Bulletin No. 35, February 2012 — Proceedings of the workshop 'Data requirements for monitoring derivative transactions', organized by the People's Bank of China and the Irving Fisher Committee, Zhengzhou, 27—29 September 2010.

Mainly, the reason for the development of foreign exchange derivatives in Chile is the presence of a large pension fund that invests overseas. Chilean pension funds are subject to investment limits and to limits on the unhedged portion of such foreign investments.

In the case of Chile, two contrasting episodes stand out and offer wider lessons. The first was in 1998–99, when hedging transactions undertaken by large Chilean corporations with dollar liabilities, coincided with Chilean pension funds undertaking investments in foreign assets. The second one pertains to the stabilizing role played by Chilean pension funds in providing dollars to dollar buyers in the wake of the collapse of Lehman Brothers in 2008.

1998–1999: The period 1998–99 was a turbulent one for emerging economies. Russia had defaulted on some of its debt and the hedge fund Long–Term Capital Management had collapsed. The Asian crisis had just peaked and there was pressure on the Brazilian real to depreciate. All these combined to exert pressure on currencies of several other emerging economies to depreciate, notwithstanding their domestic fundamentals. The Chilean peso was one of those, caught in the crossfire. Large Chilean corporations with dollar liabilities (mainly in the telecommunications and energy sector)had not hedged fully and responded to the declining peso by rushing to buy dollar forward contracts even as the dollar rose – a sort of 'dynamic' hedging (which as was seen in Chapter 6 is inherently destabilizing). At the same time, pension funds were investing abroad on a large scale (with partial or no hedging). Due to both factors, there was major pressure on the peso both on the spot and the forward market, and it weakened. This contributed to the need for a sharp macroeconomic adjustment that led to a fall in GDP of 1 per cent.[8]

The lesson in the 'dynamic' hedging programme of Chilean large companies with dollar liabilities is that external liabilities should be hedged from the time such liabilities arise. Foreign currency borrowing should not be an avenue for speculative profits for corporations whose real businesses are something else. Their profits should derive from their core operations. Should they wish to speculate in financial markets (through derivatives or unhedged loans or otherwise), they should do so out of a separate defined and limited budget for such activities with appropriate risk controls as are expected of financial institutions. (Indian corporations with US dollar borrowings ignored this rule to their peril as will be seen later in the chapter.)

2007–08: During the global funding crisis triggered by the collapse of Lehman Brothers in 2008, Chilean pension funds continued to hedge their exposure to foreign assets. Chile is one of the few emerging markets in the world that has a relatively large positive net long international investment position of the non-bank financial sector (see table 11.5).

Table 11.5: Net international investment position of emerging market economies by sector (end 2007 as percentage of GDP)

	Monetary authorities	Government	Banks	Non-bank financial sector	Non-financial sector	Total
Argentina	17	-6	0	2	10	24
Chile	10	9	-8	26	-42	-5
Colombia	10	-7	-1	3	-30	-25
Israel	17	-7	2	10	-30	-9
Mexico	8	0	-10	1	-38	-40
South Africa	11	-1	3	24	-61	-24
Other emerging markets	19	-3	-4	3	-63	-39

Source: *'Hedging in derivatives markets: the experience of Chile'*, Fernando Avalos and Ramon Moreno, BIS Quarterly Review, *March 2013.*

In their hedging of foreign exchange exposure, the Chilean private pension funds went beyond government stipulations. That helped Chilean financial institutions and large corporations who needed to cover their short (loan) positions in foreign currencies by buying dollars forward. So, there was a perfect match. Chilean pension funds sold dollars forward and Chilean banks and large corporations bought them forward. The market was 'completed' locally and this avoided instability in exchange rates.

Avalos and Moreno suggest that the Chilean case study answers in the affirmative the question of whether a large and liquid domestic derivatives market reduces the risks associated with financial stress in sudden stop or capital flow reversal episodes.[9] Specifically, the foreign exchange derivatives market addresses the exchange *rate* risk whereas large international reserves with the central bank can address the foreign exchange *funding* risk.

An added lesson arises from this case: that at the macroeconomic level, two way flows may provide a natural hedge against exchange rate fluctuations. The policy implication for emerging market governments is that they should create avenues for two-way flows. If all that they do is to liberalize overseas borrowings for their corporations but not liberalize overseas investments for domestic financial and non-financial corporate sector (or even individuals), they have to depend on the mercies of financial markets to meet their foreign exchange needs in crises. In crises, markets either freeze or several other considerations come into play in determining who gets funded on what terms. The case of India in recent times comes to mind. India had liberalized external borrowings only to find itself scampering for dollars in 2012 and 2013, having to pay a heavy price for them. India's response to its dollar shortage was to curtail overseas investment by Indians further. The Chilean case-study suggests a different approach.

Derivative risks to domestic and foreign companies in a controlled economy: The case of China

China has overtaken Japan to become the world's second largest economy. Its nominal GDP was estimated to be $8.2 trillion in 2012 by most multilateral institutions. Yet, its financial markets are rudimentary. China practices 'financial repression'. If excessive financialization has been the bane of Anglo-Saxon economies – particularly the US and UK – financial repression is the bane of most developing economies where the state exerts control over capital markets and savings and investment choices available to residents. China has kept a tight leash on interest rates. Both lending and deposit rates are regulated. Gradual liberalization of interest rates began after 2012. Although China has several stock exchanges, they are dominated by state-owned enterprises and free float has been a problem. China is one of the few countries where, even in the boom years of 2002–06, the stock market performance bore no resemblance to the underlying vigour of the economy (see Figure 11.2).

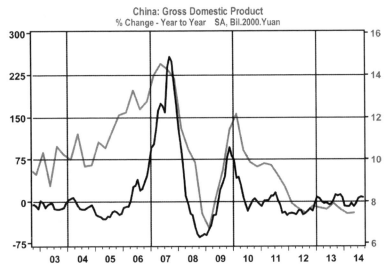

China: Stock Price Index: Dow Jones Shanghai
% Change - Year to Year AVG, Dec-31-93=100

China: Gross Domestic Product
% Change - Year to Year SA, Bil.2000.Yuan

Figure 11.2: China-stock market prices decoupled from high economic growth
Note: GDP/Stock price change on right/left hand scale respectively. AVG/SA denote Average/Seasonally Adjusted respectively.
Source: Haver Analytics

For this reason, the market for derivatives in China has not been that well developed.[10] Due to the 'financial repression', a tendency to engage in risky and speculative activities flares up whenever the government loosens controls. That is what happened with the Shanghai Stock Exchange 'which became the world's largest exchange that traded 4 million government bond futures in one day on February 23, 1995 and then collapsed when price manipulation caused over $10 billion of losses in just eight minutes' (see Box 11.1).[11]

Box 11.1: The 1995 collapse in the Shanghai stock exchange

'China established the Shanghai Stock Exchange in 1990 and opened the trading of government bond futures through 50 brokerage firms to the general public in October 1993. In a short period, over 30 exchanges opened up and over 50 futures contracts were traded in a casino-like atmosphere. In 1994, hot money migrated from equity to futures markets for government bonds, which were traded mostly in Shanghai, but also in Beijing, Shenzhen, and Wuhan. New regulations and position limits were then announced by various regulators. Government bonds were issued as zero-coupon bonds with three or five year maturities, some at variable interest rates that were adjusted discreetly with so-called "inflation subsidies", and they were settled with physical delivery that often caused shortages because open interest in futures markets far exceeded the physical amount of outstanding bonds. On February 23, 1995, the day before inflation subsidies were announced for illiquid bonds issued in 1992, one small brokerage (which was owned by the Ministry of Finance) took long positions in these bonds, that caused losses from short positions at the largest broker, Shanghai International Securities, which then tried to corner the market by selling short these futures in the amount of $26 billion, exceeding position limits by 20 times. Illegal transactions were continuing over the next three months, and the government then suspended all bond futures trading on 18 May 1995. The hot money then immediately returned to equity markets, which posted their largest gain of 31 per cent on the same day.'

[Reproduced verbatim from Oliver Fratzscher, 'Emerging Derivatives Market in Asia', Chapter for *Asian Financial Market Development*, World Bank, March 2006.]

Fratzscher suggested the following lessons (among other things) from this episode:

1. There needs to be an economic rationale to establish new derivative products that focus on hedging (rather than purely speculation).

2. Derivative markets can create systemic risk if prices of underlying instruments are not market-determined. For example, administered commodity prices or interest rates invite speculation in derivatives that often lead to overshooting once policy constraints are removed (as was the case in Chinese commodity and bond futures markets).

3. Chinese interest rates need to be fully liberalized and the two segmented bond markets need to be integrated before trading in government bond futures can resume.

In 2013, it moved to abolish the 'floor percentage', the minimum rate that banks need to charge, for borrowers which had earlier been set at 90 per cent of the benchmark lending rate. However, deposit rates remain controlled and banks cannot offer more than 110 per cent of the benchmark deposit rate to their clients. At the time of writing, the benchmark is 3 per cent and hence the ceiling on deposit rates is 3.3 per cent.

In the meantime, the government has permitted the resumption of trading in government bond futures and they resumed in September 2013. To begin with, only brokerages, mutual funds and wealthy retail investors will be allowed to trade government bond futures. The market was not opened to banks and insurers, which account for nearly three–quarters of China's outstanding bond holdings.[12]

If the ban on trading of government bond futures was due to speculation gone wrong, then the case of China Aviation Oil was a case of risk management, reporting and disclosure gone wrong (see Box 11.2). This case assumes significance since the stock of China Aviation Oil was listed in Singapore, regarded as a well regulated financial centre. The reputation of offshore financial centres rests on their disclosure, reporting and monitoring standards and compliance. This must have surely served as a wake-up call for Singapore.

Box 11.2: Transparency of OTC derivatives: The case of China Aviation Oil

China Aviation Oil Holdings Company (CAOHC), a state-owned company in Beijing, is the monopoly importer of jet fuel and in 1997 posted Mr. Chen Jui-lin to head its new Singapore subsidiary, China Aviation Oil (CAO). By 2001, CAO had prepared its initial public offering with its prospectus describing its business as oil derivatives trading, and its share price tripled after the IPO listing. Subsequently, CAO announced half-a-dozen acquisitions under the slogan "Leveraging China, Going Global". Chinese regulators had prepared an elaborate set of rules, including People's Bank of China (central bank) regulations that limit derivative transactions by state companies outside China to hedging, China Securities Regulatory Commission regulations that prohibit speculative derivative trading overseas, and State Council regulations that explicitly prohibit any OTC derivatives trading for state companies overseas. CAO itself had also invested in risk management systems, developed elaborate VAR models, and established

---

three internal controls with senior traders having strict limits, a risk control committee, and an internal auditing department. CAO won awards for its corporate governance, and Singapore investors honoured CAO as "one of the most transparent listed companies" and widely admired Mr. Chen who was the fourth highest paid CEO in Singapore. Its spectacular collapse with over US$ 550 million in derivative losses in November 2004 can only compare to the collapse of Barings in 1995.

Three factors contributed to the collapse: first and foremost was the lack of supervision from both home and host supervisors. CAO disregarded Chinese regulations and engaged in OTC derivatives trading of oil futures, taking short positions which were highly speculative (opposite of hedging), and misrepresenting its financial position with accounting gimmicks that extended loss-making futures contracts in order to avoid reporting incurred losses. Accounting standards were weak as International Accounting Standard 39 was not applied and derivatives positions were not marked to market. If these derivatives had been traded on an exchange, accounting and transparency would have been much stronger.

Second, non-regulated OTC derivative markets failed in this case, as self-regulation and internal risk management proved to be inadequate. CAO had developed elaborate value at risk (VAR) models that were built on historic oil price data, showing that prices rarely rise above $34, and were unable to predict oil prices rising to $55 in 2004 with any reasonable level of confidence. Traders' incentives created moral hazard to double up and ignore position limits, which increased short futures positions from 2 million tons of crude oil to 52 million tons, or the negative equivalent of about four years of China's total jet fuel imports. All internal controls failed, and nothing was reported to the parent company until margin calls exploded. Several commercial banks collaborated, offering unsecured credit lines, cheap financing, low margin requirements, and moral suasion to keep the speculation going.

Third, the weakening of disclosure rules by the Singapore exchange and very poor corporate governance contributed to the ultimate sin: after the Chinese central government refused to inject additional funds, the parent company CAOHC sold 15 per cent of the CAO shares in a block trade to Deutsche Bank in late October 2004. Deutsche Bank passed them on to institutional investors after having conducted 'due diligence'. The $120 million proceeds were directly lent to CAO in order to cover overdue margin calls, but eventually banks forced CAO to cut positions and realize losses of over $230 million. In November 2005, CAO had filed for bankruptcy with losses exceeding $550 million, and its assets estimated at $150 million.

Source: Oliver Fratzscher, 'Emerging Derivatives Market in Asia', Chapter for *Asian Financial Market Development*, World Bank, March 2006

China Aviation Oil was not the first large Chinese company to lose money on derivatives nor would it be the last one. In 2009, the China Banking Regulatory Commission (CBRC) came down hard on both local banks and foreign financial institutions that sold complex derivatives to Chinese companies. In August 2009, CBRC banned domestic banks from trading derivatives attached to overseas financial institutions. CBRC also said banks should assess the risk of domestic derivatives, as well as their relevance to the needs of the real economy, and provide clients with monthly updates on the status of their contracts. The losses imposed by overseas financial institutions re-opened wounds in China's psyche which date back to the days of colonialism and the Opium War: a spokesperson of the CBRC labelled these derivative products 'financial opium'.[13]

The CBRC measures were a reaction to the losses incurred in two high-profile cases. Citic Pacific, the Hong Kong-listed arm of China's largest investment conglomerate, lost $1.9 billion in 2008 on bets against the Australian dollar, while Air China, the country's flag carrier, lost $1.1 billion on oil derivatives.[14] Mushtaq Kapasi, a lawyer-turned banker who helped write these derivative contracts explained the losses incurred by China Eastern Airlines in a three-part 'confession' or 'investor education' article he wrote for the *Caijing* magazine in May 2009:[15]

China Eastern Airlines is one notorious case of a perilous hedge. Quite sensibly, the airline bought derivatives that would pay if oil became more expensive. But to make the hedge cheaper in the short term, China Eastern agreed that if oil prices dropped past a certain point, then it would have to pay double what the bank would have to pay if the price of oil went up. After the oil bubble burst last year, the company admitted these derivatives cost them 6.2 billion yuan and obliterated their profits for 2008. Of course, China Eastern is a huge company with government support. Most small investors are not as lucky.

Many small Chinese companies had taken out loans and wanted to protect themselves against changes in interest rates. A simple hedge would have worked fine. Instead, the banks sold complex derivatives called 'cost reduction swaps' that were linked to such obscure factors as differences in euro interest rates. When the credit crunch hit Europe, Chinese clients suddenly had to pay millions of dollars to their investment bankers.

Or consider what happened last summer, when the world believed that the yuan would appreciate. Small manufacturers who earned revenue in foreign currencies worried that their yuan expenses would remain constant while the yuan values of their sales would fall. Banks were eager to help these factories hedge their currency risks, but because everybody in the world believed the yuan would appreciate, it was very expensive to hedge.

Seeing these losses, the State-owned Assets Supervision and Administration Commission of the State Council (SASAC) declared its support for legal efforts by some state-backed Chinese companies to break loss-making contracts with foreign banks. It sent notices to six foreign financial institutions informing them that several state-owned enterprises reserved the right to default on commodities contracts signed with those institutions. It was interesting to note that the first report in *Financial Times* on this matter in September 2009[16] spoke of how it would be hugely damaging to China's reputation, etc. However, by the time the newspaper followed up this story in November 2009,[17] the tone had shifted to one of reconciliation.

Sample these sentences from the September 2009 report:

'Stiffing the foreigners in pursuit of domestic policy goals is a time—honoured practice here,' says Arthur Kroeber at Dragonomics, a research company in Beijing. Most global investment banks have been involved in the selling or structuring of these derivative trades and remain cautious about airing their views on the matter. Privately leading bankers rate it unlikely that contracts will be torn up. Some speculate that the political jockeying has been spurred by senior Sasac officials keen to enhance their nationalist credentials ahead of the next round of government promotions. In the event of a default, a global bank would have little choice but to go to court in London or Singapore, where most of these contracts are governed, even though any victory could prove pyrrhic. 'Assuming that the Chinese company loses in court, enforcement would be an issue,' says one senior executive of a global investment bank based in Hong Kong. 'No foreigner could take and sell an airline's assets, so China's sovereign rating would end up being downgraded.'

Analysts believe that mainland companies will have to continue dealing with western banks to hedge their exposure to commodities such as oil. But doing so could become more expensive if the risk of government intervention in the market continues to rise. 'The announcements this week can only introduce uncertainty,' says Paul Browne of law firm Simmons & Simmons in Hong Kong. 'And that is not helpful for the market.'

Notice how the tone changes in the November 2009 reporting:

Chinese regulators suspect that in some instances companies used derivatives as a way to speculate, rather than hedge, while banks frequently sold overly complex products – the most profitable – without fully explaining the potential downside.

Products with names such as 'snowballs' and 'snowblades' proliferated, many with so-called 'zero cost' structures that failed to live up to their name. Dealers say billions of dollars of trades are being renegotiated in private, some under pressure from Sasac, the shareholder and regulator of hundreds of state companies.

As well as banning the practice of intermediary trades, the CBRC now requires that banks ensure clients only buy derivatives that are appropriate for their hedging needs. The rules make it 'virtually impossible to do some of the hairier trades and will really chill the market for anything but vanilla trades in future', says Fred Chang, an industry veteran who now works for the law firm Lovells in Beijing.

In spite of grumbling among some bankers, most market participants believe that the regulations, while a stumbling block for the time being, are necessary foundations for the growth of a market that traders expect to be enormous within a decade.

David Liao, head of global markets at HSBC China, says the rules would be 'a short-term sting in terms of revenue' but would be helpful over the longer term. Most market participants expect a solution to the deadlock to emerge in time, most likely with foreign banks backing down on their positions.

What is clear is that foreign banks, while bruised, are unwilling to let either regulatory clampdown or local competition drive them out of the market. As one western banker in China says: 'You have to be in this market. You can't afford to stay out of it.'

These two news reports are an interesting case study on the dynamics of the relationship between a host government and multinational businesses, financial or non-financial. Whether the market makers end up bearing the losses or the customers do, so seems to be a function of the relative bargaining power of the host government vis-à-vis multinational corporations. Smaller countries may not be able to get away with the stance adopted by China. In very different circumstances, this is illustrated by the European Union's approach to Cypriot banks vis-à-vis banks in other countries.

For the banks themselves, the risk of a regulatory backlash like the one they faced in China is real. If they are unable to make good on their claims against their counterparties, they have to write off the losses. They may still be obligated to another party (a financial institution, perhaps with whom they had hedged their exposore. If the banks are incorporated as separate legal entities in third countries, then it might wipe out their capital. The threat of such a possibility could make them behave more responsibly towards their customers.

That most of these stories have a complex ending (or no ending at all) and that there are no clear villains (it is certain that there are no heroes!) is evident in an interesting sequel. In 2012, both Air China and China Eastern – the companies whose fuel hedging strategies made them lose substantial sums of money in 2008 – reported that their profits declined in 2011 because they were no longer hedging their fuel costs under instructions from the SASAC issued in 2009![18]

Gradual expansion and regulatory caution: The case of India

Indian derivatives markets present a very varied picture. Unlike most developing countries, India had active futures markets in commodities as far back as the 1870s, just 10 years after the Chicago Board of Trade became active. It had an indigenous form of forward trading in individual shares known as 'badla' for over a century till the late 1990s. It was replaced by modern equity derivatives (futures and options) in 2000–01. Currently, India's equity derivatives are among the most active and well-regulated in the world, spanning not only index futures and options but also futures and options in individual shares. It has active commodity futures in some commodities with bans in others, with infant and not very active futures markets in currencies and interest rates. It has tightly regulated OTC markets in interest rates, credit derivatives and foreign exchange.

In 2012, the National Stock Exchange of India (NSE) proudly announced that it figured in the top three of the global league tables in the volume of index and single stock options and future contracts traded (see Table 11.6). While the preamble stressed the hedging role of derivatives, the fact that volume in the derivatives market far outstrips the volume in the cash market is ample proof that the hedging role of derivatives has been relegated to a minor status in India, as it is almost everywhere else. The turnover of derivatives on the NSE increased from Rs. 24 billion in 2000–01 to Rs. 313,497 billion in 2011–12, i.e., an increase of 13 times in 12 years. Even discounting for inflation, this is a phenomenal increase in volume.

Table 11.6: India's National Stock Exchange: rank among international equity derivatives exchanges

Top 5 Exchanges by number of single stock future contracts traded in 2011 (in million)

Rank	Exchange	No. of contracts (in million)
1	NYSE Liffe Europe	250
2	Eurex	174
3	**National Stock Exchange of India**	161
4	Korea Exchange	60
5	Johannesburg Stock Exchange	48

Top 5 Exchanges by number of single stock option contracts traded in 2011 (in million)

Rank	Exchange	No. of contracts (in million)
1	BM & F BOVESPA	838
2	NASDAQ OMX PHLX	701
3	NYSE Euronext US	634
4	Chicago Board Options Exchange (CBOE)	516
5	International Securities Exchange (ISE)	454

Top 5 Exchanges by number of stock index option contracts traded in 2011 (in million)

Rank	Exchange	No. of contracts (in million)
1	Korea Exchange	3672
2	**National Stock Exchange India**	871
3	Eurex	468
4	Chicago Board Options Exchange (CBOE)	320
5	TAIFEX	126

Top 5 Exchanges by number of stock index futures contracts traded in 2011 (in million)

Rank	Exchange	No. of contracts (in million)
1	CME Group	736
2	Eurex	486
3	**National Stock Exchange of India**	156
4	Osaka Securities Exchange	137
5	NYSE Liffe Europe	97

Source: *National Securities Market Review (2012), National Stock Exchange of India*

The spectacular success of India's equity-related derivatives may be linked to the high rates of return on equities. In the first decade of the new millennium, India's corporate sector witnessed phenomenal growth in revenue, profits and in their national and global reach and influence, though this changed after 2011. The hitherto high returns attracted foreign investor interest. For the most part, despite being classified as volatile, foreign institutional investors (FII) have been giving a liberal benefit of doubt to the potential of Indian shares. Hence, outflows have been limited and brief and inflows have dominated (see Figure 11.3).

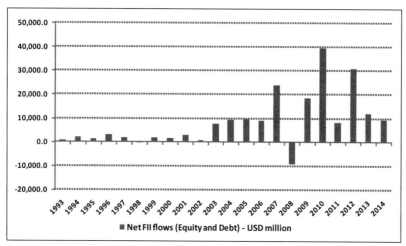

Figure 11.3: Foreign institutional investment flows into India

Source: SEBI

Note: Portfolio investment: annual net foreign investor inflows into India (Equity and Debt) in USD millions. Data for 2014 is up to March. Data for other years are calendar years.

Ample foreign portfolio investor interest in India, steps taken all around the world to liberalize capital account for financial flows and the liberalization of derivatives markets had their effect on India too. Hence, equity derivatives became a permanent and growing fixture in the Indian capital market landscape. The Securities and Exchange Board of India (SEBI), the capital markets regulator, has also played a catalytic role in the growth of equity index and single stock derivatives in India. Nevertheless, it is not obvious that high equity returns would necessarily lead to such spectacular growth in derivatives trading rather than in the stock market itself.

In December 2011, the Reserve Bank of India (RBI) expressed concern on the rising share of derivatives trading over cash trading in Indian equities and observed that 'in the interest of financial stability, these micro-level developments need to be monitored as potential sources of systemic risk.'[19]

When it comes to interest rate futures, India has had very limited success. It had to abort two attempts in 2003 and 2009 because of what market participants perceive as 'faulty designs'.[20] A fresh start was made in 2014.

A paradox with the expansion of derivatives markets in emerging economies, illustrated by India, is that though the case for new derivatives markets is always based on the 'need for hedging', the markets often end up being overwhelmingly used for speculation with little or no hedging activity. A Reuters report (for instance) mentioned that '[a]lthough India has active derivatives markets in currencies and equities, it has struggled to develop liquidity in debt derivatives, depriving banks and other financial firms of a hedging opportunity'.[21] The same report noted that 'India has a vibrant exchange-traded equities derivatives market, with turnover about 14 times that of cash markets, reflecting the potential demand for rate derivatives.' It was noted in Chapter 7 that speculative volume is essential for a well-functioning derivatives market, but the required level of speculation (going by empirical studies) is of the order of 1.5 times the hedging volume. Speculation amounting to 14 times the potential hedging demand is clearly in excess of what is needed for a liquid market and creates the likelihood of destabilization of the underlying market.

RBI is both India's central bank and the regulator for the banking sector. Derivatives on foreign exchange and interest rates come under its purview. Over the years, RBI has taken a cautious view on enabling trading in foreign exchange and interest rate derivatives: Growth of the financial market and availability of new financial instruments to market participants should be permitted only to the extent that they do not, in their judgment, undermine systemic stability and the health of the banking system. This cautious attitude has come under criticism from some quarters but appears well justified: as a regulator, a central bank is responsible for the stability of the economic system and the banking sector. In May 2011, RBI issued guidelines on the operational framework for the issuance of plain vanilla OTC single-name CDS for corporate bonds in India.[22] Two good features of the guidelines issued by RBI are that:

- Entities are permitted to buy credit protection (buy CDS contracts) only to hedge their underlying credit risk on corporate bonds. Such entities are not permitted to hold credit protection without having eligible underlying as a hedged item. Users are also not permitted to sell protection and are not permitted to hold short positions in the CDS contracts. However, they are permitted to exit their bought CDS positions by unwinding them with the original counterparty or by assigning them in favour of buyer of the underlying bond.

- The users cannot buy CDS for amounts higher than the face value of corporate bonds held by them and for periods longer than the tenor of corporate bonds held by them.

In essence, RBI has restricted the use of CDS to genuine hedging needs and prohibited the use of naked CDS as a speculative device.

RBI also requires Indian banks operating overseas to adhere to the guidelines of their host countries if those are stricter than the RBI guidelines. It also notified capital adequacy and exposure norms for CDS on the same date while clarifying the reporting platform to which CDS trades must be reported by market makers. While the May 2011 guidelines restricted the use of CDS to banks and to bonds issued by certain kinds of companies, these were later extended gradually to other financial institutions and other kinds of bonds.[23]

The Reserve Bank of India Act of 1934 was amended in 2006 to give legal sanction for OTC derivatives, as the extant Indian laws did not explicitly do so; they were not valid contracts under the Indian Contract Act of 1872 as they were deemed wagering contracts. Shyamala Gopinath, then Deputy Governor of RBI set out nine key principles that marked RBI's regulation of OTC derivatives.[24] A few innovations that the RBI made in regulating OTC derivatives which are worthy of wider adoption, especially in emerging markets, were:

- *'For an OTC derivative transaction to be legally valid, one of the parties to the transaction has to be a RBI-regulated entity.'* (This provides the regulator with direct visibility of every transaction.)

- *'Derivative structured products (i.e., combination of cash and generic derivative instruments) are permitted as long as they are a combination of two or more of the generic instruments permitted by RBI and do not contain any derivative as underlying.'* (This prevents the evolution of non-transparent complex and exotic derivatives whose pay-offs are difficult to determine.)

- *'The responsibility for assessment of customer suitability and appropriateness is squarely on the market maker.'* (In other words, the *caveat emptor* or 'buyer beware' principle was explicitly avoided as losses incurred under OTC derivatives quickly become systemic issues. This is particularly important in the developing country context as the Chinese examples above and Indian examples below illustrate.)

- *'All OTC forex and interest rate derivatives attract a much higher credit conversion factor (CCF) than prescribed under the Basel framework and all exposures are reckoned on a gross basis for capital adequacy purpose.'* (The prudent conservatism in the RBI's approach is evident here too.)

In spite of the central bank's caution on the introduction of derivatives in India, instances of wrongful selling of derivatives have surfaced periodically in India too (see Boxes 11.3 and 11.4). Complex structures involving option writing by a 'hedger' have frequently been the culprit. These structures look very attractive at the time of initiation. Non-financial companies, poorly informed about the risks, fall for this illusion quite easily (just as the treasurer of Orange County, California did in the 1990s albeit in different circumstances and for a different derivative). Companies buying these products often think that they are being clever in receiving payment from (instead of paying a premium to) the banks for hedging their risks. They do not understand or do not evaluate correctly the risks they are taking. Sellers of complex structures (looking for lucrative fees) have incentives to downplay the risks; the buyers conclude that the scenarios that would result in them suffering losses have trivial probabilities attached to them. They forget the oldest adage in finance and economics: that there is no free lunch. Hedgers would do well to remember that if something looks too good to be true, it is indeed not true.

Box 11.3: Wockhardt Pharmaceuticals

A prominent case was that of Wockhardt Pharmaceuticals, an Indian pharmaceuticals exporter whose export turnover involves an intrinsic long position in the dollar / short position in the rupee. In the years just before the financial crisis of 2008, the rupee had appreciated against the dollar. The company bought complex derivatives structures with the ostensible intent of guarding against a decline in the exchange rate of the rupee vis-à-vis the dollar. The authors do not have access to contract details and the following reconstruction is based on newspaper reports.

The contracts appear to have been designed in such a way that the hedges would compensate the hedger (Wockhardt in this case) in the event of US dollar weakness, but the hedger would end up paying proportionately more to the counterparty were the rupee to weaken against the US dollar. The structure appears to have involved the hedger writing a put option to the counterparty against rupee weakness. At the time of initiation of the contract, this would have appealed to the hedgers because they received

---

option premium for writing puts and this would have lowered the overall cost of the hedging structure. In some cases, such structures could also result in positive initial pay-offs to the hedger.

During the global crisis of 2008 the rupee, contrary to expectations, weakened. The hedger ended up paying more to the counterparty (banks) than it gained on the underlying exposure.

Box 11.4: The Tirupur textile exporters

A case that has assumed more serious overtones than the Wockhardt case, and which is still mired in a legal process, is the case of the textile exporters in Tirupur (a town in Tamil Nadu, India) suffering heavy losses in foreign exchange hedging. A newspaper article in the *Business Line* recalled the terms of the options contract (USD denotes US dollars and CHF denotes Swiss Francs):

An illustrative derivative deal dated July 3, 2007 (with 'Tokyo cut' 'European style option' and 'American barriers' as features) expiring on May 23, 2008 reads: 'The exporter buys (and the bank sells) USD Call/CHF Put at strike 1.2300 for USD4 million with Knock Out @1.2400; The exporter sells (and the bank buys) USD Put/CHF Call at strike 1.2300 for USD8 million with Knock Out @ 1.24, Knock In @1.12'; Double One touch option with trigger 1.2270 and 1.2330 with pay off USD 50000 on maturity'[25]

The key is in the notional amounts involved – USD4 million and USD8million – and the differential strike prices with knockout and knock-ins. In one part of the contract, the client agrees to buy a Call Option but the Call Option automatically gets cancelled if the US dollar rises above 1.24 CHF. He just makes 40,000 US dollars. The other part is the key – the client sells a PUT contract (he receives a premium) expressing a willingness to buy US dollars at 1.23 if it fell below 1.12 CHF. The notional size is USD 8 million.[26] The premium they received for this part might have exceeded the premium thay paid for buying the USD call and thus provided them with a 'free income'. As it happens in such cases, the dollar weakened well below 1.12 CHF and the Tirupur exporters had to buy dollars at 1.23 CHF.

Another newspaper article in the *Mint* observed:

'Exporters that Mint spoke to said they were aggressively wooed for months by several banks to buy complex financial instruments to hedge their losses from a rising rupee, and the only reason most of them stayed away from buying them was because the banks themselves often couldn't explain to the exporters how the derivatives worked. But, they say, that still didn't prevent the banks from trying every sales trick to try sell them.'[27]

The question that arises is: Why were these Indian traders (whose currencies are either US dollars or the Indian rupee) being sold derivative contracts involving US dollars and the Swiss franc in the guise of 'hedges'? The exporters were not receiving Swiss francs from their exports. They were getting paid in US dollars. So, they could not have delivered these currencies to the banks under the terms of the contract. That was against the prevailing Indian laws. This and several other legal transgressions have been identified in the Tirupur case. The RBI levied fines on the banks that sold the derivative structures in 2011, clearly indicating that it found the banks' conduct unacceptable and that it was not in conformity with established rules and procedures for selling of derivatives.[28] The case is pending before India's Supreme Court on whether the exporters or the banks should bear the losses.

The RBI's OTC regulations now impose on market-makers the obligation to ascertain and confirm the user's suitability for trading in derivatives and the appropriateness of derivatives-based solutions recommended to them and this should reduce the risk of a repetition of cases like the Tirupur exporters (Box 11.4). Nevertheless, the key lesson is for buyers: that if they cannot understand a derivative transaction, they should refrain from it.

Notes and References

1 Cem Saatcioglu, Iskender Karagul, Ara G. Volkan, 'Usefulness of Derivative Instruments in Emerging Markets: Turkish Experience', *International Business & Economics Research Journal*, Vol. 4, No. 2, February 2005.

2 The total for Asian, Latin American and 'Other Equities' markets comes to $1.027 trillion, but this includes developed countries like Australia.

3 Tony Freeman, 'Brazil a Possible Model for Derivatives Reform', *Financial Times*, 19 August 2011.

4   Jeffrey Frankel, 'What Small Countries Can Teach the World', *Business Economics*, Vol. 47, No. 2, April 2012, 97–103.

5   R. French-Davis, *Economic Reforms in Chile: From Dictatorship to Democracy*. Palgrave Macmillan, September 2010.

6   R. French-Davis, 'The Chilean Model', 17 March 2011.

7   Luis A. Opazo R., *Derivative Market: The Experience of Chile*, Irving Fisher Committee (IFC) Bulletin No. 35, February 2012, Proceedings of the workshop 'Data requirements for monitoring derivative transactions', organized by the People's Bank of China and the Irving Fisher Committee, Zhengzhou, 27–29 September 2010.

8   R. Dodd and S. Griffith-Jones, *Report on Derivatives Markets: Stabilizing or Speculative Impact on Chile and a Comparison with Brazil*, Economic Commission for Latin America and the Caribbean (ECLAC), May 2007.

9   F. Avalos and R. Moreno, 'Hedging in Derivatives Markets: The Experience of Chile', *BIS Quarterly Review*, March 2013.

10   Jinan Yan, *Development and Utilization of Financial Derivatives in China*, Paper presented at the proceedings of the workshop 'Data Requirements for Monitoring Derivative Transactions', organized by the People's Bank of China and the Irving Fisher Committee (BIS), Zhengzhou, 27–29 September 2010. Available at: http://www.bis.org/ifc/publ/ifcb35c.pdf. Accessed on 14 July 2014.

11   Oliver Fratzscher, 'Emerging Derivatives Market in Asia', Chapter for Asian Financial Market Development, World Bank, March 2006.

12   'China Reopens Government Bond Futures Market', *Financial Times*, 6 September 2013. Available at: http://www.ft.com/cms/s/0/94600a40-16cf-11e3-9ec2-00144feabdc0.html. Accessed on 14 July 2014.

13   *CBRC Moves to Regulate Derivatives*. News story by Staff Reporter Zhang Man, Caijing (English). Available at: http://english.caijing.com.cn/2009-08-06/110221312.html. Accessed on 5 January 2014.

14   Robert Cookson, Patti Waldmeir and Jamil Anderlini, 'China Derivatives Rule Change Hits Banks', *Financial Times*, 23 November 2009. Available at: http://www.ft.com/cms/s/0/20eb4ca6-d861-11de-b63a-00144feabdc0.html. Accessed on 5 January 2014.

15   'Confessions of Chinese Derivatives Deals, Parts 1 to 3'. Caijing (English), available at: http://english.caijing.com.cn/2009-05-13/110165078.html . Accessed on 5 January 2014.

16   Sundeep Tucker and Robert Cookson. 'China Talks Tough on Foreign Bank Derivatives', *Financial Times*, 14 September 2009. Available at: http://www.ft.com/cms/s/0/0bf37b92-a149-11de-a88d-00144feabdc0.html. Accessed on 5 January 2014.

17   Robert Cookson, Patti Waldmeir and Jamil Anderlini. 'China Derivatives Rule Change hits banks', *Financial Times*, 23 November 2009. Available at: http://www.ft.com/cms/s/0/20eb4ca6-d861-11de-b63a-00144feabdc0.html. Accessed on 5 January 2014.

[18] 'Chinese Airlines Hit by Dispute Over Hedging', *Financial Times*, 27 March 2012. Available at:http://www.ft.com/cms/s/0/ffe9bca2-782e-11e1-b237-00144feab49a.html. Accessed on 14 July 2014.

[19] *Financial Stability Report* of the Reserve Bank of India, December 2011.

[20] Archana Narayanan and Suvashree Dey Choudhury. 'Exclusive: India Gears Up to Launch Interest Rate Futures', Reuters, 18 October 2013. Available at: http://www.reuters.com/article/2013/10/18/us-india-bonds-futures-idUSBRE99H07M20131018. Accessed on 5 January 2014.

[21] *Ibid.*

[22] See, http://rbi.org.in/scripts/NotificationUser.aspx?Id=6432&Mode=0 for the announcement of the release of guidelines and http://rbidocs.rbi.org.in/rdocs/content/PDFs/FGCD240511A.pdf for the guidelines. Accessed on 14 July 2014.

[23] http://www.rbi.org.in/scripts/NotificationUser.aspx?Id=7793&Mode=0. Accessed on 14 July 2014.

[24] S.Gopinath, 'Over-the-counter derivative Markets in India – Issues and Perspectives', *Financial Stability Review*, Bank of France, July 2010.

[25] 'Will the RBI Probe and Unravel the Derivatives Scam?', *Business Line*, 5 July 2008. Available at: http://www.thehindubusinessline.com/todays-paper/will-the-rbi-probe-and-unravel-the-derivatives-scam/article1630785.ece. Accessed on 14 July 2014.

[26] These ranges are usually set based on probabilities computed on the assumption that changes in prices of financial assets (including currencies) are normally distributed. The Black-Scholes Option Pricing Formula is based on the assumption of normality of price changes. That means that extreme events are rare and have very low probability. In reality, however, extreme movements in prices turn out to be more frequent than a typical normal distribution would suggest. Financial market price changes are thus, said to have fat tails. Normally distributed price changes will not have fat tails.

[27] 'Close Shave for Textile Exporters in Tirupur', *Mint*, 26 March 2008. Available at: http://www.livemint.com/Companies/BVLAlkypInBaPI0KMLxdqL/Close-shave-for-textile-exporters-in-Tirupur.html. Accessed on 14 July 2014.

[28] 'The Reserve Bank had issued Show Cause Notices to these banks. In response to this, the banks submitted their written replies. On a careful examination of the banks' written replies and the oral submissions made during the personal hearings, the Reserve Bank found that the violations were established and the penalties were thus imposed.' Available at: http://www.rbi.org.in/scripts/BS_PressReleaseDisplay.aspx?prid=24300. Accessed on 14 July 2014.

12

Derivatives and Emerging Markets – Part II

The sight of bankers from the rich industrial countries capturing their home governments is bad enough. To watch them attempting to capture or bully foreign governments, often in emerging markets or developing countries, is truly objectionable. It is time to play the international lending game with an honest deck.

Willem Buiter(2009)[1]

The previous chapter looked at derivatives markets *in* emerging economies. This chapter examines

- the use of derivatives *by* emerging economies (especially by governments) as risk management tools; and

- issues arising from derivatives which have emerging market risks as the underlying.

Like the previous chapter, case studies are used to illustrate more general issues.

Use of derivatives by emerging economies

For decades, economists have suggested that developing countries could use international commodity markets to hedge commodity price risk. In recent years, with the introduction of catastrophe derivatives and weather derivatives, the same has been said about natural disaster risks. Though successful cases of actual use have been relatively few, there is concrete evidence that the potential can be, and is being, translated into reality.

Hedging macro-economic risk from commodity prices: The Mexican case

Mexico has, for many years, followed a policy of hedging its oil output in order to reduce budget uncertainty and instability. Oil has for many years occupied a crucial position in the Mexican economy. In the 1980s, it accounted for over 50 per cent of exports (see Figure 12.1). The importance of oil has waned over the years for Mexico as its oil production has declined and other exports have grown. Its oil production peaked in 2003 at 3.37 million barrels per day and in 2012, it was 2.548 million barrels per day. Total exports were $ 371 billion in 2012 with crude petroleum exports constituting $ 47 billion – about 13 per cent, still significant but not critical.

Mexico Petroleum Export/Overall Export Ratio

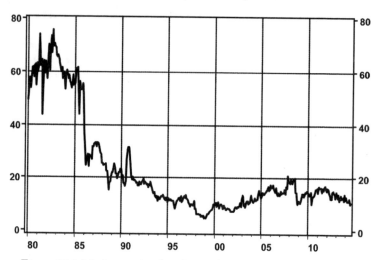

Figure 12.1: Mexico – ratio of crude petroleum exports to overall exports
Source: Haver Analytics

Yet, Mexico has continued with its practice of hedging its oil revenues from a possible reduction in the global price of crude oil every year. One reason is that oil continues to account for a large share of government revenues, estimated at a third. Under this programme, Mexico fixes the price for the oil that will be exported in the forthcoming year by *buying put options and by selling futures*. Through this mechanism, the government acquires a high degree of certainty over its oil revenues and this enables it to plan government expenditures within a stable framework.

The oil hedge paid off rather well in 2008 when the price of crude oil reached a historical high only to slump in 2009. According to the press release of the government in December 2009, the Mexican government profited from its purchase of put options on crude oil in 2009 to the tune of $5.085 billion. The hedge cost was only around $1.5 billion and hence the profit was more than three times the premium paid.[2] Such big windfall gains are rare and the last time Mexico earned such a windfall profit was in 1991 when it reportedly earned some $800 million (in 1991 prices).

Subsequent to the huge gains realized in 2009, the Mexican government did not have to exercise its put options on crude oil as oil prices ruled firm in 2010–12. For the year 2013, it engaged in a slightly different strategy. It bought puts on crude oil at the strike price of $85 per barrel and it sold puts on crude oil at a strike price of $60 per barrel, thus creating a 'put spread'. The put spread structure would have been much less expensive than the annual premium outgo of $1–1.5 billion that Mexico used to pay, but limited the gains to Mexico to a maximum of $ 25 per barrel (the difference between the two strike prices of $85 and $60 per barrel), regardless of how far the oil price (on the maturity date of the option) fell below $60. It thus exposed Mexico to a drop in the price of crude oil below $60 per barrel. Parsons and Mello felt that Mexico might have adopted the put spread strategy because it had seen its put positions expire worthless in the previous three years and hence might have wanted to limit the premium outgo; but in the process it also exposed itself to the worst case scenarios similar to the one experienced in 2009. As they put it, '*Insurance always looks expensive after a run of years when it turned out the insurance was not needed.*'[3]

Mexico hedged the oil output for 2014 at a high price of $90 per barrel.[4] Since the strike price of the option was close to the spot price of crude oil, the premium outgo for Mexico would have been higher than in the previous years. At the same time, the hedge made sense, given that, after firm prices for the last few years, statistically, the chances of a swift and deep correction would have been higher in 2014.

Besides trying to protect itself against *falling* prices of crude oil, Mexico also used the derivatives market to protect itself against *rising* prices of corn in 2011. In December 2010, it was reported that Mexico had bought call options on corn for 4.2 million tonnes in the Chicago Mercantile Exchange.[5] It is reported that Qatar joined Mexico in hedging a portion of its oil production in 2011.

The Mexican oil hedge programme and its use of corn options to hedge import costs, are prime real life examples of the classical economic function of derivatives viz. risk-reducing hedging. The aim is not to increase the revenue from exports or to reduce the cost of imports but to make it less uncertain. The short run certainty provided for budgeting purposes has important positive macroeconomic effects. However, as the preceding narrative shows, even within the overall risk-reducing approach there is always room to 'time the market' to secure the 'best' possible price or to structure the hedge to 'reduce' the cost.

Such adjustments inevitably involve taking some risk and obviously can also go wrong. Governments are subject to legislative and audit scrutiny and public accountability and this can sometimes lead to hindsight-based criticism when such optimization attempts go wrong. It is therefore important for governments who use derivatives as hedges to have a clear written policy on how and when hedging will be done so that their actions are then measured against that standard rather than the standard of hindsight.

Using complex derivatives to hedge weather risks: The case of Uruguay

Uruguay is dependent on hydro-electric power for 80 per cent of its total power needs. When hydro-electric generation falls because of inadequate rainfall, the state-owned electric utility Administración Nacional de Usinas y Trasmisiones Eléctricas (UTE) is forced to purchase alternative fuel (mostly oil and natural gas) to use as inputs for electricity generation affecting both consumers and the exchequer. If this happens when the price of oil is high, the adverse effect is exacerbated. In 2012, because of water shortages, the cost of supplying electricity reached a record US$1.4 billion, far exceeding the company's original projections of $953 million. In order to cover the gap, UTE borrowed funds from the market, drew down the country's US$150 million Energy Stabilization Fund, and increased rates to consumers.

In December 2013, Uruguay entered into a weather index derivative transaction through the World Bank which provides short-run cost certainty to the energy company, budget stability to the government, and price stability to consumers.[6] The transaction has been called a 'weather insurance' transaction but in effect is a derivative because the pay-off is triggered by the level of a weather index and is not based on measurement of actual loss. Under the transaction, UTE paid a premium and in return obtained risk cover for a period of 18 months under which it would receive a payoff depending on the extent of drought and the level of oil prices.

To gauge the occurrence and extent of a drought and potential payouts to the company, daily rainfall data is collected at 39 weather stations spread throughout the two river basins on which UTE depends (the Rio Negro and the Rio Uruguay). The rainfall data is used to compile a weather index. UTE will receive a payout from the World Bank if the weather index is below the predetermined trigger. The trigger was fixed by UTE, based on coverage and cost considerations. The amount of the payout depends on the level of the rainfall index and market oil prices at that time, with a maximum pay out of $450 million. If precipitation falls below the level set up as trigger of the contract, UTE will receive a payout of up to $450 million based on the severity of the drought and oil price levels. If oil prices are high, the payout will be larger to offset the higher cost of fuel purchases. The World Bank provided technical support to the government and UTE in designing the terms of the transaction, the protocol for the future collection of hydrographical data through Uruguay's National Meteorological Service, and legal aspects of a weather derivative contract and acted as UTE's counterparty for the transaction.[7]

The World Bank entered into an agreement with Nephila/Allianz and Swiss Re and effectively transferred the risk onto these entities. For the insurance companies, the involvement of the Bank meant that they were dealing with an AAA-rated entity rather than a developing country utility and this reduced the cost of the arrangement, the benefit of which accrued to Uruguay.[8]

The Uruguay case follows a similar but smaller transaction in Malawi where risks arising from maize crop failure (which would necessitate higher imports) were similarly covered by a weather index derivative intermediated by the World Bank, which has been a pioneer in this field. It falls into a category known as 'index insurance'. Index insurance is a 'simplified form of insurance in which indemnity payments are based on values obtained from an index that serves as a proxy for losses rather than upon the assessed losses of each individual policyholder'.[9] Payouts are made based on a pre-established scale set out in the 'insurance' policy.

Weather index 'insurance' can be applied at macro level (as in the Uruguay and Malawi examples) but also at lower levels. For example at the micro level it can be used as a method of crop insurance but without having to assess losses by each individual small farmer. Traditional insurance products are often not viable for developing countries, where limited commercialization and small average farm sizes are a major hindrance. The Indian micro-finance institution BASIX in collaboration with ICICI Lombard Insurance has been issuing weather index insurance to peasant farmers since 2003. It is estimated that more than 539,000 Indian farmers have purchased weather index insurance to date and the Indian experience has given rise to similar pilots and feasibility studies in many countries around the world, including Thailand, Indonesia, Malawi, Kenya, and

Nicaragua.[10] Weather index insurance works well for highly correlated risks, such as drought and temperature whereas localized or independently occurring risks, such as hail or fire, do not lend themselves to index insurance. Weather index insurance can also be used at 'meso' level, e.g. to provide risk cover to a financial institution which lends to small farmers.

While these transactions are publicly characterized as 'insurance', in substance, they are derivatives and not insurance. This is because there is no requirement of an insurable interest and no requirement that loss be established or measured before a pay-out is made. If the index reaches a particular level, a pay-out is triggered. They do have a lot of parallels with insurance and the ultimate counterparties (as in the Uruguay case) are often insurance and re-insurance companies rather than banks.

Derivatives with emerging market risks as underlying: economic effects

Economic entities usually assume that risks arise from derivatives transactions they have themselves entered into. However, recent experiences indicate that in some circumstances, *derivatives transacted between two parties on risks regarding a third party can affect that third party even if it is not privy to the transaction.* This has implications and economic effects on that party. Example 12.1 illustrates this contrast.

Example 12.1:

Bank B based in Europe makes a loan to D, a debtor in a developing country. B then enters into credit default swap with counterparty C, a financial institution in the USA. Under the terms of the swap, C will pay a fixed amount to B in the event of default by D. Note that the contract is between B and C and even though the pay-off is triggered by a default committed by D, D is not a party to the transaction.

However, if the existence of such a swap influences B's behaviour with D then D is in fact affected by this transaction even though it is not party to it.

Effects of foreigners' CDS transactions on domestic banks: The case of Kazakhstan

BTA Bank, Kazakhstan's largest bank, had been an 'up-and-coming darling of the capital markets world, with investment bankers furiously competing to float its bonds, provide loans, and much else'.[11] In 2009, after the financial crisis and its effects on major western banks, funding suddenly evaporated. BTA was nationalized in response to the problems. According to Gillian Tett of the *Financial Times*:

> 'Initially, BTA wanted to keep servicing its loans, and its creditors, such as Morgan Stanley, appeared happy to play along. But last week Morgan Stanley and another bank suddenly demanded repayment. BTA was unable to comply, and thus tipped into partial default. That sparked fury among some other creditors, and shocked some Kazakhs, who wondered why Morgan Stanley would have taken an action that seemed likely to create losses.
>
> One clue to the US bank's motives, though, can be seen on the official website of the International Swaps and Derivatives Association. One page reveals that just after calling in the loan, Morgan Stanley also asked ISDA to start formal proceedings to settle credit default swaps contracts written on BTA.
>
> For it transpires that while the US bank has a loan to BTA it also has a big CDS position on BTA, that pays out if – and only if – the Kazakh bank goes into default. Indeed, some of Morgan Stanley's rivals suspect that notwithstanding its loan, Morgan Stanley is actually net short the Kazakh bank.
>
> As a result speculation is rife that Morgan might have deliberately provoked the default of BTA to profit on its CDS, since a default makes the US bank a net winner, not a loser as logic might suggest.
>
> Morgan Stanley, for its part, refuses to comment on this speculation (although its officials note that the bank does not generally take active 'short' positions in its clients.) And I personally have no way of knowing whether Morgan is short or long, since Morgan refuses to disclose details of its CDS holding.'[12]

Example 12.2 illustrates the point.

Example 12.2:

Assume a bank B has made a loan of $X to a debtor D. As a creditor to D, B would normally want to avoid a default by D, as B would not get paid in full. Assume that B has also bought CDS in amount $Y to cover the risk of default on D's debt. As long as X>Y, B has a net long position in D's debt, and it will lose if D defaults. The purchase of CDS therefore is the purchase of insurance: B has an insurable interest.

However, in most countries, there is no limit on the amount of CDS which can be bought. If B had bought CDS contracts for a larger amount of D's debt than it owns, i.e., Y>X, then B has a net short position in D's debt. It is better off if D defaults than if it does not default. In this case, B is not insuring against default by D, it is actually betting on default by B.

The absence of insurable interest may not matter if the bank had no way of affecting the likelihood of default by the debtor. In that case it would resemble betting on a cricket match without match-fixing. But *if the banker can influence the likelihood of default of the debtor*, it would be equivalent to betting on a cricket match where the gambler is also playing in the match and thus has the ability to change the result.

Commenting on the same case, Willem Buiter, formerly Chief Economist of the European Bank for Reconstruction and Development, wrote:

> ...When it became clear that BTA, like most of Kazakhstan's banks was tottering on the edge of the precipice, the foreign unsecured creditors of the bank began to lobby the Kazakh government to guarantee the bank's unsecured liabilities. Pledging the resources of Kazakhstan's National Oil Fund to rescue the unsecured foreign creditors is an option that is especially popular with those who were caught with their pantaloons down. There is no insurance like ex-post insurance.

> When first BTA and then a second Kazakh bank, Alliance Bank, went into partial default, the sound of foreign bankers lobbying the Kazakh government became a mighty roar. Those doing the lobbying were presumably those long in Kazakh bank debt, that is, creditors whose credit exposure exceeded their holdings of CDS contracts written on Kazakh bank debt and the writers of the CDS. About 40 per cent of the liabilities of Kazakh banks are held by foreigners, mainly by banks and investment banks. State ownership of a bank does not, of course, mean that the state guarantees any of the liabilities of that bank. Limited liability means that the exposure of the state, like that of any owner, is limited to the state's equity in the bank.

> The foreign creditors ... are sophisticated, professional financiers, who earned very handsome spreads over US Treasury bonds by lending to Kazakh banks. This lending became grossly undisciplined and led to a massive investment, construction and real estate boom as the world economy thundered along and the prices of oil and gas (Kazakhstan's main exports) skyrocketed.

> A mole wearing sunglasses could have seen the Kazakh boom was

unsustainable and would crash. There never were creditors more undeserving than the creditors of Kazakh banks. The spread between US Treasury bonds and US\$-denominated Kazakh bank debt is called a (differential) credit risk spread. When you see it, it means that there is likely to be greater credit risk associated with the security earning the higher yield. The spread is the reward for bearing that risk. Sometimes that risk comes home to roost. Then you have to eat it. That's known as the rules of a capitalist market economy.

In Kazakhstan, some of the foreign banks that lent unsecured to the Kazakh banks are not only lobbying furiously – they are playing hardball, threatening to invoke assorted cross-default clauses in loan contracts that could bring down most of the Kazakh banking system. There is no financial upside for the creditors from following through on that threat, but there is, of course, considerable downside for the Kazakh government and people. Such behaviour is deeply unethical and should be illegal. I hope the home governments of the foreign banks that are financially exposed in Kazakhstan have the good sense either not to get involved at all, or to take the side of the Kazakh tax payers.

The sight of bankers from the rich industrial countries capturing their home governments is bad enough. To watch them attempting to capture or bully foreign governments, often in emerging markets or developing countries, is truly objectionable. It is time to play the international lending game with an honest deck.[13]

The Kazakh case raises and illustrates a lot of important issues. One of the main criticisms against CDS contracts is that buyers of CDS contracts do not just take insurance against default but *develop an incentive for default to occur* since they get paid in full when default occurs. An ordinary creditor has an incentive to restructure debt and receive payments should the borrower get in trouble whereas a CDS holder could, potentially, act to create trouble for the borrower so that the 'credit event' occurs that triggers a pay-out on the CDS contract.

It would be incorrect to conclude that the kinds of CDS deals surrounding BTA were peculiar to emerging markets. John Paulson a leading hedge fund manager, through Goldman Sachs as intermediary, shorted CDS on US home loans, in a transaction which ended up threatening the German banking system[14] and is the subject of a prosecution.

While the foregoing discussion has focussed on the negative aspects of naked CDS, it should be noted that even naked CDS and other shorting instruments may have a legitimate hedging use: they may serve as proxy hedges for risks that may not have a direct hedge. Investors might not have readily lent to the Kazakhstan government had it not been for the availability of CDS on BTA. CDS on BTA served as a proxy hedge on the Kazakh sovereign itself. Availability of indirect hedges may facilitate flow of capital that some sovereigns or corporations might otherwise be shut out of.

Naked CDS as short-selling instruments

Naked CDS contracts (i.e., CDS without an exposure to the underlying) are not insurance but vehicles to speculate against the debt servicing abilities and solvency of borrowers. At one level, a naked CDS may appear similar to a put option on stocks used to speculate on a drop in value of the shares. But an important difference is that put options are mostly exchange-traded while CDS are not. It is possible to see the number of put options outstanding because the options are exchange traded. The disclosure of a large number of put contracts having being entered into on an underlying stock sends a signal to market participants, to auditors, to regulators, to competitors (and even to potential bidders).

In another way, naked CDS ownership is akin to short sale of a stock. The buyer of a put option on a company's shares or a short seller of those shares both stand to benefit from poor performance by the company, just as the holder of naked CDS profits if the borrower defaults.

Is short speculation bad?

As was seen in Chapter 7, short selling is a normal part of the working of derivatives markets and a reflection and reinforcement of the fact that asset prices are a two-way street; indeed restrictions on short selling can be a destabilizing influence. Short positions in bonds or in stocks are the equivalent of 'anti-incumbency' in a democratic political setup. In a sense, they are to financial markets what the opposition and media are in a democratic polity. They are tools to amplify the expression of dissatisfaction with the way a corporation or a sovereign is managed. (Without them, only existing holders of stocks or bonds would be able to sell them and this might have less effect on the price.) In the long run, that is arguably a positive and not a negative for shareholders' interests, systemic stability, improved governance, economic growth and economic well-being even if there is volatility, turbulence and dislocation in the short run. Without those, lasting changes for the better seldom occur. Many examples can be given.

George Soros' bet against the British pound in 1992 might have been a humiliation at a personal level for Norman Lamont, the then Chancellor of the Exchequer and for the leadership of the Bank of England. But, it allowed the currency to break free of the shackles of being tied expensively to the German mark. The substantial depreciation of the pound that followed reflected the British economic fundamentals at that time and facilitated an economic recovery. Similarly, speculators forced the Scandinavian currencies and the Italian lira to exit the European Exchange Rate Mechanism (ERM) in 1992 and in 1993. That too restored monetary policy autonomy for these countries and facilitated an economic recovery. In fact, without the economic recovery that followed their ejection from the ERM, some of them may not have been able to meet the criteria set for joining the European single currency[15].

More recently, without the short speculators' attention on the sovereign debt situation in Greece, Spain and Portugal in 2010–11, it is inconceivable that these countries would have embarked on a severe and difficult but inevitable fiscal restructuring and austerity. It is not without risks but without painful fiscal reconstruction and restructuring it might well be impossible for these nations to have a stab at returning to economic growth in the medium term.

In environments of Greenspan puts, U.S. and European quantitative easing and Japanese monetary 'arrows', it is almost as though asset prices, stock and bond owners and issuers have an unfettered right to see their prices appreciate; short selling provides a much-needed corrective. Though there have been calls to ban short-selling, it rightly remains legal in many countries. Further, the United States has not made it mandatory that the short-sellers must actually have borrowed the security and show proof of it before placing an order to short-sell the stock.[16,17] (Selling a stock without having borrowed is called 'naked' short selling.). The European Union (EU) too has not banned the short sale of shares or sovereign debt but imposed restrictions on it.[18] (Indeed from an economist's point of view even those restrictions are a destabilizing influence.)

In that light, short selling is a part of the 'checks and balances' that markets legitimately exercise and can be considered a means of encouraging emerging market governments to adopt prudent economic policies.

However, while short selling is a necessary and desirable feature of most markets, *naked CDS represents a special case*. In this case, the moral hazard and the wider systemic implications of that moral hazard outweigh the stabilization benefits that short selling offers. The EU introduced a ban on uncovered sovereign CDS in November 2012[19] thus addressing the cause of the Kazakh issue. Implementing the ban across the world on institutions that do not come under EU regulations might be tricky because it is not clear how sale and purchase of naked CDS in offshore locations can be monitored and regulated by the EU.

Policy implications for emerging markets

Snap judgements and placing of derivatives and the associated market practices into neat 'good' and 'evil' buckets are as tempting as they are difficult. The key lesson from the Kazakh case is not that all CDS or even all naked CDS can adversely affect the domestic economy: the adverse effect only occurs when the holder of the *naked* CDS has a direct link with, and can influence, a non-derivative local transaction.

An obvious implication for central banks and regulators in emerging economies is that they need to be watchful of the effects of derivatives transactions based on risks in their countries even if they are not party to them. In a sense, they are fish in a fish bowl, but they need to watch the behaviour of the people outside who are looking into the fish bowl. They will need to look for ways to avoid moral hazard and perverse incentives without necessarily stopping (or being able to stop) the use of such instruments. For instance, they may wish to put in clauses in loans taken by borrowers within their jurisdiction whereby the lender is obliged not to take CDS beyond the value of the loan and if it does, that would allow the borrower to escape liability to that extent. This may not always be enforceable but will strengthen their case in the event of a default and reduce the moral hazard for lenders. It will help confine *naked* CDS to those buyers that cannot influence the occurrence of default.

Emerging market regulators also need to be vigilant about being taken in by high pressure advocacy and sweeping ideological statements from big developed country financial institutions and their affiliates. What must surely rankle for many neutral observers is that these institutions are inconsistent in their responses to free market practices. There should be no ambiguity in condemning, penalizing and punishing such double standards on the part of the financial sector. When it hurts them, financial institutions are quick to turn their back on laissez-faire economics and markets. In the height of the global financial crisis in 2008, Morgan Stanley (among many others) rushed to regulators to seek a ban on short-selling of its shares by hedge funds and speculators. The SEC in the US agreed.[20] That was the same time that it might have had a net short position on the debt of BTA and just before it sought the triggering of a default event. The 'icing on the cake' (or, the last straw depending on one's point of view) was that, just a few months after it lobbied to get short sale of its stock banned, Morgan Stanley was actively soliciting its clients' shares of Ford Motor Company in 2009 to be able to short that stock two days before Ford announced a major debt restructuring.[21] It offered its clients a huge fee of 13 per cent (when interest rates were less than 1 per cent in general) if they allowed their shares to be borrowed and replaced later.[22] Regulators have a lot to do to keep capitalism safe from capitalists and financial markets safe from financial institutions.

Notes and References

[1] W. Buiter, 'Derivatives and attempted state capture in Kazakhstan', FT Blogs, 1 May 2009.

[2] 'Mexico Reveals $85 a Barrel Oil Hedge', *Financial Times*, 31 January 2012. Available at: http://www.ft.com/cms/s/0/c07f47e6-4c35-11e1-bd09-00144feabdc0.html. The government press release detailing the gains made under the oil hedging programme can be found at: http://www.shcp.gob.mx/SALAPRENSA/doc_comunicados_prensa/2009/Diciembre/comunicado_075_2009_ingles.pdf. Both accessed on 14 July 2014.

[3] J. E. Parsons and A. S. Mello, 'Prepare for the Bad, Close Your Eyes to the Worst?' Available at: http://bettingthebusiness.com/2012/09/26/prepare-for-the-bad-close-your-eyes-to-the-worst/. Accessed on 14 July 2014.

[4] http://www.ft.com/cms/s/0/ec038a60-206b-11e3-9a9a-00144feab7de.html. Accessed on 14 July 2014.

[5] http://www.ft.com/cms/s/0/7fc26d7c-0e02-11e0-86e9-00144feabdc0.html. Accessed on 14 July 2014.

[6] S. Romig, 'Uruguay Hedges against Weather with World Bank – State-Run Utility Inks Weather Insurance Deal', *Wall Street Journal*, 19 December 2013.

[7] World Bank Treasury, *Mitigating the Impact of Drought on Energy Production and Fiscal*

Risk in Uruguay, Case Study. Available at: http://treasury.worldbank.org/bdm/pdf/ Case_Study/Uruguay_Weather_Derivative.pdf. Accessed on 14 July 2014.

8   *Ibid.*

9   World Bank, 'Weather Index Insurance For Agriculture: Guidance for Development Practitioners', Agriculture and Rural Development Discussion Paper 50, December 2011.

10 *Ibid.*, 16.

11 Gilian Tett, 'Kazakh Bank Falls Foul of CDS', *Financial Times*, 30 April 2009. Available at: http://www.ft.com/cms/s/0/fa0428ee-35a7-11de-a997-00144feabdc0.html. Accessed on 14 July 2014.

12 *Ibid.*

13 W.Buiter,*op.cit.*

14 Reuters, 'Factbox: How Goldman's ABACUS Deal Worked' Available at: http://www.reuters.com/article/2010/04/16/us-goldmansachs-abacus-factbox-idUSTRE63F5CZ20100416. Accessed on 14 July 2014.

15 'A Healthy Regime', A survey of Italy, *The Economist*, 6 November 1997. Available at: http://www.economist.com/node/105180. Accessed on 14 July 2014.

16 'US Short Selling Regulation'.

17 'Regulation SHO'. Available at: http://goo.gl/SqhJXq. Accessed on 14 July 2014.

18 'EU Short Selling Regulation'. Available at: http://www.aima.org/en/regulation/markets-regulation/short-selling-/eu-short-selling-regulation/index.cfm. Accessed on 14 July 2014.

19 'Short Selling Bans'. Available at: http://www.aima.org/en/regulation/markets-regulation/short-selling-/short-selling-bans.cfm. Accessed on 14 July 2014.

20 'SEC Temporarily Bans Short Sales of Financial Stocks', *New York Times*, 19 September 2008. Available at: http://www.nytimes.com/2008/09/20/business/20sec.html. Accessed on 14 July 2014.

21 'John Mack's Short Selling Hypocrisy'.

22 'Morgan Stanley's 13% Payout offer to short Ford Stock'.

13

Regulation of Derivatives

...[A] man firing a rifle goes through the same motions whether he is aiming at a target on a rifle range, at a deer, or at a man across the street. And there apparently are some people who can shoot at a man with as little feeling as at a practice target. It is nevertheless profitable for society to distinguish among different uses of a rifle, and among different uses of risk-taking for monetary gain. Nor do we have any real difficulty in drawing these distinctions when we reject sophistry and apply common sense. We call a man an entrepreneur when he takes risks in a clearly useful type of business venture; a gambler when he takes risks of a nature that clearly serve no substantially useful economic purpose; and a speculator when he takes risks of another sort, that some people do not recognize as economically useful, though others regard them as highly useful.'

Holbrook Working[1]

Derivatives are (economic) tools and, like most tools, can be used as well as misused. In the most elementary sense, it is to prevent misuse – to prevent the use of the rifle to commit murder, in terms of Working's analogy – that a need arises for regulation.

Kahn, in his seminal work on the economics of regulation (largely in the context of public utilities) made the interesting point that 'economics emerged in the eighteenth and nineteenth centuries as an attempt to *explain* and to *justify[2]* a market system'[3]. Therefore, to classical economists, regulation would clearly represent an exception to standard economic prescriptions. Kahn regarded regulation as, in essence, the 'explicit replacement of competition with governmental orders' as a means of ensuring 'good performance'[4].

Overall, economic theory suggests that regulation is justified in three kinds of situations:

- to prevent serious distortions to competition and the abuse of monopoly power;

- to protect ordinary people in circumstances where information is difficult or costly to obtain and mistakes could seriously affect their welfare; and

- to compensate for externalities in situations where the social costs of market failure exceed the private costs after factoring in the costs of regulation.[5]

In the narrower context of derivatives, Natu, a former Chairman of the

Forward Markets Commission and one of the pioneer futures regulators in India, provided a short exposition in layman's terms of the rationale behind regulation[6]. He identified two main problems. Firstly, there is a danger that too many operators with insufficient means may participate in the market, and at a time of adverse price movement, default on their obligations. Apart from creating problems of fulfilment of contracts, default could also lead to panic sales or purchases which would have a demoralizing and destabilizing influence on the market. The second danger is the potential for unscrupulous speculators to manipulate the market and thereby distort the market, and move prices beyond all justification. Natu summarized the need for regulation in the following words – '*The private interest of an operator can thus be at considerable variance with the interest of the trade and public interest. It is because of this divergence that the need for regulation arises.*'

Contrary to Natu's view on the need for regulation to protect the public interest, there was a strong school of thought for several years in the western countries (until the financial crisis in 2008), which felt that regulation of derivatives was contrary to public interest and indeed a hindrance to the economy. This is, given Kahn's view on the role of economics, not surprising. It does however mean that one must first consider the fundamental issue of whether there is a sound economic case for regulation. This chapter therefore begins with an overview of the theoretical rationale for financial regulation in general, and derivatives regulation in particular.

Economic rationale for financial regulation

What is the theoretical justification for financial regulation? There are, as noted above and as will be discussed later, economists who believe that markets should generally be left alone, that market forces are self-policing, and that regulation will do more harm than good.[7]

Based on the work of Llewellyn[8] and others, the economic rationale can be summarized as comprising the following main elements:

Externalities

The social costs of failure of financial institutions are larger than the private costs. For example, when a bank fails, it is not just the shareholders of the bank or only its own depositors who are affected. Many others with no say in the decisions of the bank – including depositors of other banks – may be adversely affected and, if the bank is large, the whole economy may shrink with many people becoming unemployed. In a run on banks, even solvent banks may fail. In economic terms, the failure of a financial institution can have large negative externalities, i.e., costs to parties outside (external to) the narrow market in question. In the case of a large financial institution, the negative externalities may be so large as to endanger the whole financial system, and this is referred to as 'systemic risk'. The negative externalities will not be considered by individual private actors in making their decisions. Economics shows clearly that goods or services which have negative externalities tend to be 'over-supplied' relative to the social optimum[9]. Therefore, regulation is necessary to deal with this negative externality, i.e., with systemic risk.

There are several sources of negative externality in banking[10]. When a distressed institution is forced to sell assets to augment liquidity, that very sale may reduce the market price of the asset below what it would otherwise have fetched. For instance, assume a bank is forced to suddenly sell a large volume of corporate bonds in order to meet a loss on a particular loan. The very sale may reduce the price of the bonds below the price assumed in its balance sheet before the sale. This is the 'fire sale externality' – the fact that valuation is done without considering the effects on market value of a large distress sale. The second negative externality arises from the fact that banks are more interconnected than most other companies. (As Brunnermeier *et al.* put it, 'hotels and steel mills do not have significant inter-hotel or inter-furnace markets'. [11]) The point is that an individual institution is oblivious to the costs that its actions inflict on others whereas in practice those actions do affect other institutions. Another negative externality is 'informational contagion'. When Northern Rock in Britain failed, it created more doubts on the solvency of other British banks and these doubts caused withdrawals in those other banks affecting them adversely. A similar logic does not apply to other types of companies – if Ford were to close down it does not necessarily adversely affect General Motors and in fact may (by reducing supply of cars) benefit it. Yet another externality is that the failure of a bank adversely affects its borrowers because they may (at least temporarily) lose their ability to raise finance; banking relationships depend critically on client-specific information which is gathered over a period of time and which cannot overnight be acquired by or transferred to another bank.

Market failures and imperfections

Financial markets are sometimes characterized by *imperfect or asymmetric information*. A financial intermediary or institution may have much more information than the investor to whom it is selling an investment. The consumer in the financial market may not be capable of verifying quality at the time of purchase. For example, the buyer of an insurance policy will have less information about the solvency of the insurance company than the seller. Also, the quality may change substantially after purchase. This may warrant regulation to protect the consumer. When buying consumer goods, these considerations do apply but usually to a lesser extent and the proportion of a person's income or wealth involved in financial transactions is often larger than in a single consumer transaction.

Secondly, in the absence of regulation, consumer confidence in the product may be so low that the market may cease to function. The century-old market for mutual benefit fund investments (known as '*Nidhis*') in South India is an example where (after many investors were cheated in the 1990s) even good and solvent institutions faced difficulties in raising funds. This is sometimes known as the 'lemon problem', faced in the market for used cars (known as 'lemons' in the US), where buyers' lack of confidence in the information provided (on the road-worthiness of a car) makes it difficult to sell even a good quality used car.[12] The presence of regulation, by giving confidence that information is reliable, may revive such a market or enable it to function.

Economies of scale in monitoring

It is very difficult for individual investors to seek information on and monitor the performance of financial institutions. There are major economies of scale when monitoring is carried out and enforced by a regulatory authority. This benefit accrues not only to the consumer but even to the suppliers of financial services because it enlarges the market size. Thus, as Stiglitz points out, 'monitoring is a public good and needs to be publicly provided'[13]. For instance, if banking companies were not required by law or rules to publish certain kinds of information, it would be very expensive for individual investors to find the same information. Through regulations on information disclosure, the overall economic cost of information on the functioning of banks is reduced and this increases economic welfare.

Collective action problems

There are many situations in financial markets where the herd instinct and competitive pressure may induce individual firms to adopt hazardous strategies in order to avoid losing to their competitors. In such situations, a common regulator is able to prescribe and enforce common standards which may be collectively beneficial to all since they bind all the participants. The LIBOR rate-fixing scandal is an example of how the absence of an external regulator can lead to persistence of wrong policies because of competitive pressure.

Moral hazard arising from investor protection

If deposit insurance or other forms of state-sponsored investment protection exist, private institutions may have a 'moral hazard' whereby they can get the benefits of taking more risk but if the risk materializes, the costs are borne by the exchequer. To prevent or minimize this type of socially inefficient and excessive risk-taking, regulation is necessary.

Most economists therefore agree, on the basis of sound economic principles, that financial regulation is necessary and indeed beneficial. Readers will notice that several of these justifications – market failures and externalities for instance – are not peculiar to financial regulation and form part of the justification for regulation or government intervention in almost any sector.

General issues in financial regulation

This section deals with issues that relate to financial regulation in the broader sense while the next section examines issues that are more particularly relevant to derivatives.

Types of regulation

The main types of financial regulation can be summarized as:

- Prudential regulation, which requires regulated institutions to be prudent by anticipating future problems and providing for them. This comprises two sub-components:
  - Micro-prudential regulation which deals with the safety and soundness

of individual financial institutions including banks, insurance companies, depositories, stock or derivatives brokers or clearing houses;

○ Macro-prudential regulation (also known as 'systemic regulation') to preserve the stability of the financial system *as a whole* and prevent the failure of one institution from triggering problems throughout the financial system.[14]

• Investor/consumer protection regulation (also known as 'conduct of business' regulation) designed to protect investors, especially small and individual consumers and investors, from fraudulent or incomplete information, unfair or misleading selling practices etc.

• Competition regulation to promote or preserve adequate competition in the market and prevent anti-competitive practices.[15]

Regulations can also be distinguished on the basis of the type of financial service into banking regulation, insurance regulation, securities regulation, derivatives regulation etc. Another distinction, which existed in the erstwhile Financial Services Authority in Great Britain, is between 'retail' and 'wholesale' or 'institutional' clients of financial institutions.

Given the complex nature of the different types of regulation and the different financial services, there are often multiple agencies involved in regulating financial markets. For example, in India, the respective roles of the Reserve Bank of India and the Competition Commission of India in regulating competition among financial institutions were at one time a matter of disagreement. In China, there has been disagreement on the roles of the The People's Bank of China (PBOC – the central bank) and the China Banking Regulatory Commission and the relationship was reported, in 2014, to be strained[16]. In the specific case of derivatives too, there are jurisdictional issues between the various regulators and ministries. As issues of jurisdictional limits inevitably arise, regulated entities do seek to find loopholes that exist in the ambiguities and gaps. However, it is now generally agreed that macro-prudential regulation falls mainly to the central bank.

The boundary problem

An interesting problem in regulation is the so-called boundary problem. Effective regulation *ipso facto* implies that because of the regulation, the regulated institutions have had to forgo some profit-making opportunities. (If the regulation is so loose that it does not affect in any way the behaviour of institutions, it is clearly superfluous and not 'effective'.) This then implies that the rate of return achievable in the regulated sector will be lower than in the unregulated sector, and therefore the unregulated sector will grow at a faster rate. This will also induce the regulated sector to seek opportunities in the unregulated sector through affiliates or subsidiaries. For example, if regulated banks are prohibited by rules from engaging in certain kinds of profitable investments, they may seek to create Special Investment Vehicles or investment funds which are not subject to the rigours of banking regulation, i.e., which fall outside the boundary of regulation. Because it is not subject to regulation, the unregulated activity falling outside the boundary tends to have a higher growth rate than the regulated activity. Eventually the unregulated sector becomes larger and also connected to the regulated sector. Thus *over time, the area which is under regulation shrinks relative to that which is unregulated.* At this stage, a need arises to consider widening the boundary of regulation. However, widening the boundary increases costs to the regulator. It may also imply increasing the government's contingent liability involved in the protections offered to investors in the regulated sector – for instance deposit insurance. Therefore the boundary problem is one which regulators face willy-nilly and need to be aware of.

Brunnermeier *et al.* point out that '[a]lthough Boundary problems are a generic consequence of effective financial regulation, it does not mean that all such regulation is a waste of time nor that such problems cannot be mitigated by sensible design.[17]' They identify another generic issue which is worth highlighting in their own words:

> A major problem is that the more effective regulation becomes, the more unpopular it will be, since it will prevent the regulated from doing what they want to do. The boundary problem will worsen such unpopularity. It leads to the following claims that such regulation is:
>
> a) Ineffective and unfair, resulting in disintermediation
>
> b) Inefficient and cost enhancing
>
> c) Complex and capable of being subverted.
>
> … If there is a Boundary problem, (and regulation within the boundary is effective) then, almost by definition, there can be no level–playing–field. The

unregulated outside the Boundary have a stronger competitive position than those within…What the regulators will have done is to take the business away from the regulated (the good guys in white hats) and given it to the unregulated (the bad guys in black hats)…The point is that the aim of the exercise is to prevent the key financial institutions from overstretching themselves, and so failing, rather than preventing any financial institution from doing the business[18].

Pro-cyclicality or anti-cyclicality of regulation

When formulating or changing regulations, it is important for regulators to be conscious of the cyclical effects of the rules. Do the regulations tend to worsen the extremes (i.e., promote even greater expansion during a boom and contraction during a bust)? If so they are known as 'pro-cyclical'. For example, the shift from Basel I norms for capital adequacy of banks to Basel II and the change of accounting policies under the International Financial Reporting Standards, have both had a 'pro-cyclical' effect. Basel II tied the risk-weighting of assets to credit ratings; during a boom, the credit ratings of many borrowers tend to increase. This reduces the level of capital which a bank has to hold against the asset and hence enables it to expand lending. But in a bust, credit ratings tend to fall and the capital requirements increase – at the worst possible time for the bank. The International Financing Reporting Standards (IFRS) required a larger portion of bank assets to be marked to market: as a result when markets were booming, the 'capital' of the bank also boomed enabling it to lend even more. But when bad times arrive and market prices fall, the capital shrinks rapidly. As Goodhart points out, taken together, these were a major source of instability.[19] By contrast, the older capital adequacy and accounting rules, while less sophisticated, were not pro-cyclical and in some cases anti-cyclical. Paradoxically, writing several years before the crisis, Stiglitz had argued in favour of mark-to-market accounting on grounds of the need for transparency[20]. Recent experience suggests that the pro-cyclicality of mark-to-market and fair value accounting may create more harm than the benefit from transparency.

Regulation, monitoring, supervision and enforcement

While the loose term 'regulation' is often used to cover all forms of government-sponsored intervention in financial markets, a distinction can be drawn between four kinds of regulatory work. The first is *regulation* per se: this, to quote

Llewellyn, is the 'establishment of specific rules of behavior'. The second is *monitoring* which is to observe whether the rules are being followed. The third is *supervision*, which is general observation, collection of information and giving of clearances when so required, going beyond just observation of compliance with rules. The fourth, which is often ignored by theoretical economists but occupies an important place in the real world, is *enforcement*, which is action to make entities conform to the rules when monitoring or supervision shows that they are not complying with rules. Prosecuting those who violate regulations is one element of enforcement.

Generalized (rules-based) vs. customized (principles-based)regulation

Conceptually there are two approaches to regulation, not just financial regulation. One is the prescription of a clear set of generalized rules that all regulated entities have to follow with only limited scope for differentiation. Another approach is to formulate a set of principles and then customize the specific regulatory requirements based on the specific nature of each regulated entity. In practice, most regulatory regimes (within and without the financial sector) involve a combination of both these approaches. For example, a general rule may apply but the regulator may be able to grant a case-by-case exemption. Consistency, reduced regulatory discretion (which reduces the risk of corruption), and reduced need for a detailed understanding of each entity by regulatory staff are the benefits of the first approach, but its drawback is its rigidity and resulting inefficiency. The customized approach is more efficient if administered well but is more prone to corruption and also requires a much more intimate knowledge of the inner workings of each entity on the part of the staff of the regulator. Therefore, a customized approach requires a greater degree of supervision (see previous paragraph for the meaning of supervision).

Structure and multiplicity of regulators

Conceptually there are several approaches to regulatory structure:

- *The Legalistic or Institutional Approach:* This is an approach where the legal status of an institution determines its regulatory supervision. For instance, an insurance company would be regulated by the insurance regulator regardless of the precise nature of a particular line of business the company may be engaged in. This approach has serious weaknesses in a country with sophisticated financial markets, because companies which in law are either insurance or banking or stock-broking companies may be engaging in transactions which have elements of other businesses and may escape effective regulation. Its main benefit is simplicity in identifying jurisdiction and, for regulated entities, the fact that they each need to deal with only one regulator.

- *The Functional Approach:* The functional approach seeks to regulate financial institutions based on the type of business they undertake, irrespective of the legal status of a company. Therefore, various branches of the same institution could be under the purview of different regulators as a result of the business that they conduct. Successful regulation under this approach requires close coordination between regulators. It does increase costs and compliance burdens for regulated entities.

- *The Integrated or 'Single Peak' Approach*: Under this approach, a single regulator oversees all types of financial institutions and provides both prudential regulation and consumer protection regulation. The UK, till recently, was the most prominent example of this approach.

- *The Twin Peaks Approach:* The twin peaks approach relies on two regulators: a prudential regulator and a consumer protection regulator. Its biggest strength is the presence of a separate and specialized focus on protecting investors and on the conduct of institutions.

A purely legalistic approach does not fit the requirements of well-developed financial markets and is thus suitable only for underdeveloped or emerging markets where product overlaps and financial innovation are absent.

The three remaining approaches have advantages and disadvantages and are to be found in several developed and emerging markets. The UK presents an interesting case where it moved to a single regulator, removed the central bank from the regulation of financial markets and then did a 180 degree turn, reinstated the central bank's role and installed two regulators (see Box 13.1)

Box 13.1: The UK experience

In 1997, as soon as the new Labour government took office, the UK decided to move to a system of an integrated financial services regulator, called the Financial Services Authority (FSA). This supplanted a multiplicity of market regulators and the banking regulation role of the Bank of England.

At the time this was lauded as a major modernization of the regulatory framework and in particular a response to the blurring of lines between banking, insurance, derivatives and other forms of financial transactions. It was seen as the cutting edge structure for the 21st century and influenced institutional design in several other countries. The FSA made a major move towards principles–based regulation. [While the approach was that of a 'single peak', rather confusingly the system was also known as one with 'tripartite authorities' whereby the FSA regulated financial markets, the Bank of England had control of monetary policy and maintaining market stability (but not bank regulation), and the Treasury (finance ministry) had responsibility for financial and economic policy as well as the institutional structure of the overall financial system.]

However, the 2007–08 financial crisis affected the British banking system more severely than several others and led to a re-evaluation of the approach. The FSA clearly failed to detect or prevent the failure of several banks. It turned out that Northern Rock, the bank that triggered the banking crisis in the UK, had not been inspected by the FSA for 3 years at the time it failed[21].

The UK has now given up the single peak approach and reintroduced the central bank (the Bank of England) in a big way into the regulatory arena. The new structure took effect in March 2013. There are now two separate regulatory agencies – one dealing with prudential regulation known as the Prudential Regulation Authority and another called the Financial Conduct Authority which regulates conduct-of-business (investor and customer protection). While this bears strong resemblance to the 'twin peaks' approach, a clear difference is that both of these regulators are subordinate to the overall regulatory jurisdiction of the Bank of England and indeed one of them is headed by a Deputy Governor.

Advantages of a single regulator

A structure with a single regulator:

- Reduces scope for 'regulatory arbitrage' or 'forum shopping' (where regulated entities choose one regulator over another based on which has the 'easier' regulation). This is the biggest advantage of this structure.

- Reduces the need for, and costs of, multi-agency coordination.

- Makes the best use of staff with specialized regulatory expertise; this is important everywhere but can be even more important in emerging markets and countries with limited regulatory capacity.

- Enables the regulator to readily spot and appreciate the cross-cutting issues that affect multiple parts of the financial sector. (Reddy also points out that a single regulator is better placed to respond to innovations as there are no gray areas[22].)

- [For the regulator] may produce economies of scale with respect to the administrative costs and overheads of the regulatory apparatus.

- [For the regulated] may minimize compliance costs and what (in India) is called the 'inspector raj' (i.e., where inspectors from different agencies keep coming over and looking at the books).

- Facilitates international cooperation between regulators because there is a single point of contact[23].

- There is less risk of 'over-regulation' (regulation exceeding the optimum); overlaps can be spotted and the overall regulatory burden assessed better.

Disadvantages or limitations of a single regulator

The single regulator structure has the following disadvantages:

- 'All eggs are in one basket' and if the single regulator fails to catch a big regulatory risk, there is no fall back or second opinion. This appears to have partly been the case in the UK under the FSA.

- The type of supervision and expertise needed for micro- and macro-prudential regulation may be different; there may be no synergies and indeed there may even be 'diseconomies of scope' in bringing them together (and hence advantages in separating them).

- Merely placing different functions under one umbrella is not a guarantee of coordination or an integrated view. Internal coordination needs are greater under single regulator. (The FSA experience showed that even though it was theoretically a single entity, in practice there was poor coordination between the difference wings dealing with different sectors. Thus, theoretical benefits were not realized.)

- In the event of regulatory capture, the negative effects are greater because the captured regulator would be virtually omnipotent; with multiple regulators it is more difficult for all of them to be 'captured' by a particular regulated entity.

- If the super-regulator is also 'independent', there is (as Reddy pointed out[24]) a risk of an undemocratic concentration of power without accountability to the public. Large organizations also tend to be more bureaucratic.

- The risk of 'under-regulation' (less regulation than optimal) is greater under a single regulator, inasmuch as specialized or esoteric aspects of one particular line of business, say, insurance, may receive less attention under an omnibus regulator than under a specialized regulator.

An important consideration often ignored by economists is the effect of 'turf' warfare which – reflecting a principal-agent problem within the government – often has a big role to play in determining the actual institutional structure. As an example, in the context of the USA, Fresh and Baily noted that

> Any agency that has been around for a long time has developed its defenders. Its leaders do not want their agency to disappear, and they feel strongly about preserving the jobs of their employees. The congressional committees that oversee the agencies develop relationships with them, and do not want the scope and power of their committees reduced.[25]

This problem is present worldwide (except in underdeveloped countries or emerging markets where institutions are being created from scratch), and any reform attempts which ignore this reality are unlikely to be successful.

Regulatory capture and intellectual bias

The term 'regulatory capture' is used frequently and often loosely. A simple but effective definition is that it is 'subversion of regulatory agencies by the firms they regulate'. Another is that it is 'a process by which regulation is, by intent and action of the industry regulated, directed away from the public interest toward the interest of the regulated industry.' Posner made the important point, often overlooked in popular writing, that a successful attempt by an industry to change regulations in its favour is not, in and of itself, evidence of capture.

The classic form of regulatory capture is when the regulator is captured by the regulated on the basis of materialistic gain or 'illicit gratification'. At one end of the spectrum this may involve criminal acts of bribery or corruption. This is not unknown either in developed or developing countries. In 2014, an opposition party in India, for instance, openly alleged that oil and gas regulation has been 'captured' by a large corporate house. However, that is not the form of capture that is relevant here: that is a known problem for which there are known (though not easy) solutions through the criminal justice system.

Another form is where regulators are captured through the creation or exploitation of conflicts of interest without explicit criminality. Examples of at least the appearance of conflict of interest are frequently found in developed countries. For instance, Ritholtz pointed out that the Wendy Gramm, wife of Senator Phil Gramm was on the board of Enron (a major user of OTC derivatives) at the time he piloted the Commodity Futures Modernization Act or CFMA, which liberalized OTC derivatives.[26]

A more subtle form of capture is through sub-conscious intellectual or 'cognitive' bias, whereby the regulator begins to subscribe to the intellectual framework of the regulated even though that framework is flawed and contrary to wider public interest. This is also called 'cultural capture'.[27] This too appears to have been a major force at work in several countries.

Capture may affect not just regulators but the academics who influence them. To some extent, the writings of academic economists have sometimes displayed (at the very least) appearance of conflict of interest and yet there has not been much academic or regulatory attention to this. For instance the most influential paper on the benefits of commodities as an investment class was written by a Yale professor who is also a partner at a major commodity fund management company.[28] Another academic paper providing empirical evidence of the price stabilizing effects of commodity fund investing was sponsored by another commodity fund manager. Economists are loathe to admit that there is such a thing as 'economist capture' but it clearly exists. Zingales brought out both the sources of such bias and provided credible empirical evidence by looking at the positions taken by economists on certain issues.[29] He advocated several measures (such as a reform of the publication process, allowing multiple contemporaneous submissions, restricting the outside activities of editors, a data policy for field experiments and proprietary datasets, minimizing the ability of companies to influence the published results of research, and a mechanism of shaming of academic economists who take 'unreasonable' positions in the media or in expert testimony). He added:

> Ultimately, however, the most important remedy to reduce capture is awareness by economists that this risk exists. Until we admit that we can be captured by vested interests as much as regulators, the risk of capture

cannot be addressed. For this reason, the most important remedy is to start talking about this problem.

Issues in derivatives regulation

This section focuses on issues that apply to a greater degree to derivatives markets.

Financial innovation

A major challenge for regulators is the rapid speed at which new derivative instruments are created by banks and financial institutions. For a time, as mentioned in earlier chapters, there was a sense (at least in the USA and UK) that such innovation must be good with the market completion argument discussed in Chapter 4 providing (as has been shown, erroneous) intellectual support. That has changed and there is now a clear recognition that innovation needs to be monitored and regulated.

Financial innovation arises from many sources. It may originate in a request from a bank's client for help in dealing with a particular risk and a bank may design a derivative instrument to meet the need. Alternatively, the idea may strike a strategist within a bank and may then be marketed to a customer who has a need that the bank is aware of. When the transaction is put through, it gradually becomes known more widely in the markets. In some cases, the innovation may remain a one-off transaction but in other cases it may be replicated by the same institution for other customers. Other institutions and /or customers may begin to enter into similar transactions. In some cases, the original issuer or another bank may create a variant with slightly different features. When the volume of transactions on the original or mutated instrument reaches a certain size, the market makers, with or without regulatory intervention, may begin to evolve standardized terms for the instrument, to make it more liquid and to reduce transaction costs. Standardization may in turn create a secondary market where the original buyers of the instrument can resell. Banks now begin to actively market the instrument to their customers. Over a period of time, standardization and enhanced liquidity begin to increase the volumes of transactions. As volumes grow, there is possibility that the size of the market becomes large enough to create systemic risk.

Since such structured products typically produce large fees, and the remuneration of staff is tied to fee income, there is a strong incentive to sell. Some of the selling may well be to customers who are not properly informed or equipped to handle the risks in the transaction. This creates risks of misconduct in terms of customer protection. Figure 13.1 is a diagrammatic summary of the links between financial innovation and regulatory risk.

Financial Innovation and its implications for Regulation: A Diagrammatic Summary

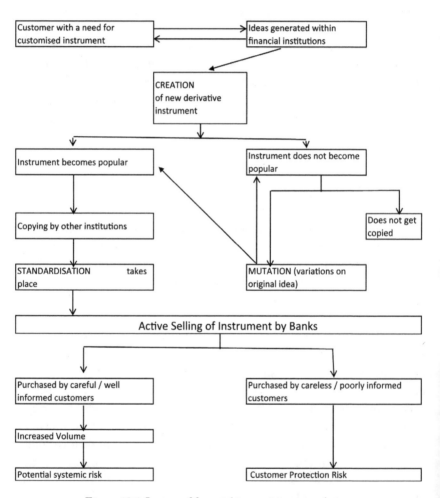

Figure 13.1: Impact of financial innovation on regulation

The above description assumes that banks are free to sell the innovations—obviously that can only happen if regulators permit them to or if they contravene regulations. The issue for regulators is the extent to which they permit it. One approach (typically found in the US especially since the CFMA) can roughly be characterized as 'everything is permitted which is not prohibited'. The other approach (typified by India) is that 'everything is prohibited which is not permitted'. The former approach produces both a higher 'return' in terms of potential economic benefits and higher risk; the latter is a lower return/ lower risk approach. Both can be rational. The choice should, in concept, depend on the expected size of the returns from innovations versus the potential risks. Since these are subjective assessments at best, there is ample room for regulators to differ in their approaches.

Posner and Weyl went as far as to suggest an agency (similar to the American Food and Drug Administration that screens pharmaceutical innovations) to scrutinize financial innovations after evaluating the net social benefits before approving it for public distribution. The test would be based on the central question of whether the product was more likely to be used for hedging or speculation. A detailed examination of this idea is beyond the scope of this book[30].

Regulatory competition

The globalization of derivatives markets poses a new challenge to regulation: that of regulatory competition between countries accompanied by 'regulatory arbitrage' by participants. One of the motivations for Britain's move in 1997 to principles–based regulation under a single regulator was a desire to remain an attractive location for the financial services industry especially vis-à-vis New York where a more rigid rules-based system was in force then (especially prior to the CFMA 2000). Some countries – with relatively small domestic participation – benefit by creating a less-regulated environment and this makes it more difficult for other countries to regulate effectively. This problem is analogous to the problem of tax havens. For example, in early 2012, the Monetary Authority of Singapore floated a consultation paper which indicated that Singapore might not require mandatory exchange listing and trading of derivatives on exchanges, running directly contrary to the lessons learnt from the 2008 crisis.

Self-regulation and the risk of manipulation

Until recently, regulators in developed countries have been relatively sanguine about 'self-regulation', the practice of members of an industry themselves deciding on the rules they would voluntarily and collectively abide by. There was also a general belief that the larger financial firms had too much at stake in terms of reputation to indulge in manipulative behaviour. They might lobby for their interests, but would not actually break the law. A certain degree of trust was part of the regulatory approach.

Faith in self-regulation has been shaken by a series of scandals in recent years involving manipulation by seemingly respectable companies and of widely used and almost-venerated benchmarks. These involve the manipulation of the LIBOR, the London gold bullion market's 'gold fixing' and of the foreign exchange options market (see Boxes 13.2 to 13.4).

Box 13.2: The LIBOR scandal

In 2012, it was disclosed that leading banks had been rigging the level of the LIBOR. The rate is supposed to reflect the rate at which banks lend to each other and is used as a benchmark for interest rates around the world. Most floating rate loans and interest rate derivatives are priced with reference to LIBOR (e.g. 'LIBOR + 0.75 per cent). The disclosures were the culmination of a probe started by the US Commodity Futures Trading Commission (CFTC) after it noticed as far back as 2005, that something was amiss in the LIBOR-setting process.

It emerged that traders at leading banks would manipulate rates to help each other and reduce their borrowing costs or help their valuations. In one Email, a Barclays Bank employee asked a derivatives trader to submit a lower LIBOR rate and when the trader obliged, wrote: 'I owe you big time! Come over one day after work and I'm opening a bottle of Bollinger [champagne]'. Barclays Bank was the first to admit guilt and pay a fine of $450 million to the CFTC and FSA in June 2012. It also emerged that Barclays had deliberately undercut its submissions on interest rates (which form input into the setting of LIBOR) in order to paint a better picture of its financial health during the financial crisis and that this was based not on actions of individual 'rogue' trades but of internal instructions from managers.[31] The Swiss bank, UBS, was also found guilty and paid a $1.5 billion fine. In all about $6 billion in fines were levied from various institutions.[32] However, while the banks were fined (and costs borne by shareholders), no employees were jailed.[33]

REGULATION OF DERIVATIVES

Box 13.3: Allegations of rigging in gold and foreign exchange markets

In late 2013, regulators in the US, UK and Switzerland began investigating 15 banks, including such leading names as Barclays, Citibank, UBS, Goldman Sachs, Deutsche Bank, HSBC, J.P. Morgan, Morgan Stanley, Royal Bank of Scotland and Standard Chartered in connection with rigging of the foreign exchange market.

Despite its huge size, the foreign exchange market is run by a small group of global traders and the $2 trillion spot market is controlled by a group of fewer than 100 individual traders at a handful of large banks. As in the case of LIBOR, the allegations centre around the determination of a benchmark, in this case the 'WM/Reuters 4pm fix'. The fix is a time of day when banks guarantee their customers a certain rate for their currency trade. Normally trades are done immediately when they are placed and there is a bid/offer spread whereby the trader will offer a higher price for buying and a lower price for selling, with the spread being the bank's legitimate income. Alternatively the customer can wait for the fix. At the fix, the customer is guaranteed the mid-rate between the bid and the offer price. However dealers know in advance what volumes the customer wishes to trade at the fix; it is alleged that there was collusion by the banks to determine the fix at levels favourable to them and unfavourable to their clients. The fix also acts as the benchmark for currency valuation of portfolios and this is one reason many mutual funds would ask for their transactions to be put through at the fix rate. While the variations in rates were small, the enormous volumes make them very lucrative. As of November 2013, at least 12 foreign exchange traders had been suspended. In March 2014, it emerged that a staff member of the Bank of England had also been suspended in connection with this matter.

In March 2014, a New York resident filed a suit as a class action against Societe Generale, Deutsche Bank, Barclays, Bank of Nova Scotia and HSBC alleging that they had colluded to manipulate yet another benchmark - the London gold fix. Gold fixing happens twice a day based on a teleconference between banks. At the start of each fixing, the chairman announces an opening price to all members who relay that to their customers and based on orders received from them, instruct their representatives to declare themselves buyers or sellers at that price. The price is adjusted up or down until supply and demand match and that price is declared as the fix. The fixings are used globally as benchmarks. Bafin, the German financial regulator, and the UK's Financial Conduct Authority began a probe into the matter.

Box 13.4: Allegations of metal supply and price manipulation against leading banks and exchange

In August 2013, suits were filed against J.P. Morgan, Goldman Sachs, the London Metal Exchange and Glencore in the United States, alleging that they were artificially inflating aluminium prices.[34] Among other things, the investment banks were accused of colluding with the London Metal Exchange to restrict metal supplies, hoard them and create artificial scarcity.

Regardless of the actual outcome of the cases, it is significant that several of these entities not only trade commodities on the derivatives markets but also own warehouses in which commodities are stockpiled. This combination of ownership of the physical commodity, proprietary and other trading and market-making in derivatives produces monopoly power and gives rise to potential for manipulation. There are strong reasons for holding that banks should not be engaged in non-financial businesses, especially because they are all partly under-written (especially post-2008) by public funds.

Underestimation of risk

Regulations usually require the holding of reserves (capital) in proportion to risk. This in turn hinges on the 'correct' measurement of risk. The Gaussian or 'normal' distribution has an exalted place in mathematics and statistics for its elegance and its adaptability to a wide range of practical problems. It has become almost ubiquitous in risk measurement in finance. However, as experience has repeatedly shown, financial uncertainties are very often not normally distributed and hence for purposes of derivatives it would be better to consider the Gaussian distribution to be the 'abnormal' distribution! This applies *a fortiori* to the more complex derivatives. Index CDS swaptions – options to purchase or sell CDS based on an index[35] – are an example of a relatively new instrument that has extraordinarily high risks, which are easily under-estimated.[36] Hutchinson, an experienced fund manager (albeit, a self-professed 'bear') has argued that 'traders benefit enormously by finding instruments where conventional risk management grossly understates the risk of the instrument[37]. They are able to trade much larger volumes of the instrument than they could if it was managed properly'.[38] The short point is that regulators need to be aware that traders have a vested interest in underestimating risk and that most models, especially those based on 'normality' are likely to contribute to this underestimation.

Regulation of derivatives: Lessons from America

Internationally, attitudes to regulation of financial markets, and derivatives in particular, have undergone major changes over the last two decades. The discussion in this section centres on events in the United States of America because, as the largest global financial market, the opinions and actions of American policy makers have been the prime movers of attitudes elsewhere.

The environment till the 1990s

Under the principles of English common law, which largely applied to the U.S, gambling contracts were considered contrary to public policy and hence these contracts were unenforceable. The nature of many derivative contracts was such that they fell in a grey area. If one enters a speculative contract to buy wheat in six months but without intent to take delivery, is that a gamble or not? Gambling in the US is regulated at the state level. In most states, the rules were such that speculative contracts might have been unenforceable.

This changed in 1936 when the statutory framework for derivatives regulation in the USA was provided by the Commodity Exchange Act 1936 (CEA). A basic requirement of the Act was that futures be traded on a regulated exchange with full transparency, and this is commonly known as the 'exchange trading requirement'. Contracts traded through exchanges were recognized as legally binding. The CFTC was the regulatory agency established for the enforcement of the CEA. This created a stable regulatory environment for futures trading and it extended to financial futures as well as to options in general.

At the time the Act was passed and for many years afterwards, swaps were not a major element in the financial markets. As the swaps market grew in size, the CFTC began to look seriously at the regulatory issues that arose. The first issue that came up was whether swaps were subject to the exchange trading requirement. In 1989, the CFTC exempted swaps from the requirement *provided they were negotiated individually based on non-standardized terms*, and they were *not marketed to the public*. Following further legal clarifications and amendments, it was notified in 1993 that swaps which were, *inter alia*, 'not part of a fungible class of agreements that are standardized as to their material economic terms' would be exempted. Clearly the exemption was intended only for bilateral OTC deals and not for standardized transactions in a secondary market.

However, as Greenberger brings out clearly,[39] the market gradually shifted to standardized terms through the 'master agreement' of the International Swaps and Derivatives Association (earlier called the International Swap Dealers Association). Under the ISDA master agreement, even electronic trading by multiple parties (not just one-to-one) was taking place. Thus by the late 1990s, the market had evolved to the stage where it was no longer truly compliant with the exemption. In 1998, the CFTC proposed to bring swaps under regulation and put out a discussion paper on possible regulatory instruments and methods.

In 1994, the United States' Government Accountability Office (GAO – the American equivalent of the Auditor-General in Commonwealth countries) brought out a 200 page report on financial derivatives entitled *Financial Derivatives: Action needed to protect the financial system*. The report itself was a response to major derivatives-related losses announced by Procter and Gamble and by Orange County in California. In fact, an inquiry commission report suggested that these losses were not unrelated to the exemptions that CFTC had granted in 1993 to certain non-standardized derivatives from being traded only on recognized exchanges. The GAO stated bluntly that it 'found that no comprehensive industry or federal regulatory requirements existed to ensure that U.S. OTC derivatives dealers followed good risk-management practices.'

While government agencies like the CFTC and the GAO were seeking more regulation, the intellectual climate among economists and bankers that prevailed at the end of the 1990s, was largely in favour of keeping swaps (and indeed virtually all derivatives) away from any form of regulation. The release of the GAO report provoked a barrage of counter-arguments. Three examples will show the extent of deeply held belief about the self-regulating nature of the financial industry. The first was a paper by Merton Miller (co-author of the Modigliani-Miller theorems).[40] Two observations of his are important. One is that he sincerely believed that no serious danger of a derivatives-induced financial collapse really existed. Second, he believed that once a whole new generation of corporate leaders who have grown up with derivatives and computers took over, corporate losses involving derivatives would become a thing of the past. Thus he believed the problem was one of lack of understanding by an older generation.

The second example is the paper by Siems, a senior economist and policy adviser at the Federal Reserve Bank of Dallas in 1997[41] which argued that regulators should leave derivatives alone because,

> ... coercive regulations intended to restrict banks' activities will be unable to keep up with financial innovation. As the lines of demarcation between various types of financial service providers continue to blur, the bureaucratic leviathan responsible for reforming banking regulation must face the fact that fears about derivatives have proved unfounded. New regulations are unnecessary. Indeed, access to risk-management instruments should not be feared but, with caution, embraced to help firms manage the vicissitudes of the market ... A careful review of the risks and rewards derivatives offer, however, suggests that regulatory and legislative restrictions are not the answer. To blame organizational failures solely on derivatives is to miss the point. A better answer lies in greater reliance on market forces to control derivative-related risk taking.

Although he was writing in his personal capacity, it is a reasonable conclusion that the official establishment held not-very-dissimilar views.

A third and more extreme example was the following quotation from Wallison, a Fellow of the American Enterprise Institute:

> ... there is little reason, from an economic perspective, for the regulations. Incentives exist, or can be created through private systems, to protect against the risks that are usually cited in defense of banking regulation. Moreover, the private systems would remove much of the cost and risk created by current government regulation. This suggests that the only reason we regulate banks is because we want to, not because we have to.[42]

In the same year, in testimony to the U.S. Congress, Greenspan, the then chairman of the Federal Reserve, made the following comments:

> ....I would argue that the first imperative when evaluating market regulation is to enunciate clearly the public policy objectives that government regulation would be intended to promote. What market characteristics do policymakers seek to encourage? Efficiency? Fair and open access? What phenomena do we wish to discourage or eliminate? Fraud, manipulation, or other unfair practices? Systemic instability? Without explicit answers to these questions, government regulation is unlikely to be effective. More likely, it will prove unnecessary, burdensome, and perhaps even contrary to what more careful consideration would reveal to be the underlying objectives.

A second imperative, once public policy objectives are clearly specified, is to evaluate whether government regulation is necessary for those purposes. In making such evaluations, it is critically important to recognize that no market is ever truly unregulated. The self-interest of market participants generates private market regulation. Thus, the real question is not whether a market should be regulated. Rather, the real question is whether government intervention strengthens or weakens private regulation. If incentives for private market regulation are weak or if market participants lack the capabilities to pursue their interests effectively, then the introduction of government regulation may improve regulation. But if private market regulation is effective, then government regulation is at best unnecessary. At worst, the introduction of government regulation may actually weaken the effectiveness of regulation if government regulation is itself ineffective or undermines incentives for private market regulation. We must be aware that government regulation unavoidably involves some element of moral hazard – if private market participants believe that government is protecting their interests, their own efforts to protect their interests will diminish to some degree.

The intellectual case for de-regulation or non-regulation of financial market activity rested on the belief that, in a well-functioning market economy, the rational self–interest driven actions of market participants would ensure that systemic risks are either diversified or eliminated, or protected against through self-regulation. This intellectual case was a very weak one conceptually but it was espoused by people like Greenspan who (at the time) had enormous credibility, and hence this school of thought had clout far beyond its intrinsic merits.

The de-regulation of 2000

As was seen earlier, by 1998 the CFTC had come to the conclusion that the swaps markets needed to be brought under some form of regulation. At the time, the size of the OTC derivatives market was $80,000 billion. However, given the intellectual climate described above, and the strong support from those in powerful regulatory positions, the proposal faced vehement opposition. Even within the government, the U.S. Treasury (finance ministry), the Federal Reserve (central bank) and the Securities and Exchange Commission (stock market regulator) all opposed the proposals. So powerful was the sentiment, that the CFTC's attempt to bring swaps under regulation led, in an unexpected and unintended twist, to the diametric opposite result: the passing of a new Act *completely exempting swap transactions from any kind of regulation.* This Act, the Commodity Futures Modernization Act 2000 (CFMA), removed OTC derivative transactions from all exchange trading requirements so long as the counterparties were either large participants with more than $10 million in assets or were individuals using it for risk management. Thus OTC derivatives were now 'exempt from capital adequacy requirements; reporting and disclosure; regulation of intermediaries; self-regulation; any bars on fraud, manipulation and excessive speculation; and requirements for clearing'. Also, it exempted them from the state regulations on gambling, thus making them fully enforceable even though they were not traded on an exchange.

It is noteworthy that credit default swaps are not really swaps at all because they are not an exchange of cash flows. Instead, they involve payment of a premium in return for a contingent payment by the other side in case of default – this is nothing but insurance. Yet the term insurance was deliberately eschewed to avoid coming under the capital adequacy requirements of insurance regulation[43]. Thus, through the passing of the CFMA, swaps in the world's largest and most sophisticated economy were:

- though derivatives in every sense of the term, not regulated as derivatives by the CFTC and did not need to be traded on exchanges;
- though often essentially insurance contracts in substance, not regulated by state insurance regulators and required no reserves to be held against them[44];
- though akin to wagers, not subject to the rules and restrictions on gambling under common law or state regulations.

The CFMA created a 'regulatory black hole' where 'almost no law applied to this market'.[45] From the point of view of those who believed that regulation is unnecessary and that markets can regulate themselves, this was the attainment of utopia. It did provide a clear practical test of the 'no need for regulation' school of thought.

The post-2008 backlash

The events of 2007 and 2008 delivered a decisive empirical verdict against the 'no regulation' school. A backlash against de-regulation followed. Stout's testimony to the US Congress is worth quoting *in extenso* and reflecting upon:

...Studying the history and theory of derivatives regulation inevitably leads to four basic conclusions. First, despite industry claims, derivative contracts are not new and are not particularly innovative. Second, derivatives trading may provide some benefits to the overall economy. It is important to note, however, that while the industry routinely claims the social benefits from derivatives trading are substantial, there is no empirical evidence that supports this claim or establishes the magnitude of the supposed social benefits. A third basic conclusion that can be drawn from studying the history of derivatives is that healthy economies regulate derivatives trading. Fourth, history teaches that successful derivatives regulation generally does not take the form of either a heavy-handed ban on all derivatives trading, or direct monitoring by some omniscient government overseer. Traditionally, derivatives markets have been successfully regulated through a web of procedural rules that include reporting requirements, listing requirements, margin requirements, position limits, insurable interest requirements, and limits on enforceability.[46]

Specifically on the question of whether derivatives are used for insurance (hedging) purposes or for speculation, she emphasized, that it can be difficult to prove that any particular transaction is not a hedge, because traders are 'usually clever enough to hypothesize some underlying risk they are supposedly exposed to that the derivative supposedly offsets'. She added that by 2008, it was a mathematical certainty that the market for CDS, for example, was primarily a speculative market because by 2008, the notional value of the CDS market was more than four times larger than the size of the market for the underlying.

Stout added that derivatives speculation can be criticized for reducing real economic productivity by diverting valuable resources, especially human time and creativity, away from industries and activities that contribute more to sustainable economic growth and to social welfare.

Greenberger pointed out that if, without the de-regulation by the CFMA, the norms of market regulation been applicable, 'these swaps transactions would have been adequately capitalized by traditional clearing norms; and the dangers building up in these markets would otherwise have been observable by the transparency and price discipline that accompanies exchange trading'.[47] He added that while the inadequate capitalization triggered the meltdown, the crisis was aggravated by the opaque interconnectedness of large financial institutions emanating from interest rate, currency, foreign exchange and energy swaps. Quoting him *in extenso*,

Because there was no road map outlining interdependency of those financial transactions, the worst was feared ... Institutions became too big to fail because of these uncharted and feared interdependencies; and the fear that unwinding of these institutions (as proven in the Lehman bankruptcy) would be hampered by the lack of reliable pricing of the instruments in question.

The darkness of this huge multi-trillion dollar unregulated market not only caused, but substantially aggravated, the financial crisis. And, the American taxpayer funded the bailouts and rescued the economy from Depression. The banks are now stronger than ever. The taxpayer, however, is burdened by high unemployment, job insecurity, depleted pensions, and little access to credit....[48]

Post-2008 there has been a big shift to re-regulation in the US, particularly through the Dodd-Frank Law (Wall Street Reform and Consumer Protection Act 2010) and the various regulations under it. New regulations include the 'Volcker Rule', named after former Federal Reserve Chairman Paul Volcker, which (in essence) bans banks from proprietary trading. Proprietary trading is trading by banks for their own account (i.e., where the profits and losses accrue to them) as against trading as intermediaries for their clients.

The 'derivatives lobby' has been credited with diluting a lot of the new regulations including the details of the Volcker Rule. The industry has lobbied with regulators themselves (the CFTC and SEC) and with the legislature. At one stage, 3500 people were involved in the lobbying effort with the CFTC alone![49] In the year after the enactment of the Dodd-Frank law, the Securities Industry and Financial Markets Association paid more than $ 3 million to law firms working on regulations and individual banks paid much more.[50] (It would be wrong to assume that lobbying only happens in the US – it is simply larger and more transparent than elsewhere.)

Suffice it to say that the 2008 crisis established conclusively the error of the belief that rational self-interest of market participants obviates the needs for regulation. The classic justification for regulation on grounds of externality (because the gains to risk taking activity on the part of any financial market participants are private and the costs may be public) is by itself a necessary and sufficient case for government regulation. If taxpayers are going to be billed – as happened in the 2008 crisis – then the government, as their representative, ought to make sure that market participants (whether they are intermediaries or originators or investors) do not undertake risks whose consequences would exceed their capacity to bear. To that extent – the divergence between private and public interest that Natu referred to many years earlier – regulations are warranted.

In sharp contrast to the US was the situation in India where regulators, and in particular the Reserve Bank of India, had taken a very conservative approach to derivatives. That conservatism served the country well. Three critical regulatory requirements imposed by the RBI insulated India from the CDO/CDS mess in the first decade of this century:

- Firstly, the insistence that OTC financial derivatives must be used as hedges of an underlying exposure, and not as speculative investments, kept volumes down to the level needed for hedging.

- Secondly, the insistence that at least one party to such deals must be an RBI-regulated entity ensured that the prudential regulations were much better followed in spirit. It also gave the RBI access to information since regulated entities have reporting requirements.

- Thirdly, the RBI had much better and more comprehensive information on the volume and impact of the OTC market than elsewhere because of its wise insistence on centralized clearing.[51]

Admittedly, India is vastly different from the United States in terms of size and stage of development. Nevertheless, it is interesting to note that almost any 'mainstream' Western expert on the financial sector, if asked to advise India in 2007, would have opposed the first two if not all three of these requirements. Yet, the fact that the RBI, with its very different streams of recruitment (its key policy makers are usually not from the Ivy League or Oxbridge), has much larger diversity of thought (and hence less 'groupthink' and 'intellectual capture') than most central banks, and its strong leadership at a critical time, meant that it had the intellectual independence to contradict the conventional wisdom. This was one case where being 'behind the curve' and 'away from the cutting edge' was wise. Interestingly, India is a country far behind the US in the 'Corruption Perceptions Index' published by Transparency International. This may suggest that intellectual bias and intellectual capture can be more dangerous for market stability than traditional criminal acts of corruption.

Causes of the regulatory failure

Why, in spite of a strong body of theory suggesting that regulation was a definite necessity (on the intellectual grounds already described above), did intelligent, well-read economists of the anti-regulation school go so wrong?

Firstly, the assumption by financial economists that market-determined pricing is always 'right' and that credit rating agencies are accurate predictors of default proved incorrect. Whatever the reasons, it is beyond dispute that the pricing of U.S. mortgages in the mid-2000s proved to be wrong by a large margin. Secondly, the advocates of de-regulation ignored or did not grasp the extent of negative externalities arising from the shifting of risk when that shifting becomes large and widespread. The near ubiquity of the use of credit derivatives, CDOs, etc. meant that many companies who had no intention to assume American real estate price risk were in fact doing so. Thirdly, unlike the real sector of the economy where risks are a combination of both systematic (macroeconomic risk) and unsystematic risks (firm or sector-specific), risks in the financial sector are predominantly *systemic* (cf. systematic)[52] because finance permeates every sector of the economy and financial asset prices are linked to economic fundamentals and economic policies – fiscal, monetary and others. The failure of a large bank has effects going far beyond the staff, depositors and shareholders of that institution and affects confidence in the entire banking system. Arguably, because systemic risk varies directly with size of the financial sector vis-à-vis the rest of the economy, the greater the number of participants, the greater the need for regulation! This is contrary to the normal belief that in a widely dispersed and competitive market, the need for regulation is less. (This is a reminder that laws and principles of economics are not equivalent to those of the physical sciences.)

Secondly, there is strong evidence of various kinds of intellectual and cultural capture, not only of regulators but also of academics of the kind discussed earlier in this chapter (see Box 13.5).

Box 13.5: Conflicts of interest

The documentary 'Inside Job' won an Oscar for the best documentary in the Academy awards presented in February 2011. The movie was about the financial crisis of 2008. In the process, it deals with and mostly destroys many reputations. *Time* magazine once called Rubin, Summers and Greenspan the 'committee to save the world'. Their reputations and even conflicts of interest

---

are highlighted and questioned in the documentary. The documentary also states that the former governor of the Federal Reserve (Fred Mishkin) co-authored in May 2006 a report titled, 'Financial Stability in Iceland', that the report was written in conjunction with the Icelandic Chamber of Commerce and he was paid a substantial sum which was not disclosed in the report. It goes on to state that, on the person's CV, the report title was changed to 'Financial Instability in Iceland'.[53]

Quite apart from subtle forms of 'capture', there is a lot of self-interest in de-regulation within the financial services industry. In a paper published – with a great sense of timing - in December 2008, Philippon and Reshef showed that the relative wage rate in the US financial industry has been directly correlated with the level of de-regulation (see Figure 13.1). The index of de-regulation peaked before the Great Depression. De-regulation gave way to re-regulation from then on until the 1980s and since then, the second wave of deregulation started and in the twenty-first century, exceeded the previous peak.

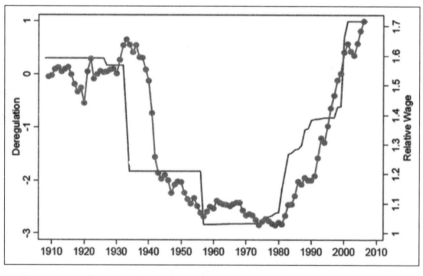

▬▬▬▬▬▬ Financial De-regulation index

━━━●━━━ Relative wage in financial sector

Figure 13.2: Relative wage in the financial sector vis-à-vis level of de-regulation

Source: Wages and Human Capital in the U.S. Financial Industry: 1909–2006, Thomas Philippon and Ariell Reshef, New York University and University of Virginia respectively, December 2008

The dangers of over-regulation

So far, this chapter has shown that regulation of derivatives is unavoidable and an absolute necessity, and that there are strong economic reasons to justify it. However, it is important to recognize that over-regulation can also pose dangers. Over-regulation can not only drive market activity underground, it may impede even the normal functioning of the primary market. Over-regulation will reduce economic efficiency and slow down growth and ultimately affect the welfare of the common citizen.

Goodhart *et al.*[54] and Benston[55] eloquently bring out some of the dangers. Firstly, the intended costs of regulation are often exceeded by the unintended costs and in the long run, regulatory compliance can become a big drag on the regulated industry. Secondly, because consumers do not pay for regulation and it is supplied free of cost at the margin, it is seen as a free good and the demand for further regulation is more than the optimal level. Thirdly, existing market participants have a vested interest in preventing new entrants and a high regulatory burden acts as a potent entry barrier to competition. Apart from regulatory capture there is another mechanism which gives an advantage to existing participants: complying with regulations involves considerable and lumpy fixed costs, for example the cost of staff and computer systems for regulatory compliance. Any new entrant will have to incur these fixed costs, whereas an existing firm can expand by incurring a lower level of variable costs.

Benston also deals with the natural tendency of regulation to expand beyond the optimal level:

> ... the greater the extent of regulation, the greater the possibility for [legislators in] serving and doing favors for regulated firms in return for campaign contributions...The staffs and leadership of the regulatory agencies also extend the reach and depth of regulations. Therefore the degree of regulation has an almost in-built tendency to escalate. In part they do this to satisfy the firms they are charged with regulating. This tendency is enhanced by the regulators' regular contact with the regulated firms rather than with the consumers and unregulated firms, and by a 'revolving door' whereby professionals move from and to regulated firms and regulatory agencies. Thus the regulators are 'captured' by the regulated ... Whether or not they are captured, regulators benefit from extending their budgets and their bureaucracies.[56]

Note that Benston does not refer to corruption *per se* though this is a definite risk, and corruption is not unknown, especially in the developing country context.

Benston also makes the highly perceptive observation (which one of the authors as a former government official and regulator can corroborate) that regulators face an asymmetry in their incentives. If they de-regulate and the results are positive, credit goes to the captains of the regulated industry. But if the de-regulation is followed by any disaster which can remotely be attributed to the de-regulation, the regulator will be severely blamed and (in countries like India) may even be suspected of colluding and then persecuted by the media and perhaps prosecuted by the state. Thus even for an honest, non-captured regulator, de-regulation is more risky than an increase in regulation.

These risks are very real. In countries like India, where there is a strong historical legacy of over-regulation, a consciousness of this risk is important. If the CFMA represents one extreme (de-regulation), the licence-permit raj which India operated for 40 years represents another (the heavy hand of government intervention in commercial decisions). Over-regulation results in wasted efforts and unproductive transaction costs, with participants expending resources in compliance activities. It prevents new and productive activities from being undertaken. In the specific case of the financial sector, it could impede capital formation and reduce efficiency in the use of capital. In addition, regulation breeds corruption which, apart from being an evil in itself, eventually makes regulation less effective. The last few years in India have seen a resurgence of detailed microregulation and a tendency towards proliferation of new rules, authorities and appellate authorities which, while serving the self-interest of retiring civil service and judicial officers, increases the potential for over-regulation. The risk in countries like India is that the clear intellectual defeat of the Western 'total de-regulation school' may be used in some quarters to justify a new financial licence-permit raj, perhaps administered by 'independent'[57] regulators rather than ministries, but with similar consequences.

At the margin, whether one de-regulates further or tightens regulation is a matter of context and the starting point. Clearly, there is more scope for de-regulation in countries that maintain severe financial repression and the opposite may be true in the case of countries that adopt a hands-off attitude.

The challenge for regulators is to steer clear of the twin dangers. The effects of over-regulation are those of a gradual debilitating affliction, like a tape worm eating away into the vitality of the system, whereas under-regulation can, like a heart attack, produce sudden death. Avoiding heart attacks is clearly the more pressing task, but that does not necessarily mean that one should extend an invitation to the tape worm.

Notes and References

1   H. Working, 'Speculation on Hedging Markets', *Food Research Institute Studies,* Stanford University, Vol. 1, Issue 2, May 1960, 187–8.

2   Emphasis his.

3   A. E. Kahn, *The Economics of Regulation: Principles and Institutions.* John Wiley and Sons, New York, 1970, 1.

4   Kahn, *ibid.,* 20.

5   M. Brunnermeier, A. Crocket, C. Goodhart, Avinash D. Persaud and H. Shin, *The Fundamental Principles of Financial Regulation.* International Centre for Monetary and Banking Studies, Geneva, 2009, 2.

6   W. R. Natu, *Regulation of Forward Markets.* Asia Publishing House, Bombay, 1962, 18.

7   G. J. Benston, *Regulating Financial Markets: A Critique and Some Proposals,* Hobart Paper No. 135. Institute of Economic Affairs, London, 1998.

8   D. T. Llewellyn, *The Economic Rationale for Financial Regulation.* Financial Services Authority, London, April 1999.

9   When producers do not pay the true costs (because some of the costs are borne by others), their marginal costs are lower than the marginal costs to society. Therefore they produce more of the good than they would otherwise. For instance, if a factory produces a product but also releases toxic effluents and does not have to treat those effluents, it will end up producing more of the product than if it were made to pay for the treatment.

10 M. Brunnermeier, A. Crocket, C. Goodhart, Avinash D. Persaud and H. Shin, *The Fundamental Principles of Financial Regulation, op.cit.*

11 *Ibid.,* 4.

12 G. A. Akerlof, 'The Market for 'Lemons': Quality Uncertainty and the Market Mechanism', *Quarterly Journal of Economics,* Vol. 84, No. 3, 488–500, 1970.

13 J. Stiglitz, 'Principles of Financial Regulation: A Dynamic Portfolio Approach', *The World Bank Research Observer,* Vol. 16, No.1, 1–18, Spring 2001.

14 M. Brunnermeier, A. Crocket, C. Goodhart, Avinash D. Persaud, H. Shin, *Ibid.*

15 D. T. Llewellyn, *Institutional Structure of Financial Regulation and Supervision: The Basic Issues,* Paper presented at World Bank Seminar on Aligning Supervisory Structures with Country Needs, Washington DC, 2006.

[16] J. Anderlini, 'China Bank Regulators Caught in Turf War', *Financial Times*, 9 April 2014.

[17] M. Brunnermeier, A. Crocket, C. Goodhart, A. D. Persaud and H. Shin, *op.cit.*

[18] Emphasis added.

[19] C. Goodhart, *Procyclicality and Financial Regulation*, Banco De Espana (Bank of Spain). Available at: http://www.bde.es/f/webbde/Secciones/Publicaciones/InformesBoletinesRevistas/RevistaEstabilidadFinanciera/09/May/Fic/ief0116.pdf. Accessed on 14 July 2014.

[20] J. Stiglitz, *op.cit.*

[21] A. Fresh and M. N. Baily, 'What Does International Experience Tell Us about Regulatory Consolidation?', *The Pew Financial Reform Project*, Briefing No. 6, 2009.

[22] Y. V. Reddy, 'Issues in Choosing between Single and Multiple Regulators of Financial System', Address by Deputy Governor of the Reserve Bank of India, Public Policy Workshop, ICRIER, New Delhi, 22 May 2001.

[23] Y. V. Reddy, *ibid.*

[24] Y. V. Reddy, *ibid.*

[25] A. Fresh and M. N. Baily, *op.cit.* 4.

[26] B. Ritholtz, 'Credit Default Swaps Are Masquerading as Financial Products – They Should be Regulated as Insurance Products', *Washington Post*, 11 March 2012.

[27] J. Kwak, 'Cultural Capture and the Financial Crisis', Chapter in *Preventing Regulatory Capture: Special Interest Influence and How to Limit it*, edited by D. Carpenter and D. Moss. The Tobin Project, Cambridge University Press, 2013.

[28] K. Geert Rouwenhorst, co-author of 'Facts & Fantasies About Commodity Futures', *Financial Analysts Journal*, Vol. 62, 2006, was on the Board of Summerhaven – see: 'Investors turn cold on commodities as rally fizzles', Gregory Meyer, *Financial Times*, 6 December 2013.

[29] L. Zingales, 'Preventing Economists' Capture', Chicago Booth Research Paper No. 13–81, University of Chicago – Booth School of Business, 2013.

[30] E. A. Posner and E. G. Weyl, 'A Proposal for Limiting Speculation on Financial Derivatives: An FDA for Financial Innovation', Institute for Law and Economics, Working Paper No. 594. The Law School, University of Chicago, March 2012.

[31] B. Masters *et al.*, 'Barclays Fined a Record $450 m: UK Bank Penalised for Rigging Libor', *Financial Times*, 28 June 2012.

[32] K. Matussek and O. Suess, 'Metals Currency Rigging Worse than Libor, Bafin Says', Bloomberg, 16 January 2014.

[33] D. Douglas, 'Libor-rate Fixing May Have Cost US Agencies $3 Billion', *Washington Post*, 20 December 2012.

[34] A. Harris and M. C. Fisk, 'J.P. Morgan Sued with Goldman in Aluminum Antitrust Case', *Bloomberg*, 7 August 2013.

35   Note that there are three distinct kinds of embedded risk – option pricing risk, credit default risk, and basis risk (i.e., the risk that the index will not move in consonance with the actual credit risk).

36   T. Alloway and M. Mackenzie, ' "Swaptions" Trade Leaps Over Regulatory Hurdles', *Financial Times*, 31 March 2014.

37   Hutchinson suggested the use of a Cauchy distribution which has a standard deviation of infinity (instead of the 'normal' distribution) to quantify risks of index CDS swaptions!

38   Martin Hutchinson, 'The Bear's Lair: The Ultimate in Foolish Leverage'. 7 April 2014. Available at: http://www.prudentbear.com/2014/04/the-bears-lair-ultimate-in-foolish. html#.U0lgr_mSy2c. Accessed on 14 July 2014.

39   Michael Greenberger, *The Role of Derivatives in the Financial Crisis*, Financial Crisis Enquiry Commission Hearing, Washington D. C., 30 June 2010.

40   M. Miller, 'Do We Really Need More Regulation of Financial Derivatives?', University of Chicago Graduate School of Business, Selected Paper no. 75. (Address delivered at the inauguration ceremony of the International Executive M.B.A. Program at Barcelona conducted by the University of Chicago Graduate School of Business, 17 October 1994.)

41   Thomas F. Siems, *Policy Analysis:10 Myths about Derivatives*, Cato Institute, Washington D.C., 1997.

42   P. E. Wallison, 'Why Do We Regulate Banks', *Regulation 2005-06*. The Cato Institute, Washington D.C., 2006.

43   Greenberger, *op.cit.*

44   This was eventually the direct cause of the collapse of American Insurance Group.

45   Greenberger, *op.cit.*

46   Lynn A. Stout, Testimony to United States Senate Committee on Agriculture, Forestry and Nutrition, 4 June 2009. Available at: http://www.ag.senate.gov/download/stout-testimony. Accessed on 14 July 2014.

47   Greenberger, *op.cit.*

48   Greenberger, *op. cit.*

49   S. Brush and R. Schmidt, 'How the Bank Lobby Loosened US Reins on Derivatives', *Bloomberg*. Available at: http://www.bloomberg.com/news/2013-09-04/how-the-bank-lobby-loosened-u-s-reins-on-derivatives.html. Accessed on 14 July 2014.

50   *Ibid.*

51   Subir Gokarn, 'Regulatory Perspectives on Derivatives Markets in India', Keynote address at World Federation of Exchanges Annual Conference. Available at: http://www.world-exchanges.org/focus/2011-06/m-2-2.php. Accessed on 14 July 2014.

52   Readers should note the difference between 'systemic risk' which is the risk posed to the entire financial *system* by (say) excessive lending going beyond the individual parties in transaction, and 'systematic risk' which is the macroeconomic risk that affects the value of a security in a portfolio. The two are connected but distinct.

[53] See, http://ftalphaville.ft.com/blog/2010/08/25/325376/mishkins-very-own-icelandic-blow-up/ and the links therein for more information. The relevant video clip from 'Inside Job' is also available through this blog post.

[54] C. Goodhart, P. Hartmann, D. Llewellyn, L. Rojas-Suarez and S.Wiesbrod, *Financial Regulation – Why, How and Where Now*. Routledge, 1998.

[55] G. J. Benston, *op.cit.*

[56] G. J. Benston, *op.cit.*

[57] 'Independence' merely means absence of political control; it does not eliminate the dangers of capture, corruption or the natural tendency of bureaucracies to grow.

14

Derivatives and Development: A Critique

[F]inancial sector size has an inverted U-shaped effect on productivity growth
S. Cecchetti and E. Kharroubi[1]

Do derivatives contribute to economic development? That is an interesting question but before even attempting to answer it, it is necessary to note that derivatives are but a part of the broader landscape of the financial sector. In economics, the 'financial sector' is often analysed separately from the 'real sector' where actual goods and services are produced. The distinction is important. As an oversimplified example, if an economy suffers 100 per cent inflation over a year because of excessive monetary expansion by the central bank, it will affect the financial sector significantly; but if incomes also grow at exactly the same rate and incomes are distributed in the same way as before, the end-result is that in real terms everyone is exactly as well off as in the previous year. (In this example the financial sector had no effect on the real sector.) A wider question, and perhaps more difficult to answer, is the question of whether finance and the financial sector of the economy contribute to development. This chapter looks at both questions without always separating them rigidly.

Chapters 11 and 12 discussed several examples where developing countries have benefited from the use of derivatives. Chilean companies had an exposure to the US dollar exchange rate because of their international investments. The forward market allowed them to hedge it. Mexico was able to avoid budgetary uncertainty by hedging its oil production through buying plain vanilla put options on crude oil. Uruguay was able to use weather index derivatives to protect against drought risk. On the other hand, there were also many examples where companies and countries hurt themselves by exposing themselves to derivatives products that they did not comprehend.

The question is, does one blame a tool for causing hurt or grief, or does one own up to one's failure to handle it safely? This debate is eternal and extends into many areas of public policy, as the American debates on gun control illustrate. At a practical level, it is useless to appeal to investors' self-control and knowledge. Most people understand these concepts and most of those who understand are unable to practise them sustainably. Derivatives cannot be an exception to basic human nature.

On many occasions, derivative users may not have a choice or scope to avoid using them. Banks deal with customers at different levels. That allows them to exert pressure on their customers on, say, using derivatives to obtain better terms on their loan facilities. Given the size of derivatives risks, at a practical level, it is not feasible for regulators to appeal to users' self-control and will power, invoke the principle of *caveat emptor* and wash their hands of the implications of losses. Quite apart from economic justifications, such an approach has proved politically unsustainable, indicating that society as a whole – to the extent that democratic politics reflects the view of a majority of people in society – is unwilling to leave derivatives risks to be dealt with by users alone. And users are not just corporations. In India for example, much of the trading in stocks, including by retail investors, has migrated to trading in single stock options and /or futures. Most individuals who trade in them may not understand that derivatives and the leverage embedded in them are double-edged swords. In a relatively poor and unsophisticated country when it comes to these matters, regulators cannot rely on individual awareness and discipline to keep out the harmful effects of derivatives. (The problem is not confined to developing countries: the SEC in the USA had to order a probe into complex derivative based 'exchange-traded notes' after unsuspecting investors lost large amounts of money.[2])

Thus, two things need to be remembered. The first is that the application of derivatives is on a scale that was not visualized when they were first developed. The second is that most of this application is for speculation, with hedging often becoming a minor and ancillary business. As has been discussed elaborately in previous chapters, speculation is not always harmful, but not always socially useful either. Speculation is useful when it imparts stability to financial markets by enhancing information flow to markets – information that enables prices to better reflect underlying economic or corporate fundamentals – and enabling correction of anomalies through arbitrage. However, recent regulatory trends tend towards protecting large institutions and providing a permanent put option on asset prices (see the discussion on short selling in Chapter 7). Regulators and regulations are encouraging, intentionally or otherwise, speculation that causes asset prices to deviate from fundamentals when they come down selectively on speculation that introduces downside risk to asset prices. Regulators increasingly see their role as one of keeping the ecosystem stable and safe enough for financial intermediaries to continue to make profits through expansion of derivatives trading, rather than ensuring that derivatives serve useful economic functions. To put it bluntly, the effect of this is to favour market intermediaries rather than market users. So, in that sense, regulators actually may be undermining the socially and economically useful functions of derivatives. Nevertheless, to the extent that large losses in the hands of inexperienced users undermine the case for derivatives, there is a political threat to the business model of financial intermediaries. Hence, it is in the self-interest of financial intermediaries that they allow regulators to develop a regulatory framework that reduces the chances of large losses.

This leads back to the point that the role of derivatives in economic development is better discussed in the context of the role of finance in economic development.

Finance and its role in development

It is important to note here the distinction between the growth of the financial sector and its growing importance or dominance in the economy, and the growth of finance (debt and equity) and its importance to economic growth. Finance, in the form of capital, is a factor of production in the real sector; the financial *sector* denotes the economic agents (financial services firms, their shareholders etc.) who enable the provision of finance. (However, it is not unusual to find the two terms used interchangeably.) In recent years, the financial sector has taken on a life of its own and its growth has far outstripped the growth of the real sector.

The growth of finance

As it happens in most cases, it all started with good intentions and sound theoretical underpinnings. Until recently, most economists believed that both finance and the financial sector were good for growth. The idea that an economy needs intermediation to match borrowers and lenders, channelling resources to their most efficient uses, is fundamental to economic thinking. Goldsmith,[3] McKinnon[4] and Shaw[5] earlier and more recently Levine *et al*[6] and Rajan and Zingales[7] provided theoretical and empirical support for this proposition. While there were dissenting voices, it was generally accepted that finance was not merely a by-product of the development process but an engine propelling growth. This, in turn, was one of the key elements supporting arguments for financial deregulation.

Innovation, investment and enterprise need finance. Hence, finance is the lynchpin that enables all other economic activity. Therefore, if finance is good, the logic went, more of it would be better. Enterprises need loans. If banks can not only make loans but can also take the loans periodically off their books, then they can make even more loans and enable even more entrepreneurial activity and capital formation. So went the thought process. (However, for every transaction, there are two sides. If banks offloaded their balance sheet risks, someone had to bear those risks. The overall economic risk cannot be diversified away. Finance cannot conjure up growth like magicians pull rabbits out of hats. But, that is almost what the world had come to expect of finance and what the financial sector implied that it could do.)

Finance, or more precisely debt, appeared to deliver economic growth after the 1980s. That it did so after the removal of any semblance of a monetary anchor restraining central banks from creating paper money is no coincidence. After the Bretton Woods systems and its US dollar standard collapsed early in the Seventies, the world experienced a period of economic stagnation combined with high inflation. After Paul Volcker abandoned targeting of money supply and began to target interest rates, the intellectual consensus in the developed ('free') world paid less attention to money supply. All that central banks had to do was to credit the accounts of commercial banks with more money. Creating base money became as easy as that. In a sense, the base money became the margin money on top of which the mountain of debt was created – many times as big.

The chart below shows the 'structural break' in the evolution of bank credit and banks' assets in the world from the Seventies and, more pronouncedly, from the Eighties. Something changed in the Eighties. Taylor[8] concedes that one of the goals of current and future research would be to pin down exactly why the period from the 1940s to the 1970s was so unusually quiescent, with no financial crisis at all.

Figure 14.1: Size of the banking sector relative to GDP – loans, assets and broad money in 14 advanced countries

Source: 'The great leveraging', Alan Taylor, University of Virginia, July 2012

He refers to the century between 1870 and 1970 as the 'Age of money'. In this age, 'the ratio of loans to money was more or less stable. Loans to GDP hovered in a range around 0.4 to 0.5, with broad money to GDP sitting a little higher at an average of about 0.6 to 0.7. From the 1970s, the picture changed dramatically, and the 'Age of Credit' started. Although broad money relative to GDP remained almost flat at around 0.7 (rising a little only in the 2000s), the asset side of banks' balance sheets exploded. Loans to GDP doubled from 0.5 to 1.0 and assets to GDP tripled from about 0.7 to roughly 2.0.'

Taylor posed the logical question as to what changed in the 1980s. He pointed to two possible factors: banks' risk tolerance changed over time as enterprises got rebuilt after the economic depression followed by the devastation of World War II and, secondly, financial liberalization played its part. He did not proceed to examine these hypotheses rigorously since the thrust of his paper was on something else. While these were indeed proximate causes, there were other equally, or more, important causes:

- *The creation of an expectation of, and appetite for, high growth*: The world economy, until the beginning of the 19th century, had not experienced (and hence not developed an appetite for) high economic growth. Thereafter technological developments – as human ingenuity grew wings – generated high growth and fostered an appetite for it. It continued into the 20th century only to be interrupted by two World Wars, the Great Depression and the stop-go adherence to the Gold Standard in the inter-war period. The destruction of enterprises and loss of people entailed by the economic depression and the two World Wars paved the way for faster economic growth post-1945. Substantial rebuilding was both desirable and feasible. Financial repression (capital controls) and low growth of broad money and bank credit did not matter. When the reconstruction era had run its course by the 1970s, it became more difficult to sustain growth in developed countries. This put pressure on governments to rekindle growth through monetary means.

- *The prevalence of fiat money unrestrained by any real anchor*: For a variety of reasons, in the early 1970s, the United States shut down the gold window and floated the dollar. Soon, the world had floating exchange rates, unconstrained monetary policies and no nominal anchor for money supply. This was different from the preceding era when countries were anchored to gold or some other constraining anchor. The absence of an anchor allowed the U.S. government to use its exclusive privilege (its ability, as custodian of the world's reserve currency, to print global public money at will) to finance (without substantial new taxes) a stupendous military-industrial complex, the Vietnam war, the space program, Lyndon Johnson's (otherwise splendid) Great Society policies, et cetera.

Thus, while financial liberalization - which in turn led to financial innovation and the derivatives explosion - played a very important role in the explosion of bank credit (especially to the private sector), unrestrained creation of fiat money was arguably just as important for the post-1980 world of global debt explosion.

The expansion of finance (through financial liberalization, derivatives and money supply expansion) extended the run of global growth aided, no doubt, by technological developments, a period of détente in global affairs and globalization of production, etc.

Of late, finance appears no longer able to drive economic growth. The years since the financial crisis of 2008 have witnessed unprecedentedly loose and cheap monetary policy and yet this has not fired up economic growth in the US and in Europe. Most cyclical economic indicators – at the time of writing in 2014 – lag well behind past economic recoveries.

In theory, equity is better than debt, for raising more equity capital improves a firm's balance sheet and reduces its overall riskiness. If institutions cannot provide all the capital that firms need, then firms could go directly to the public. Public capital markets connected savers directly to users. Financial disintermediation was assumed to be better than bank-intermediated financing, because it was democratic and it was efficient. However, the reality has turned out to be different. A review commissioned by the UK Government found that the equity markets were no longer performing the role that had been expected of them in terms of financing productive economic activity (see Box 14.1). John Kay, author of the review stated in an interview that he was beginning to wonder if the role of public equity markets was over from the point of economic value. It had become a casino activity, dissociated in large part from what these companies actually do. It was rather like betting on horses which does not actually affect the performance of the horses. He felt that investing in shares has been reduced to gambling which often made money for the house and no one else.[9]

Box 14.1: The Kay review of equity markets

The 'Kay Review of UK equity markets and long-term decision-making' (Final Report July 2012) was a comprehensive and insightful analysis of the equity markets in general and the UK in particular in relation to their impact on long term decision-making and on economic growth, commissioned by the UK Government and written by Professor John Kay of the London School of Economics. Many of the findings of the Kay review apply beyond the UK. Key insights relevant to this chapter are extracted below (numbers in parentheses are the relevant paragraph numbers from the report).

The restructuring of the financial services industry that followed deregulation and internationalisation, the development of financing techniques which made possible the takeover of even the largest companies and the erosion of the traditional resistance of UK institutional investors to hostile takeover, all led major companies to pay far more attention to equity markets and their share price. (1.18)

The unhappy shareholder exits only by finding someone else to take his or her place. This substitution does not eliminate the impact of exit, but it greatly reduces it. At the same time, the structure and regulation of equity markets today overwhelmingly emphasise exit over voice and this has often led to shareholder engagement of superficial character and low quality. We believe equity markets will function more effectively if there are more trust relationships which are based on voice and fewer trading relationships emphasising exit. (1.32)

It has long been recognised that there is a logical contradiction embedded in the efficient market hypothesis. If all relevant information were fully incorporated in market prices, there would be no incentive to obtain the information in the first place. The more efficient is the process described as 'price discovery' – the more rapid the incorporation of the views of market participants into market prices – the less the reward from engaging in the socially more important function of 'value discovery' – understanding the fundamental value of the company attributable to its potential earnings and cash flow. (4.11)

The belief that the best approach to information asymmetry is the provision of additional data may have led to a proliferation of data ill adapted to the needs of users, and to a belief that activities whose attractions are derived from the exploitation of information asymmetry are acceptable if accompanied by full, even if largely incomprehensible, disclosure. (4.16)

Regulatory philosophy has increasingly been based on a model of markets which emphasises trading over trust relationships. Regulation has been framed to excessive degree with the concerns of market intermediaries rather than market users in mind. It is a measure of priorities that regulation admits, even encourages, market participants to gain an advantage over others by reacting more quickly to data, but prohibit market participants from gaining an advantage over others by obtaining better information. Equity markets should be seen as a means of contributing to the performance of business, not as a game in which all competitors race for relative advantage when the starting gun is fired. (13.11).

Price, a long-standing fund manager and observer of financial markets, also based in the UK, put this more colourfully:

Listed stocks are second-hand assets; the primary purpose of the stock market is to raise expansion capital for young companies and simultaneously to allow founding entrepreneurs and their backers to cash in some of their chips. If you view the stock market as the default and almost exclusive choice for your savings, you are acting not as an investor but as a speculator. Nobody in their right minds would devote their life savings to hoarding second-hand cars, but then a colossal industry of vested interests and economic agents has not arisen around the second-hand car trading market, spurred on by facile second-hand car cheerleaders in the popular media.[10]

Limits to economic growth?

It is quite possible that the world might have reached, or breached, the limits of economic growth and that future growth rates will be slower than the past. While a fuller discussion of the potential for and limits to economic growth on the scale experienced in the last twenty to thirty years is beyond the scope of this chapter or the book, it is worth pointing out that global economic growth witnessed in the twentieth century (especially in the second half) and in the first decade of the twenty-first century are more anomalous than normal. Just the growth in the first decade of the new millennium is estimated to have exceeded the growth in the first 19 centuries A.D.[11] One may argue that there may be errors in GDP calculations for the distant past and even the present, especially as the calculation over periods of changing consumption baskets is not a trivial issue and the subject of much debate among statisticians. Nevertheless, the sheer enormity of the difference is such that it appears to outweigh such measurement issues and it is apparent that growth has been running at extraordinarily high levels. This surely must have consequences and not all of them will be pleasant, to put it mildly. The assumption that more finance will lead to more growth may thus run into this constraint.

While it is human nature to extrapolate the most recent trend into the future, the course of history often runs differently and things are often more circular than linear. Mean reversion may be more valid and relevant than linear extrapolation. The higher growth rates of the last few decades may have been an extraction 'from the world for the world', through the use of finance. The global crisis of 2008 may be a reminder of the folly of attempting to push the growth frontier through the relentless use of debt, facilitated by the unrestrained creation of money. Even if it produces a temporary growth spurt above the sustainable level, it may be brought back to trend by crisis-induced de-leveraging. When it takes hold, lower growth will be inevitable and perhaps even desirable. In that sense, the 2008 global economic, financial and banking crisis was one down payment. The response to the crisis – restoring growth through zero interest rates and more debt – means that more bills for the artificially induced growth spurt will become due in future.

Recent economic studies

As noted above, it was generally accepted among economists that finance made a positive contribution to growth and development both in theory and in practice. In recent years however, there has been a steady stream of studies questioning of the usefulness of finance (and the financial sector) in economic growth and development.

Cecchetti and Kharroubi of the Bank for International Settlements did a series of investigations. They found that the relationship of several finance-related variables to the real economy has an inverted U-shape. Whether it is total credit, bank credit or employment in the financial services sector, they all were positively correlated to GDP per capita and then the *correlation reaches a peak before the relationship turns negative*. They tested the correlations using econometric techniques and controlled for other factors. Their findings remained robust. They also noticed that there was a clear inverse relationship between employment in financial intermediation and economy-wide productivity growth.[12] It is this inverse relationship that they set out to investigate in a second paper.[13] They concluded that as the financial sector attracts skilled workers with higher pay, it impacts the ability of other businesses, particularly new enterprises to attract talent, adversely. Thus, with enterprises lacking skilled workers, their ability and willingness to take risks and innovate diminishes.

After all, more than the collateral, the intellectual property embedded in their skilled workers is crucial for the survival and growth of new businesses. As they lose this important factor crucial for their success, financing too becomes more difficult to obtain. That also means that industries that can more easily post collateral are the ones that obtain funding. That is why credit booms usually coincide with construction booms. The property and real estate sector, with their tangible assets, are able to post collateral more easily. The paper's conclusions are rather unambiguous:

> The growth of a country's financial system is a drag on productivity growth. That is, higher growth in the financial sector reduces real growth. In other words, financial booms are not, in general, growth-enhancing, probably because the financial sector competes with the rest of the economy for resources. Second, using sectoral data, we examine the distributional nature of this effect and find that credit booms harm what we normally think of as the engines for growth: those that are more R&D-intensive. This evidence, together with recent experience during the financial crisis, leads us to conclude that *there is a pressing need to reassess the relationship of finance and real growth in modern economic systems.* (Emphasis added).

Philippon and Reshef[14] found that '*most of the rise in living standards after 1870 was obtained with less income spent on finance and less financial output than what is observed after 1980; and the relationship between financial output and income has changed after 1980.*'

One of their conclusions is consistent with Cecchetti and Kharroubi: '*it is quite difficult to make a clear-cut case that at the margin reached in high-income economies, the expanding financial sector increases the rate of economic growth.*'

The implication is that finance is indeed good for development – but only up to a point. Too much of finance can be a drag on growth. These recent studies require a re-appraisal of the traditional position that the growth of finance and the growth of the financial sector are necessarily good for development.

The work of Cecchetti and Kharroubi suggests that there is an inverted U curve and that *until the size of the financial sector relative to GDP reaches the maximum point on a curve, finance does provide a positive impetus to growth.* In countries whose financial sectors are smaller than that level, the traditional position is likely to still be valid. However, regulators in those countries have the opportunity to learn from the experience of the developed countries in not blindly assuming that finance is always benign. They have the opportunity to use finance constructively without allowing it to reach destabilizing levels. And above all, they have the opportunity to put their domestic financial sectors on a sound footing without following the failed practices of developed countries.

Finance vs. the financial sector

As was apparent from a preceding section, in recent years, finance has not been successful in increasing growth in developed countries. It is also possible that the rates of growth that people have got used to are simply not sustainable.

However, while finance may no longer be able to generate growth in the real economy, it has itself grown dramatically and at a much faster rate than the real economy that it is supposed to support. This is where the role of derivatives becomes significant: *the derivatives explosion was a major factor that drove this differential between the rate of growth of productive finance and the rate of growth of the financial sector.* Financial markets, as they have evolved in the last three decades, have moved from their primary function of connecting capital users and savers (the basis for economic theorists to assume that Finance was an engine of growth) to a mechanism that caters primarily to the interests of financial intermediaries themselves. In other words, the process has become the goal, though the service of the end-users at both ends of the capital spectrum remains the ostensible goal or the honourable fig leaf. There have been distortions of prices of many financial assets and instruments through manipulation that borders on criminality. Regulators are probing almost all the major global financial institutions for manipulation of foreign exchange markets, the LIBOR interest rate market and the market for precious metals (see Chapter 13).

Box 14.2: Share buybacks and executive remuneration

Related to this issue of a deliberate conflation of means and ends, is the behaviour of the corporate sector with respect to executive remuneration and share price performance. Professor Michael Jensen is considered the father of Agency Theory. Agency theory was developed to stress the point that managers should act as agents of shareholders. This theory was a

---

backlash against managers' tendencies to go for acquisitions which diluted shareholder value. Executive remuneration plans using stock options have proliferated as a result of that. In truth, this has produced the worst of both worlds. Managers have not given up their tendency to build empires nor have they aligned their behaviour with long-term value creation for shareholders, but (since compensation is tied to short-term movements in stock price) boosting stock price has become an end in itself.

In a paper published in 2010, Michael Jensen and his co-author decried the tendency on the part of Wall Street analysts and managers of listed firms to feed off each other through this game of 'earnings guidance'. Companies provide earnings guidance for analysts to come up with their earnings forecasts and then companies set about beating those earnings forecasts every quarter and that provides a nice boost to the share price. They wrote, *'Rather than the forecasts representing a financial by-product of the firm's strategy, the forecasts came to drive those strategies.'*[15]

There is another example of how policies, ostensibly designed to help the real economy, are serving the interests of the financial sector and, in the process, lead to undesirable behavioural consequences that have long-term costs. Extraordinarily low interest rates in many developed countries in place since 2009, in response to the global crisis of 2008, combined with large-scale money printing has further emboldened executives to engage in buying back shares. In a speech in January 2014, Richard Fisher, President of the Federal Reserve Bank of Dallas, pointed out how the flood of easy money that the Federal Reserve has circulated since 2009 enables share buybacks. Given extraordinarily low interest rates, these buybacks, after inflation and some tax treatment have negative costs for executives.[16] Of course, this has a very pleasant effect on Earnings per Share (EPS) and, hence, on the share prices itself! It is not difficult to notice, in this sequence of actions, that there is no real economic value addition that results in a higher share price. It is financial alchemy.

It is conceded that these examples are illustrative of the behaviour of parts of the wider corporate sector and not of the financial sector alone. Nonetheless, one should not miss the role that the financial sector plays in aiding and abetting such behaviour and in being an intellectual and behavioural forerunner for such practices.

Thus, with the global financial industry operating largely in its own interest rather than in the interests of the wider economy, it is a moot point as to whether finance and financial derivatives are good for development. As with many things in the modern era, what starts out as a good thing quickly mutates into a threat to the world, through excessive use and abuse. The Nobel laureate Robert Merton, generally a strong supporter of financial innovation, had himself noted that '[a]ny virtue can readily become a vice if taken to excess, and just so with innovations.'[17] Indeed, the pursuit of innovation through derivatives and of growth of the financial sector as ends in themselves, dissociated and decoupled from real economic activity, have considerably weakened the case for finance being either a precondition or a concomitant contributor for economic development.

This also means that all countries, but especially developing countries, need to be watchful about aspects of bilateral or multilateral treaties that constrain their regulatory options in the financial sector. For instance, in the wider context of capital flows, Gallagher *et al* pointed out that the investment clauses of the proposed Trans-Pacific Partnership and other Free Trade Agreements (FTA) negotiated with the US are based on the 2012 US model Bilateral Investment Treaty (BIT) which does not provide for use of 'Capital Flows Management' (CFM) measures in times of crisis. Where safeguards exist in BIT, they are modelled on standard Generalized Agreement on Trade in Services (GATS) clauses which do provide for adoption of measures in times of 'Balance of Payments' difficulties. But, these are restricted to capital outflows and not inflows. Further, these safeguards must also comply with WTO norms of being non-discriminatory, temporary and necessary. The burden of proof on all this rests with the respondent and not the complainant. Importantly, the United States' model BIT provides for investor-state dispute settlement rather than confining dispute settlement to between states.[18]

Financial sector activity growth and financial asset prices have taken on a life of their own and, in the process, have become the veritable tail that wags the dog. The global financial crisis was an opportunity to reverse this, but global policy and corporate elites have not grasped it: as Figure 14.1 showed, the ratio of bank assets to GDP has continued to grow post-crisis. At the time of writing, six years after the crisis, Finance continues to remain a pervasive source of economic instability globally, as Lord Turner, former head of the UK's Financial Supervisory Authority reiterated.[19] It is necessary for the financial sector to become less hostile to economic stability before it can become a catalyst or positive force for development.

Notes and References

1   S. Cecchetti and E. Kharroubi, 'Reassessing the Impact of Finance on Growth', *BIS Working Paper No. 381*. Monetary and Economics Department, Bank for International Settlements, July 2012, 14.

2   K. Dugan, 'How a 56-Year-Old Engineer's $45,000 Loss Spurred SEC Probe', *Bloomberg*, 17 April 2014.

3   R. Goldsmith, *Financial Structure and Development*, Yale University Press, 1969.

4   R. McKinnon, *Money and Capital in Economic Development*, Brookings Institution, Washington D.C., 1973.

5   E. Shaw, *Financial Deepening and Economic Development*, Oxford University Press, New York, 1973.

6   R. Levine, N. Loayza and T. Beck, 'Financial Intermediation and Growth: Causality and Causes', *Journal of Monetary Economics*, Vol. 46, No. 1, 31–77, 2000.

7   R. Rajan, and L. Zingales, 'Financial Dependence and Growth', *American Economic Review*, Vol. 88, No. 3, 559–86, 1998.

8   A. Taylor, 'The Great Leveraging', National Bureau of Economic Research, Working Paper No. 18290, August 2012. Available at: http://www.nber.org/papers/w18290. Accessed on 14 July 2014.

9   'Financial System Waiting for the Next Crisis', *Financial Times*, 2 June 2013. Available at: http://www.ft.com/cms/s/0/f39bce2e-ca1a-11e2-af47-00144feab7de.html. Accessed on 14 July 2014.

10 T. Price, 'Home Truths from Abroad', *The Price of Everything* blog, PFP Wealth Management, 4 November 2013. Available at: http://thepriceofeverything.typepad.com/files/home-truths-from-abroad.pdf. Accessed on 14 July 2014.

11 'Mischarting Economic History', The Economist Blogs, 20 June 2012. Available at: http://www.economist.com/blogs/graphicdetail/2012/06/mis-charting-economic-history. Accessed on 10 November 2014.

12 S. Cecchetti and E. Kharroubi, *op.cit.*

13 S. Cecchetti and E. Kharroubi, 'Why Does Financial Sector Growth Crowd Out Real Economic Growth?', paper presented at the Institute for New Economic Thinking-Federal Reserve Bank of San Francisco conference 'Finance and the Welfare of Nations', September 2013.

14 T. Philippon and Ariel Reshef, 'An International Look at the Growth of Modern Finance', *Journal of Economic Perspectives*, Vol. 27, No. 2, 73–96, Spring 2013.

15 J. Fuller and M. Jensen, 'Just Say No to Wall Street: Putting A Stop to the Earnings Game', *Journal of Applied Corporate Finance*, Vol. 22, No. 1, 59–63, Winter 2010.

16 Richard Fisher, 'Beer Goggles, Monetary Camels, the Eye of the Needle and the First Law of Holes', speech before the National Association of Corporate Directors by President of the Federal Reserve Bank of Dallas, 14 January 2014. Available at: https://www.dallasfed.org/news/speeches/fisher/2014/fs140114.cfm. Accessed on 14 July 2014.

17 R. C. Merton, 'The Financial System and Economic Performance', *Journal of Financial Services Research*, Vol. 4, Issue 4, December 1990, 265.

18 K. P. Gallagher, S. Anderson and A. Viterbo, *Capital Flow Management and the Trans-Pacific Partnership Agreement*, G-24 Policy Brief No. 79, October 2013.

19 'Finance is Inherently Unstable: Adair Turner', *Mint*, 15 January 2014. Available at: http://www.livemint.com/Industry/FnDUFFIjcEFcUWbyHXwdTN/Finance-is-inherently-unstable-Adair-Turner.html. Accessed on 14 July 2014.

15

Regulatory Policy for Derivatives:
A Pragmatic Approach

'In theory, theory and practice are the same. In practice, they are not.'
Attributed to Albert Einstein.

Previous sections of this book have set out extensively the economic functions and implications of derivatives. This concluding chapter attempts to distil the economic theory and experience to propose some practical guidelines for policy making and regulation relating to derivatives. The recommendations in this chapter are in two parts, covering structure and philosophy respectively.

Regulatory structures and rules

This part makes some specific recommendations on regulatory rules and structures.

Insurable interest and reserve requirements for credit derivatives

It was seen earlier that a CDS is not really a swap but in substance an insurance contract. CDS is 'neither fish nor fowl; it trades like a financial product but is not a security; it is designed to hedge future prices but is not a futures contract; it pays off in the event of a specific loss-causing event but is not an insurance policy'.[1] The Kazakhstan case in Chapter 12 was an example of the moral hazard that can result from the use of CDS for speculation.

On the principle of substance prevailing over form, regulators must require the principle of 'insurable interest' (not necessarily using that term) to apply to all purchasers of Credit Derivatives. This would imply that any party seeking protection from credit risk must stand to suffer if the risk actually materializes. Also, sellers of swaps should be required to hold suitable reserves against them.

Centralized clearing for all derivatives which have a secondary market

Exchange listing and trading sheds light on the pricing model, brings about standardization and uniformity and improves liquidity. Besides ensuring that the Exchange stands behind the contracts, it also ensures that regulators will be able to respond more readily and easily to instances of abuse and violations of fair trading on the part of financial institutions. The swaps market was an example of a standardized market that pretended to be customized for regulatory purposes. As was seen in Chapter 11, Brazil has shown that moving most formerly-OTC derivatives to exchanges does not necessarily reduce volumes.

The disadvantage of exchange listing is the inability to customize the derivative to a specific need. Customization can be helpful in meeting specialized or idiosyncratic needs of particular participants. For the firm holding a customized instrument, the gains and losses can be netted out against other non-derivative investments the firm may hold. It may be possible to get a much longer tenor than an exchange-traded product. However, customized products are less transparent from a regulatory perspective and thus increase systemic risk.

In an exchange-traded transaction, one party's loss is the mirror image of the other party's gain. From a systemic point-of-view it is a zero sum game. A key and not-well-understood issue is that *pricing of OTC transactions is not necessarily a zero-sum game (unlike in exchange-traded instruments) since valuation models are neither uniform nor transparent.*[2] Thus for a given change in price, the sum of the measured accounting effects may be a plus or a minus *even though the true economic effect is clearly a zero sum.* It is even theoretically possible, though unlikely, that both the counterparties, by using different models could show a gain from the same small price movement. This poses major regulatory problems in system-wide aggregation. The experience with so-called OTC swaps, which were in fact resold and traded shows clearly the danger of allowing secondary trading of 'over-the-counter' derivatives.

To call for *all* derivatives to be exchange-traded and centrally cleared would be extreme because it would curb flexibility and customization and thus reduce welfare. With such curbs, even such obviously useful derivatives as currency or interest rate swaps might never have been invented.

The thrust of regulation has to be to promote a regime where:

- OTC derivatives are used for genuinely customized transactions; and
- all standardized transactions go through exchanges.

Therefore, *any derivative that is being resold beyond the original counterparties to the original deal must either go through an exchange or be subject to case-by-case regulatory approval.* Case-by-case approval should be contingent on at least one of the parties involved having a legitimate need to use the derivative *as a hedge* (not as a speculation) and the other party being an institution which is adequately capitalized and has the expertise to assess and manage the risk.

Centralized clearing does however create new risks of its own: with centralized clearing, the clearing house itself may become systemically important and be subjected to tighter regulatory scrutiny. The collapse of a regulated commodities exchange in India in 2013[3] (after it committed serious fraud, diverted commodities from its warehouses and failed to deliver them) illustrated that regulated exchanges are not necessarily safe. Regulators therefore need to pay attention to:

- Multiple exchanges: Having several exchanges for the same kind of derivative spreads the risk but increases the effort required in monitoring; a single one has obverse benefits and disadvantages.

- For-profit vs. not-for-profit exchanges: Is it or is it not desirable for exchanges to be profit-seeking entities? The profit motive keeps them efficient but also increases the temptation to cut corners; not-for-profits have obverse merits and demerits. There have been allegations that stock exchanges in the US have helped computerized 'high-frequency-traders' gain an edge over others because of the profits earned by the exchanges from this kind of trading.[4] Peterffy, a leading stockbroker, expressed the view that the use of computerized trading (to replace the old physical 'open outcry') initially produced an increase in transparency and a lowering of transaction costs, benefiting the economy but of late further advances in technology are fragmenting the market, taking many trades offline, impeding price discovery, reducing transparency and giving certain parties unfair advantages.[5] On the benefit-of-doubt principle (see below), not-for-profit derivatives exchanges may be preferable especially for emerging markets where law enforcement and legal deterrence is weaker.

Restraint on remuneration at top levels

The perverse incentives created by the enormous remuneration packages of employees in the financial services sector clearly played a role in creating the financial crisis of 2008. Long ago, Akerlof and Romer showed that managers of financial institutions may have an incentive to 'loot' if they felt the losses could be passed on to the exchequer and added that 'when the owners of a firm drive it bankrupt, they can cause great social harm, just as looters in a riot cause total losses that are far greater than the private gains they capture'.[6] While this was originally an argument against deposit insurance, the taxpayer financed bailouts of 2008 and the phenomenon of too-big-to-fail mean that there is now an even bigger moral hazard than that posed by deposit insurance. No executive in the financial sector had to repay a bonus after the crisis – they retained their gains. *Clearly, executive remuneration has potential negative externalities.*

The argument against remuneration control is twofold. Firstly, it might lead to firms losing their best and most talented staff to other firms. Secondly, it might take away the incentive for efficient and effective performance and operate against the interest of shareholders.

The first point actually strengthens rather than weakens the case for control: while voluntary restraints by individual firms could lead to loss of talent, a regulatory imposition of restraint would affect all participants in a given sector and thus will not facilitate 'poaching'. As regards the second, the linkage of remuneration to profits (once touted as a means of reducing principal-agent problems) has been clearly shown to be the prime cause of reckless risk taking, which in turn creates the negative externality of passing on costs to the general public.

India has, for decades, had restrictions on executive remuneration under the Companies Act for directors of companies. Ceilings are based on profits and in the case of companies with no profits, on the size of the company. (The Indian rules are only for directors; for financial institutions, it might be desirable to extend them to employees at a senior level who have the ability to take policy decisions on levels of risk.) The European Union introduced ceilings on bankers' bonuses and also regulations on the manner in which those bonuses are paid taking effect from 2014. These kinds of controls suffer from many defects, but even with their many flaws and irrationalities, it appears that there is more that is right than wrong with the Indian (and now European) philosophical approach on this question.

Since it is not so much the actual amount of remuneration as the linkage to profits that creates the negative externality, the argument that remuneration restraints would lead to loss of talent could be addressed quite easily: high absolute levels of remuneration can be permitted *without* links to short term profits and/ or with clawbacks for losses. An incentive-compatible and rational design of remuneration controls is beyond the scope of this book, but is an area for constant regulatory attention and vigilance.

Another area for regulatory attention is the incentive effects of accounting standards. Fair value accounting and the immediate recognition of anticipated but unrealized gains, with bonuses based on reported profits, creates an incentive for staff to do 'deals' rather than ensure that an instrument performs well throughout its life. The RBI in India introduced a very salutary requirement that profits on securitized assets are not recognized at the time of securitization but only as the securitized assets are realized, even though this is runs contrary to 'generally accepted' accounting practice.[7]

Multiplicity of agencies

Chapter 13 outlined the pros and cons of having a unified versus a fragmented regulatory structure. During the run-up to the 2008 financial crisis, the experience of the UK with a single regulator was not good–but the experience of the US with multiple regulators was not good either! What this shows is that, at least from the point of view of derivatives, structure *may not matter as much as is sometimes thought.* The precise regulatory structure is not so important that a lot of time, effort and political capital should be spent on achieving an 'ideal' one. *If a country has a particular structure based on history and evolution, it may be better to retain it and adapt and modify gradually rather than to replace it wholesale.*

Instead, efforts should be directed at

- getting the right type and quality of regulations and regulators within each agency;
- ensuring coordination among them; and
- monitoring what is happening 'outside the boundary'

The last point acquires increased importance because of the growing importance of 'shadow banking'. The shadow banking sector comprises specialized financial institutions (such as asset management and securities firms) that perform credit intermediation services similar to traditional banks or depository credit institutions, but without the explicit central bank liquidity support or public sector credit guarantees. (In the US it accounted for nearly 60 per cent of total financial intermediation in 2011.[8])

Composition of regulatory governance structures

In recent years, the belief that monetary policy should be left to groups of expert macroeconomists has acquired the status of axiom among most economists and financial journalists. The merits of that proposition are beyond the scope of this book. Fligstein *et al* found that the Federal Open Market Committee's consensus approach, and the lack of intellectual diversity engendered in the Federal Open Market Committee of the US Federal Reserve, contributed to the inability of the Federal Reserve to recognize danger signals ahead of the 2008 financial crisis. In their words the 'inability to make sense of this crisis seems to have stemmed directly from the cognitive limitations of a conceptual apparatus founded firstly in the training of macroeconomists and secondly in the routines of career central banking'.[9] Thus it is important that the design of governance structures for regulatory agencies should take into account the dangers of intellectual monoculture and strive for diversity of thought.

Conflicts of interest: Avoiding the revolving door

The world has widely varying practices in the way senior personnel of the regulatory agencies are recruited. In the US, the regulatory staff is often drawn from the financial services industry and it is also common for former regulators to subsequently join the boards of companies they once regulated. This two-way movement is sometimes called the revolving door. In countries like India and to an extent the UK, there has traditionally been a 'class barrier' between the regulated and the regulators who are mainly career civil servants and government economists. Each approach has strengths and weaknesses.

It is invaluable for the regulators to know and understand the world of the regulated and there is nothing better than actual experience in a regulated entity to provide that understanding. Some highly regarded and tough regulators have come from the ranks of investment banking – Gary Gensler of the CFTC for instance. On the other hand, coming from a common social background does increase the chances of regulatory capture (of the materialistic and the intellectual kind) and there is credible evidence that regulators have, at least sometimes, been excessively influenced by the entities they regulate. A retiring lawyer of the SEC had this perspective:

> The revolving door is a very serious problem. I have had bosses, and bosses of my bosses...who made little secret that they were here to punch their

ticket. They mouthed serious regard for the mission of the Commission, but their actions were tentative and fearful in many instances. You can get back to Wall Street by acting tough, by using the SEC publicity apparatus to promote yourself as tough, and maybe even on a few occasions being tough, if you pick your targets carefully. But don't appear to fail. Don't take risks where risk would count… The revolving door doesn't push the agency's enforcement envelope very often or very far. The attitude trickles down the ranks. Combined with the negative views of the civil service promoted by politicians and the beatings we take from the public, it is no surprise that we lose our best and brightest as they see no place to go in the agency and eventually decide they are just going to get their own ticket to a law firm or corporate job punched. They see an agency that polices the broken windows on the street level and rarely goes to the penthouse floors. On the rare occasions when Enforcement does go to the penthouse, good manners are paramount. Tough enforcement – risky enforcement – is subject to extensive negotiation and weakening.[10]

In this respect career civil servants and career government economists tend to do better in retaining intellectual independence and distinguishing between the interests of the financial sector and the wider interests of the public.

In the design of regulatory systems, regardless of the specific approach adopted, the most important thing is for governments to be vigilant in identifying issues of conflicts of interest and preventing or mitigating them. Among other things, a 'cooling off' requirement would be helpful; this may require that any person who has been in a senior regulatory position cannot join or rejoin any regulated entity for, say, 3 years after he or she was in a regulatory position: this reduces the incentive to do favours while in office by deferring any potential payoff in the form of lucrative jobs or board slots. For developing countries at least, the career civil service/ government economist approach does seem better; deficiencies in domain knowledge can be remedied through outside inputs whereas regulatory capture can have much more serious consequences.

Calibrated response to commodity price booms and slumps

As was seen in Chapters 5 to 7, the theory and evidence suggest that while derivatives may play a price stabilizing role, they can for extended periods of time also play a destabilizing role. This means that derivatives regulators should be watchful at times when prices – especially commodity prices – are moving substantially beyond what fundamentals appear to justify. Price rises can, in a poor country, directly affect the underprivileged while price falls can also hurt peasants and small producers.

The first step in these situations would be to try and understand whether prices are driven by clear fundamentals or are being driven (or exacerbated) by momentum trading or other destabilizing forces. In the former case, intervention against the market is not desirable, but in the latter it may be essential. If there is evidence of a generalized speculative excess, commodities regulators *should be prepared to use regulatory instruments like selective margins to make speculation more difficult and thereby reduce the extent to which destabilizing speculation occurs.* On the other hand, they should *resist the tendency to become 'price controllers'* and should not intervene just because prices have moved in an 'undesirable' direction. These judgments are difficult to make, while no firm rules can be laid down, some factors to be considered are:

- whether real interest rates are positive and high: the higher the prevailing interest rate, the lower the risk of overshooting and vice versa;

- whether the ratio of speculative derivatives trading to the size of the underlying market is rising sharply: if so the risk is higher. In this regard indicators such as the 'Working's t' (see Chapter 7) need to be calculated and monitored.

Limited reliance on models

When financial markets move up or down in lockstep, any external disturbance or shock has the potential to create spikes in volatility. Models often break down when they are most needed: at times of high volatility. When models break down, valuation and pricing become impossible and bid-ask spreads become too wide to offer a meaningful guide to buying and selling intentions.

Models of derivative pricing are models – not reality. Therefore regulators need to be wary of basing regulatory actions substantially on models. Derman has rightly argued that anyone using a model is effectively taking a speculative short position on volatility of the parameters in that model: if the parameters fluctuate more than assumed in the model, a loss will result.[11] *The more complex the model and the more difficult it is to understand, the more sceptical regulators must be and the less reliance they should place on it for regulatory purposes.*

Regulators also need to be conscious of the possible 'performative' effect of models (see Chapter 10). The Black Scholes option pricing model began as a way of understanding and describing options pricing. The authors of the model actively sold it and earned money from the propagation of it.[12] Eventually, the model became the market and instead of the model being a 'camera' casting light on what was going on, it became an 'engine' that changed what was going on.[13] Regulators need to be watchful and assess the role and performance of models.

Regulatory philosophy

This part makes recommendations on broader issues of regulatory philosophy.

Deliberate regulatory uncertainty: Avoiding rigid rules and retaining discretion

There is a widely held view among economists, especially in the West, that transparent and clear rules which can be interpreted consistently and with certainty are a good thing. Intuitively, this would seem to be right.

Chapter 13 discussed the 'boundary problem' in regulation, whereby entities seek to place themselves outside (usually, just outside) the regulatory boundary. Going outside the boundary requires knowing exactly where the boundary is. This suggests that the conventional wisdom on regulatory certainty – while indeed in the interests of the regulated entities – may not always be in public interest. Indeed, one way of mitigating the 'boundary problem' is to make the boundary not clearly defined by moving away from precise rules towards a broad public policy intent. This creates some regulatory uncertainty in the minds of those seeking to exploit the restrictions on the regulated sector. To use an analogy from India's border disputes, if the 'line of actual control' remains disputed, it may prevent people from setting up business operations anywhere close to that line since they may end up on the wrong side of it; they would be better off staying clearly in undisputed territory! Likewise, regulatory uncertainty may mean that financial firms will stay in a zone which is safely within the boundary.

This suggests an approach where policy intent is described in broad rules with discretion in terms of actual application for those administering them. The argument against this is well known: it leaves more potential for arbitrariness and corruption and for that reason is usually a bad idea. However, in the specific context of financial regulation, *it may (counter-intuitively) be a good thing*. If the banks and the non-banking financial institutions are not totally certain *ex ante* what the central bank will consider to be within/ without the scope of a particular regulation, it may dissuade them from exploiting loopholes in the way that is so common in Anglo-American systems of greater legal certainty. Taking the analogy of 'shadow' banking, discretion creates the threat that regulators can switch on the lights suddenly and this may induce better behaviour; on the other hand rules that prevent regulators from switching on the lights without prior notice (new rules) encourage bad behaviour. Concerns about misuse of discretion are legitimate but should not be overstated. They can be addressed by creating strong accountability mechanisms including internal controls, audit and legislative review.

In the highly competitive financial markets, participants are often forced to do something they do not really want to because everyone else is doing it, and to not do it would cause a competitive loss. Human beings sometimes have to be chained so that they do not cause harm to themselves (and to others) with their own behaviour: Ulysses in the Greek epic the Odyssey, asked to be tied to the mast to resist the temptations of the sirens. Regulations provide a chain but uncertainties are another chain: Kunti, the mother of the Pandavas in the Hindu epic Mahabharata, prayed to Krishna to keep her in hardship and uncertainty so that she would always need to seek his grace and blessing.

Therefore, the regulatory and policy environment should seek to maintain a prudent balance between uncertainty and certainty rather than pursue a goal of eliminating all uncertainties. In achieving that balance, regulators must remain open to empirical evidence, and fine-tune their policies, laws and regulations as required but always keeping in mind systemic (rather than sector-specific) considerations. The right approach would be to leave room in regulations for a significant amount of discretion but ensure it is exercised only at higher levels of the regulatory organization and with due internal process and appropriate external accountability.

Tailoring regulation to capacity in developing countries: Use of blunt regulation

For developing countries and emerging markets, which have many unexploited development opportunities in the real economy, the development of their own derivatives markets should generally not be a priority. For such countries there are almost certainly much higher economic welfare gains from improvements in the real economy than from improved allocative efficiency the financial sector.

Furthermore, countries with scarce human capacity should not necessarily be devoting their best brains to the task of keeping pace with the innovations of investment bankers.

Smaller developing countries may thus be better off not having their own derivative markets and/or restricting the use of derivatives by domestic entities to hedging only. Larger ones may be well advised to follow the approach of 'blunt regulation': i.e., have some simple and blunt rules that are easy to interpret and hard to circumvent. Blunt regulation tends to stifle financial innovation and to preclude the development of the more sophisticated (and thus more risky) types, but is easier to understand and enforce – which is exactly what such countries may need. The Glass-Steagall Act in the USA which rigidly separated commercial and investment banking is an example of blunt regulation.

Monitoring financial innovation: A benefit of doubt rule

Many financial innovations have had negative externalities – i.e., the costs to society have exceeded the costs to the parties involved. On the other hand, financial innovations have also improved economic welfare. As seen in Figure 13.1, financial innovation typically goes through the following stages:

- creation of a customized product;
- standardization of the product and widespread adoption; and
- mutation (as new variants are created).

The major challenge for regulators is that the innovativeness of the marketplace results in new features arising very quickly, at a pace that regulators cannot keep up with. However, so long as the product is non-standardized, the size of the market usually remains small and does not pose systemic risk. It is standardization that results in large-scale expansion. The only advantage regulators have in this unequal race is that standardization usually requires some explicit or implicit regulatory blessing. It is at this point that regulators need to be vigilant and not give their blessing until they are convinced the innovation is benign.

It is easier for outsiders to comment on regulation than it is for regulators and governments to decide on specific regulatory issues. Unlike academic economists or the authors of books like this one, they do not have the luxury of setting out various arguments and letting someone else decide. Nor do they always have the time to gather every possible piece of evidence or to carry out a literature survey. They have to decide and, sometimes, to decide quickly. Evidence, argument and expert opinion are often equivocal as this book must have amply demonstrated.

This problem is not unique to financial regulators. Judges in courts and umpires in sports face it all the time. In the Anglo-Saxon criminal law system, if there is doubt in the minds of the jury (or the judge in cases without jury trials), the benefit of that doubt goes to the accused. In cricket, when a bowler claims that a batsman is out and the umpire is unsure, there is a clear rule: the benefit of doubt goes to the batsman. This does not mean that no one is ever convicted in the courts or that no batsman is ever given 'out' in cricket.

A similar 'benefit-of-doubt' rule should be instituted for derivatives regulators. In proposing this rule, the authors were guided by two factors. First, while the contribution of finance to development may not be as significant as often thought (see Chapter 13), the potential *negative effects of a financial crisis can be catastrophic* – the long-term cost to the US economy of the 2008 crisis has been estimated as somewhere between 40 and over 100 per cent of one year's GDP.[14] Assuming a 'normal' growth rate for the US economy of 2–3 per cent, it means that a crisis of the magnitude witnessed in 2008 can push an economy back by 20 to 30 years. Against that yardstick, the potential benefits from financial innovation or new derivatives are small. Second, it is *very difficult to put a genie back into the bottle*: it is more difficult to close down an existing market than it is to start a new one.

The proposed decision guideline for regulators is that:

- if they are convinced that a new derivatives instrument or innovation is beneficial in the public interest, they should allow it;

- if they are convinced that it is not, they should disallow it; and

- if *they are in doubt* about whether or not it is beneficial, they should *disallow it* or at best allow it on a trial basis.

Regulatory competition: Be prepared to lose the battle to win the war

In a globalized world with capital free to move across borders, regulators are constantly compared with other regulators and inter-country comparisons are frequently cited by the regulated when seeking more liberal regulation. Three trump cards are usually played by the regulated entities in persuading regulators to 'keep up with the Joneses':

- The first is that not allowing a particular form of derivative will *impede real economic development* and slow down growth;

- The second is that failure to follow fashion will lead to *loss of business* to financial centres in other countries. This is believed to have played a role in the UK's headlong rush to a single regulator in 1997;[15]

- The third is that resisting fashion is *ineffective* especially for regulators in small or emerging markets: the market will still exist elsewhere and so one might as well join it since one cannot beat it. For instance, if one does not allow currency futures locally, a non-deliverable forward market will develop overseas and (so the argument goes) any deleterious effects will happen anyway.

Regarding the first point, it was seen in Chapter 13 that there is clear empirical evidence that the actual contribution of finance and of the financial sector to development is limited and indeed sometimes negative. Therefore there can be no automatic presumption in favour of allowing new derivatives. (For example, for many years, the RBI's restrictions on CDS in India were criticized for reducing the availability of finance for productive purposes and indeed they have been relaxed to an extent in recent years. Yet Ashcraft and Santos in their study of the US credit market found 'no evidence that the onset of CDS trading affects the cost of debt financing for the average borrower' and 'economically significant adverse effects to risky and informationally-opaque firms' though they did find benefits for some firms.[16])

As regards the second point, if the price of not following other countries is to lose business and jobs in the financial sector to another location, then that price may (if the systemic risks are felt to be large) be worth paying to protect the real sector. In other words, losing the financial sector battle may be necessary to win the real sector war. (However, this may be a more difficult question for a small country with an offshore financial centre where finance is the dominant economic activity.)

On the third point – that 'regulators cannot win' – the argument is exaggerated when considering systemic risk. Regulators *do* have the capacity to control the extent to which *domestic* banks participate in overseas derivatives markets, and domestic banks almost always have the largest share of the domestic banking business. If they do not, the central bank can change its bank licensing regulation to require domesticity. Sharma showed that Indian domestic regulation had remained effective even though there is a large offshore non-deliverable forward market in the Indian rupee.[17] The regulatory restriction on Indian banks prevents arbitrage from occurring between the domestic and offshore markets and thus preserves regulatory autonomy. The point is that even if 'substitute' markets develop offshore, domestic regulations have considerable effect on domestic entities.

This is not to suggest that all new ideas must be resisted: rather it is to emphasize that regulators need to ensure that *ideas are adopted only because they are assessed to be good in domestic conditions* and not merely because everyone is following them.

Differential approach to different markets

While this chapter has generalized about derivatives, regulators should discriminate between the different derivative instruments on the basis of the trade-off between social utility and social risk. Several factors are involved.

Firstly, some derivatives are more complex than others. Complexity promotes opacity and makes risks more difficult to assess. Linear derivatives (see Chapter 2) like forwards and futures are the simplest and most transparent and pose the least difficulty while exotic derivatives like swaptions and 'CDO squared' are the most opaque. Those derivatives which have a notional underlying (see Chapter 2) rather than a real and deliverable underlying, also require relatively greater regulatory attention. Secondly, some kinds of derivatives pose greater systemic risk than others – the interest rate futures market used by banks is clearly more systemically important than the turmeric futures market used by spice merchants. Thirdly, some underlyings have greater macroeconomic significance in terms of hedging needs than others (e.g., oil in Mexico, copper in Chile, foreign exchange everywhere). Fourthly, some commodities have significant effects on the poor and vulnerable either as consumers (e.g. maize in Malawi and Zambia) or as producers (e.g. cocoa in Ghana) or both (wheat in India and Pakistan).

For a regulator, the level of regulatory attention should vary positively with all of these factors – complexity, systemic risk, macroeconomic importance and importance of the underlying to the poor. To illustrate, the regulatory spectrum may span the following:

- simple foreign exchange forwards which clearly are crucial as hedging instruments for exporters and importers and have rarely been a source of regulatory problems;
- commodity futures in non-essential commodities, which are often useful hedging instruments for producers as well as industrial consumers, which generally have a neutral or price stabilizing influence but may sometimes play a price destabilizing role;
- currency and interest rate swaps which enable borrowers to hedge against currency and interest rate risk and are predominantly used for this purpose, but pose some systemic risk in the event of counter party default;
- commodity futures in essential commodities which are articles of staple consumption for the poor, where the risk of inflation from long-term speculation may be high;
- futures and options in equities which are primarily speculative instruments and where hedging volumes are relatively insignificant, and with potential systemic effects on other financial markets;
- complex financial derivatives like CDO and naked CDS which have limited or even negative social utility and create major negative systemic consequences.

The illustrative list above is organized very roughly in terms of a decreasing 'benefit-cost ratio'. Clearly, the regulatory approach has to be tailored accordingly.

As a crude rule-of-thumb, the 'social benefit-cost ratio' of a particular derivatives market varies

- Inversely with complexity (the more complex, the higher the cost vis-à-vis benefits);
- Inversely with systemic risk (greater the systemic risk posed, the greater the cost);
- Directly with the macroeconomic importance of hedging (because the welfare benefits of risk transfer through hedging are larger for macro-economically significant markets); and
- Indeterminately with the importance of the underlying to the poor, depending on whether the market is stabilizing or destabilizing in nature. However, when the poor are mainly consumers of the underlying commodity, the inflationary price destabilization risk becomes an important regulatory

consideration, especially because of the increasing tendency towards commodity investments (see Chapter 7).

Scepticism on 'cutting edge' theory and current intellectual fashions

Finally, policy makers need to exercise caution and scepticism about new theories that have not been tested over at least one full boom-and-bust cycle. Capital account liberalization, linking risk-weighted capital requirements to credit ratings under Basel II, the economic benefits of asset-backed securities and credit default swaps, marking-to-market under International Financial Reporting Standards, the tying of executive remuneration to short-term stock prices – these were all concepts that came with a bang, and were promoted with a lot of intellectual firepower; indeed to disagree was like wearing a bowler hat to an exhibition of contemporary fashion. Yet all are discredited to some degree today. (For instance, in 2012 the International Monetary Fund – for decades an implacable enemy of capital controls – finally admitted that 'there is no presumption that full [capital account] liberalization is an appropriate goal for all countries at all times' and that '[i]n certain circumstances, capital controls can be useful for supporting…and safeguarding financial system stability'[18].)

India presents an interesting case study. The slowness of the Indian regulatory system, the insularity of its bureaucracy, and the relatively small number and limited influence of think-tanks are all usually (and validly) considered bad things. Yet these very features insulated India from the vicissitudes of fast-moving Western economic fashion. This factor, along with the perspicacity of some key people in the RBI, kept India largely protected from the crisis.

When regulators are presented with innovative derivative securities that require changes in regulations, they should subject the proposals to intelligent scrutiny inviting opinions beyond persons in the specialized sector from which the innovation emanates.

Borio summarized an insightful study of the financial cycle (different from the well-known business cycle) as follows:

> Understanding in economics does not proceed cumulatively. We do not necessarily know more today than we did yesterday, tempting as it may be to believe otherwise. So-called 'lessons' are learnt, forgotten, re-learnt and

forgotten again. Concepts rise to prominence and fall into oblivion before possibly resurrecting. They do so because the economic environment changes, sometimes slowly but profoundly, at other times suddenly and violently. But they do so also because the discipline is not immune to fashions and fads. After all, no walk of life is.[19]

Perhaps regulators should, in assessing the durability of new economic ideas, drop the Gregorian calendar and adopt the Hindu cosmic calendar of Brahma, in which one day of Brahma equals a year of man.

Notes and References

[1]   B. Ritholtz, 'Credit Default Swaps are Masquerading as Financial Products: They should be Regulated as Insurance Products', *Washington Post*, 11 March 2012.

[2]   'Derivatives and US Corporations', Fitch Ratings, 7 June 2012.

[3]   The National Spot Exchange, not to be confused with the National Stock Exchange.

[4]   B. Van Voris, 'BofA, NYSE, Brokerages Sued Over High-Frequency Trading', *Bloomberg*, 19 April 2014.

[5]   T. Peterffy, 'Comments of Thomas Peterffy, CEO of Interactive Brokers Group', Before the World Federation of Exchanges, 11 October 2010. Available at: http:// www.zerohedge.com/news/2014-04-07/father-high-speed-trading-speaks-market-we-created-casino-complete-mess-rigged-game. Accessed on 14 July 2014.

[6]   George A. Akerlof and Paul M. Romer, *Looting: The Economic Underworld of Bankruptcy for Profit*, Brookings Papers on Economic Activity, No. 2, 1993.

[7]   Y. V. Reddy, 'Global Financial Turbulence and Financial Sector in India: A Practitioner's Perspective', address by Governor, Reserve Bank of India, at the Meeting of the Task Force on Financial Markets Regulation organized by the Initiative for Policy Dialogue, Manchester, 1 July 2008.

[8]   S. Antill, D. Hou and A. Sarkar, *The Growth of Murky Finance*, Federal Reserve Bank of New York, 27 March 2014. Available at: http://libertystreeteconomics.newyorkfed. org/2014/03/the-growth-of-murky-finance.html. Accessed on 14 July 2014.

[9]   N. Fligstein, J. S. Brundage and M. Schultz, *Why the Federal Reserve Failed to See the Financial Crisis of 2008: The Role of 'Macroeconomics' as a Sensemaking and Cultural Frame*. Department of Sociology, University of California, Berkeley, February 2014.

[10] J. Kidney, 'Retirement Remarks'. Available at: http://www.secunion.org/files/ RetirementRemarks.pdf and reported in R. Schmidt, 'SEC Goldman Lawyer Says Agency Too Timid on Wall Street Misdeeds', *Bloomberg*, 8 April 2014. Available at: http://www.

bloomberg.com/news/2014-04-08/sec-goldman-lawyer-says-agency-too-timid-on-wall-street-misdeeds.html. Accessed on 14 July 2014.

11 Emanuel Derman, *Models Behaving Badly*, Free Press, New York, 2011.

12 Donald MacKenzie, *Is Economics Performative?: Option Theory and the Construction of Derivative Markets*, Paper presented at the History of Economics Society, Tacoma, May 2005. Availanble at: http://www.espanet2012.info/__data/assets/pdf_file/0017/3419/is_economics_performative.pdf. Accessed on 14 July 2014.

13 Donald MacKenzie, *An Engine, not a Camera: How Financial Models Shape the Markets*. MIT Press, Cambridge, 2006.

14 T. Atkinson, D. Luttrell and H. Rosenblum, *How Bad Was It? The Costs and Consequences of the 2007–09 Financial Crisis*, Staff Paper No. 20. Federal Reserve Bank of Dallas, 2013.

15 A. Fresh and M. N. Baily, 'What Does International Experience Tell Us about Regulatory Consolidation?', *The Pew Financial Reform Project*, Briefing No. 6, 2009.

16 A. B. Ashcraft and J. A. C. Santos, *Has the Credit Default Swap Market Lowered the Cost of CorporateDebt?* Federal Reserve Bank of New York, Staff Reports, Number 290, July 2007.

17 V. K. Sharma, 'No Real Link between Offshore, Onshore Re. Markets', *Business Line*, December 20, 2013.

18 H. Schneider, 'IMF Softens Stand on Capital Controls after Surveying Financial Crisis Damage', *Washington Post*, 4 December 2012.

19 C. Borio, *The Financial Cycle and Macroeconomics: What Have We Learnt?*, BIS Working Papers No. 395, Monetary and Economic Department, Bank for International Settlements, December 2012, 1.

Index

About the Authors

T. V. Somanathan is Director at the World Bank, Washington and a member of the Indian Administrative Service. His doctorate in economics was on the subject of commodity and financial derivatives. He is a Chartered Accountant, Chartered Management Accountant and Chartered Secretary. With over 27 years of experience in the World Bank and in the Union and State Governments of India, he combines academic rigour with practical experience in economics, finance, public policy and regulation. His publications include a book titled *Derivatives* (1998) and more than 80 papers, articles and book chapters.

V. Anantha Nageswaran holds a doctorate in finance (on exchange rate behaviour) and has over two decades of experience in global capital markets with leading financial institutions such as UBS, Credit Suisse and Bank Julius Baer. He is an adjunct faculty on international finance and economics at the Indian Institute of Management Bangalore (IIMB) and Singapore Management University. He is a weekly columnist for *Mint*, a regular contributor to CNBC, Reuters and Bloomberg television networks and is also a co-founder of the Takshashila Institution.